"To my knowledge, this is the most comprehensive and analytically refined exposition and critique of postmodernism."

Douglas Groothuis, professor of philosophy, Denver Seminary, author of *Truth Decay*

"*Understanding Postmodernism* is the best one-stop introduction to postmodernism from a conservative evangelical perspective. It describes and evaluates postmodernism from historical, theological, and philosophical perspectives and does so in a lucid and accessible manner."

Bruce Riley Ashford, provost, professor of theology and culture, Southeastern Baptist Theological Seminary

"The gospel is never preached in a vacuum. It is always heard against the backdrop of the culture's collective mindset and mood. Well, the cultural mindset and mood is steeped in postmodern thought that relativizes truth, knowledge, and value. As a result, people today are morally confused and biblically illiterate. Confusion, darkness, and disintegration reign. Kelly and Dew cut through the confusion, ably dissecting postmodernism and demolishing its credibility. As the smoke clears, a vision of shalom emerges where Christianity is seen as true and Jesus is seen as the fount of all wisdom and knowledge. A must-read book for all who need to be reminded of the objective goodness, truth, and beauty of Christianity."

Paul M. Gould, associate professor of philosophy and Christian apologetics, Southwestern Baptist Theological Seminary

"Ours is a world of skepticism, irony, and intellectual despair, all of which tempt us away from the kingdom of God. This book is a profoundly Christian antidote: a way to analyze our postmodern context, accept its fresh insights, identify its missteps and downright errors, then move on to a mature, thoughtful grasp of the truth in Christ and actively live out its implications. A profound book in lucid prose!"

James W. Sire, author of *The Universe Next Door* and *Apologetics Beyond Reason*

"Postmodernism is no longer a youthful upstart but has now reached middle age. If we take 1968 as its date of birth, the revolution is now fifty years old, which explains the philosophical paunch and aching cultural joints. *Understanding Postmodernism*, similarly, is a mature evangelical response, more interested in showing charity and asking what we can learn from the postmodern protest to modernity than in knee-jerk reactions. The authors stay calm and carry on reasoning. In particular, they examine ten major themes, including language, rationality, and truth (they're analytic thinkers, after all), bringing both clarity and charity to bear on a movement that has affected the academy, society, and church like no other in recent memory."

Kevin J. Vanhoozer, research professor of systematic theology, Trinity Evangelical Divinity School

"Critics regularly compare defining postmodernism to 'trying to nail Jell-O to the wall.' If this cliché is true, Kelly and Dew have done the inconceivable: they have successfully nailed the postmodern ethos to the cross. *Understanding Postmodernism* is a clear, appreciative exposition and critique of the tenets of postmodernism. This distinctively Christian introduction also provides much-needed historical framing and real-world application for college and seminary students. Highly recommended."

Rhyne Putman, associate professor of theology and culture, New Orleans Baptist Theological Seminary

"Why is the Western world involved in such a monumental collision of ideas today? What about the claims disputed hotly but seriously every day on news broadcasts, heard from college students and even professors alike, assuming, questioning, or denying the presence of any knowable truth in the world? Like the old saying states, 'ideas have consequences.' In this volume, philosophers Stewart Kelly and James Dew explain where this trend came from—why and when it emerged—as well as providing a detailed response to these ideas. Painstakingly documented and carefully reasoned, this volume provides the critique that this generation sorely needs. Highly recommended."

Gary R. Habermas, distinguished research professor, chair of the department of philosophy, Liberty University and Baptist Theological Seminary

"*Understanding Postmodernism* is an important book that helps readers navigate between the extremes concerning truth: taking a completely neutral, unbiased, infallible God's-eye view of reality or stepping into the destructive quicksand of relativism. In an age in which professing Christians are increasingly embracing postmodern assumptions, this book is a proper corrective in its overview and assessment of the key themes of postmodernism as well as a defense of a gospel-centered understanding of truth."

Paul Copan, Pledger Family Chair of Philosophy and Ethics, Palm Beach Atlantic University, author of *An Introduction to Biblical Ethics* and *A Little Book for New Philosophers*

UNDERSTANDING

POSTMODERNISM

A CHRISTIAN

PERSPECTIVE

STEWART E. KELLY
WITH JAMES K. DEW JR.

IVP Academic

An imprint of InterVarsity Press
Downers Grove, Illinois

InterVarsity Press
P.O. Box 1400, Downers Grove, IL 60515-1426
ivpress.com
email@ivpress.com

InterVarsity Press® is the book-publishing division of InterVarsity Christian Fellowship/USA®, a movement of
students and faculty active on campus at hundreds of universities, colleges, and schools of nursing in the United
States of America, and a member movement of the International Fellowship of Evangelical Students. For
information about local and regional activities, visit intervarsity.org.

All Scripture quotations, unless otherwise indicated, are taken from The Holy Bible, New International Version®,
NIV®. Copyright © 1973, 1978, 1984, 2011 by Biblica, Inc.™ Used by permission of Zondervan. All rights reserved
worldwide. www.zondervan.com The "NIV" and "New International Version" are trademarks registered in the
United States Patent and Trademark Office by Biblica, Inc.™

While any stories in this book are true, some names and identifying information may have been changed to protect
the privacy of individuals.

Cover design: David Fassett
Interior design: Daniel van Loon
Images: Portrait of René Descartes by Frans Hals at the Louvre, Paris, France / Bridgeman Images

ISBN 978-0-8308-5193-5 (print)
ISBN 978-0-8308-8908-2 (digital)

Printed in the United States of America ∞

InterVarsity Press is committed to ecological stewardship and to the conservation of natural resources in all our
operations. This book was printed using sustainably sourced paper.

Library of Congress Cataloging-in-Publication Data
A catalog record for this book is available from the Library of Congress.

P	23	22	21	20	19	18	17	16	15	14	13	12	11	10	9	8	7	6	5	4	3	2	1
Y	36	35	34	33	32	31	30	29	28	27	26	25	24	23	22	21	20	19	18	17			

FROM STEWART KELLY:

*In honor of Shirley Lachs, for her kindness,
generosity, and encouragement*

FROM JAMES DEW:

*To TD and the Dew Crew—my greatest
joys this side of heaven*

CONTENTS

ACKNOWLEDGMENTS

There are many people who contributed to making this book possible. We would like to thank Wesley Davey, Alex Oakley, and Tara Dew for their labor in helping us read and edit the manuscript. We also thank two anonymous reviewers for many helpful suggestions and substantive comments—the book is better for their efforts. We are grateful for the work of David McNutt for overseeing our book and being a pleasure to work with. The staff at IVP was a model of grace and efficiency. Finally, we would like to thank our wives and children for their love and support all along the way.

1

INTRODUCING POSTMODERNISM

*Our society is in the throes of a cultural
shift of immense proportions.*

STANLEY J. GRENZ, *A PRIMER ON POSTMODERNISM*

SEISMIC CHANGES

Many older Americans have fond memories of the 1950s into the 1960s. The
Korean War had ended, the economy and suburbia were booming, we were
not at war, television was on the scene, and much in American life seemed
good and decent. Unfortunately, this happy time was not to last. The 1960s
saw the assassination of President Kennedy, race riots in numerous cities, the
Vietnam War and the protests against it, the civil rights movement, the assas-
sinations of Dr. Martin Luther King Jr. and Robert Kennedy, a brutal Democratic Convention in 1968, and an unraveling of the tightly woven fabric of
American peace and prosperity. The American landscape had drastically
changed between 1960 and 1970, in part for the better and in part for the worse.

But the Western world and the United States changed in other important
ways in the '60s. The traditional and dominant ways of approaching history,
philosophy, theology, and other disciplines came under a sustained assault.
The traditional ways involved a worldview commonly known as the Enlightenment.[1] The Enlightenment (and its corresponding worldview, modernism)

---

[1]There is *not* a single Enlightenment, but rather different Enlightenments at different times. For
example, there is a British Enlightenment, a French Enlightenment, a Dutch Enlightenment, and
so on. It should also be noted that each Enlightenment divides into radical, moderate, and

dominated Europe from around 1660 until the start of the French Revolution in 1789. It introduced a number of ideas that challenged traditional Christian ideas, and contributed significantly to the rise of modern science. Christian thinkers were increasingly challenged to defend the faith against a growing secular revolution.

Given that the Enlightenment worldview was often known as modernism, many thought an appropriate label for the new view was postmodernism, based on the simple ideas that it both came after modernism and that it seemed to reject key modernist beliefs. Postmodernism, whatever exactly it was, caught on in literary circles, philosophy, theology, history, and the social sciences. Through the work of the philosopher Thomas Kuhn, it was also seen as attacking the central ideas of science and its claims to certain knowledge and truth. Depending on who and what you read, after the smoke had cleared it didn't seem like much was left standing. These radical changes in culture and the world of ideas happened simultaneously in both North America and much of Europe, with the year 1968 as the pivotal turning point in the final transition from modern to postmodern.

Throughout the 1950s the Western world was still dominated by Enlightenment modernism. By the end of the 1960s this was no longer the case. In this book we will attempt both to give an overview of modernism and then to seek to define postmodernism in a manner that does justice to its breadth and variety. We intend to aid the reader in understanding postmodernism, and we hope to thoroughly and fairly evaluate postmodernism from a Christian perspective.

We will limit how much we write about leading postmodern thinkers such as Friedrich Nietzsche, Michel Foucault, Jacques Derrida, Jean-François

---

conservative elements. Still, all of these Enlightenments had some broad trends in common. This general Enlightenment is often dated from around 1660 (with the work of the philosopher Benedict Spinoza) until 1789 (the beginning of the French Revolution). But the influence and dominance of leading Enlightenment beliefs would continue up until the 1960s. The best single volumes on the Enlightenment(s) are Jonathan Israel, *Enlightenment Contested: Philosophy, Modernity, and the Emancipation of Man 1670–1732* (New York: Oxford University Press, 2006); Margaret C. Jacob, *The Radical Enlightenment: Pantheists, Freemasons, and Republicans*, 2nd ed. (Lafayette, LA: Cornerstone, 2006); Roy Porter, *The Creation of the Modern World: The Untold Story of the British Enlightenment* (New York: Norton, 2000); Peter Gay, *The Enlightenment: An Interpretation, vol. 1, The Rise of Modern Paganism* (New York: W. W. Norton, 1977); Darrin M. McMahon, *Enemies of the Enlightenment: The French Counter-Enlightenment and the Making of Modernity* (New York: Oxford University Press, 2002); and J. G. A. Pocock's three-volume work on the Enlightenment, *Barbarism and Religion* (Cambridge: Cambridge University Press, 2001).

Lyotard, and Richard Rorty. We do this not because they are not worth studying, but because they are difficult to write about in a manner that is both clear and accessible to those without a substantial amount of background knowledge. Rather, we will focus on the major themes of postmodernism and weave in some of these thinkers along the way. We believe this topical approach makes the understanding of postmodernism an easier task than an approach that focuses on leading postmodern thinkers. Postmodernism has challenged how evangelical Christians think about the gospel,[2] about the Scriptures as the inspired Word of God, about knowledge, and about truth itself. If the leading postmodern theologians are correct, then traditional Christianity needs to be overhauled in some significant ways.[3] This overhaul would involve more than mere cosmetic surgery, but rather a radical reorientation and revisioning of the whole of Christian theology and Christian life. In 1 Peter 3:15, Peter writes that we should "always be prepared to give an answer to everyone who asks you to give the reason for the hope that you have. But do this with gentleness and respect." And Paul writes in 2 Corinthians 10:5 that "we demolish arguments and every pretension that sets itself up against the knowledge of God, and we take captive every thought to make it obedient to Christ." So both Peter and Paul call on us as Christians to use our minds well in the defense of the faith and in our examination of various philosophies and theologies.

DEFINING POSTMODERNISM

Before we are in a decent position to present and evaluate postmodernism, we first need to know what it is. One cannot think clearly about a belief or worldview that cannot first be defined. But a number of definitions have been suggested,[4] and there are even some thinkers who aren't sure it *can* be carefully defined.[5] It should also be noted that a number of books and articles on postmodernism never get around to giving a

---

[2]See Jon Hinkson and Greg Ganssle, "Epistemology at the Core of Postmodernism: Rorty, Foucault, and the Gospel," in *Telling the Truth: Evangelizing Postmoderns*, ed. D. A. Carson (Grand Rapids: Zondervan, 2000), 68.

[3]See particularly the work of Stanley Grenz, John Franke, Brian McLaren, and James K. A. Smith here. All advocate some version of what can be termed postmodernism.

[4]For a number of different approaches to postmodernism, see Stewart E. Kelly, *Truth Considered and Applied: Examining Postmodernism, History, and Christian Faith* (Nashville: B&H Academic, 2011), 49-65.

[5]See Ernest Gellner, *Postmodernism, Reason, and Religion* (London: Routledge, 1992), 22.

definition of it, perhaps because they think it is obvious or because they themselves are not sure exactly what it is. In this book we will understand postmodernism both as a worldview (which includes a number of beliefs about the nature of knowledge and reality) and as the worldview that follows Enlightenment modernism. In the first sense, postmodernism can be understood philosophically, while in the latter sense it is better understood historically—as a particular worldview that follows in time another particular worldview.

Before we attempt an initial definition, one more matter needs to be discussed. This involves what has often been called the principle of charity. The basic idea here is that when we read and seek to understand a differing view, we should always give the benefit of the doubt (act charitably) toward the view and its author. If there are two ways to read a particular page or passage, and one of them makes the author look like an idiot while the other one does not, the kind or charitable thing to do is to understand them in the second sense. In an important sense this is simply applying the basic message of 1 Corinthians 13 to our fellow humans. It is kind and charitable to give someone the benefit of the doubt, and unkind not to do so. In what follows we will make every effort to read and understand with this principle in mind. A simple example is as follows: a few years back, Larry King of CNN fame made the following comment about some people filling sandbags to aid in flood control: "It's wonderful that we have eight-year-old boys filling sandbags with old women." We suspect that what he meant to say was something like the following: "It's wonderful that we have eight-year-old boys and old women filling sandbags together." Given the principle of charity, we understand King to mean that people were working together rather than that boys were stuffing sandbags with the elderly. Similarly, advocates of postmodernism will be understood as trying to make sensible (rather than ridiculous) claims, unless we have good evidence to the contrary.

Now we are in a position to offer an initial definition of postmodernism. We believe that postmodernism is committed to all of the following beliefs:[6]

---

[6]Though not necessarily to only these beliefs. Even in a book of some length we are being selective in what we write about and what we don't. We think what we have selected are the core or essential components of postmodernism. We also readily confess that some difficult matters will be simplified, though hopefully not to the point of distortion.

1 *Postmodernism challenges the Enlightenment confidence in human reason.*
This tenet involves rejection of the key beliefs of Enlightenment modernism, especially the confidence in human reason and René Descartes's conviction that we could achieve certain knowledge by following his method. Descartes's thought is still admired by many, though we believe he set his sights too high, demanding a level of certainty only rarely attained by humans.

2 *Postmoderns believe the human person is heavily situated rather than a neutral observer.*
Postmoderns place heavy emphasis on the fact that our beliefs, values, and worldviews are all significantly, if not entirely, shaped by our situation in life. The big word for this is *situatedness*—the idea that we humans cannot look at the world/reality with complete objectivity, but only from a particular point of view that shows the massive influence of culture and the environment we grew up in.

3 *Postmoderns reject the idea that language simply and transparently captures the world around us.*
Modernism had a good deal of confidence in the ability of language to capture or mirror the external realities to which it referred. So the claim "The cat is on the mat" captures the ideas that there is a cat (external to our minds), a mat, and that the cat has a particular relation to the mat (she is on it). Such an understanding views language as stable and unchanging over time. Many postmodern thinkers reject the idea that language accurately represents external realities and the idea that language is stable over time. If the modernist view of language is mistaken, it undermines some of the main tenets of the Enlightenment.

4 *Postmodern thinkers view truth as something that is created/constructed by human beings, rather than something discovered that is (in some sense) already out there.*
Descartes, John Locke, and many other later philosophers viewed truth as something that exists prior to humans' thinking about it. So, for example, the claim "dinosaurs existed" was thought to be true even if no human ever thought about it. This is because dinosaurs existed well before humans ever came on the scene. But suppose this understanding of truth is mistaken? Suppose truth is created (or "constructed") rather than discovered. Many postmoderns claim that we humans build or construct truth, rather than

discover some truth which already existed. This is a complicated matter, one we will develop in more detail later in the book.

5 *Postmodern thinkers reject the idea that the human self is stable and continuous over time.*

Descartes and his fellow moderns[7] believed that the human self endured over time, was relatively unchanging, and had a relatively fixed human nature. Postmoderns, following Friedrich Nietzsche and David Hume, think the idea of an enduring self is a fiction. They see the self as ever changing, as constructed by both our choices and the constant environmental influences around us, and they reject the idea of the self as conceived of both by many moderns and by traditional Christianity.

6 *Postmoderns have gnawing doubts as to whether the methods used by historians and those in the social sciences provide any hope of arriving at objective truth.*

In the 1950s the great majority of historians and social scientists still believed that certain methods carefully followed would lead us to some degree of objective knowledge and to truth. This view is sometimes labeled methodological objectivity. A historian carefully following methodological objectivity would be in an excellent position to know various historical truths. Such truths were better described as discovered than created. Postmoderns, however, see the idea of methodological objectivity as very much worthy of our rejection. The results of such methods, they argue, are primarily reflective of our environment and our subjective choices (the idea of situatedness again), and are thus not scientific or purely reasonable.

7 *Postmoderns challenge the traditional idea that Europe and North America are somehow (morally) superior to countries in Asia, Africa, and so on.*

One of the central claims of most postmodern thinkers is that human history, rather than being marked by fairness and decency, has instead been characterized by massive oppression. So though the United States is founded on some very impressive documents (the Constitution and the Declaration of Independence), American history has often failed to live up to those ideals. Not everyone has been treated well. For example, African Americans, women, Native Americans, Asians, Hispanics, Jews, Catholics, the Irish, laborers, the

---

[7]Not all moderns agreed with Descartes. David Hume is a notable exception here.

poor, and the disabled[8] have all been the victims of significant oppression over a long period of time. History texts in the past often turned a blind eye to this oppression,[9] and instead focused on the achievements of an elite few, usually white men. Beginning in the 1960s many historians began to focus on how common, ordinary people lived from day to day, writing rich histories about women, African Americans, the poor, and many others.[10] There was an emphasis on a plurality of voices and a number of perspectives rather than the single (sometimes elitist) voice of the most powerful groups in society.

8 *Postmoderns have come to increasingly see truth as more therapeutic in nature than as static and objective.*

Prior to the 1960s those who doubted the existence of truth were still a distinct minority.[11] The rise of postmodernism has changed all that. Richard Rorty, for example, began his academic career teaching philosophy at Princeton. By the end of his career he had moved away from Princeton and away from traditional ideas of truth to teaching comparative literature. He was convinced that rather than possessing truth, all we humans have left is local stories (what life seems like from some particular point of view) rather than a larger story (sometimes called a metanarrative; see number 9 below) that is true for everyone. Rorty hoped that people would adopt a politically liberal humanism, but he himself admitted that it was no truer than any other view. Rorty and others saw human situatedness (or embeddedness) as making it impossible for any human to be in a position to make claims that are genuinely true. So better views are not any "truer" than any other view, but they could better help us cope with the difficulties of life. On this view coping takes the place of truth, and better views are seen as *therapeutic.*

---

[8]This list is not intended to be exhaustive.

[9]For example, most American history textbooks in the 1930s have little to say about the treatment of African Americans, women, organized labor, or other groups mentioned above.

[10]See Leon Litwack, *Trouble in Mind: Black Southerners in the Age of Jim Crow* (New York: Knopf, 1998); William H. Chafe, *The American Woman: Her Changing Social, Economic, and Political Roles, 1920-1970* (New York: Oxford University Press, 1972); and Michael Harrington, *The Other America: Poverty in the United States* (New York: Scribner, 1997). For a textbook with a nontraditional approach, see Nelson Lichtenstein et al., *Who Built America? Working People and the Nation's Economy, Politics, Culture, and Society*, 2 vols. (New York: Worth, 2000).

[11]The noted American historians Charles Beard and Carl Becker both embraced some form of relativism in the '20s and '30s, only to be "cured" of their views by the obvious evil of Hitler and the Nazis. The traditional line is that there are no atheists in foxholes. One can also make the case that there aren't any relativists there either!

9 *Postmoderns see metanarratives as inherently oppressive and as generally beyond the ability of humans to grasp them.*
Lyotard is perhaps best known for defining postmodernism as "incredulity towards metanarratives."[12] A metanarrative is an overarching story or worldview, a story that claims to describe the main elements of reality in one big story. Possible examples of metanarratives include Marxism, Enlightenment humanism (or modernism), scientism,[13] Christianity, and Buddhism. Some have understood Lyotard's claim to rule out Christianity, while others[14] have claimed that Lyotard did not have Christianity in mind when he made this claim.

10 *Postmoderns reject what has been called the omnicompetence of reason.*
Enlightenment thinkers clearly display a significant confidence in human reason and its ability to know truth, to know it with certainty, and to use those truths to bring about the steady improvement of the human race. Thus reason properly applied leads to the progress of civilization. Alister McGrath has referred to this confidence as a belief in the omnicompetence of human reason.[15] Descartes, Locke, Gottfried Wilhelm Leibniz, Thomas Reid, the French philosophes, and Kant all possess large measures of this faith in reason.[16] Postmodern thinkers, on the other hand, challenge and/or reject this confidence as unwarranted. Thinkers from Nietzsche to Foucault to Derrida led the assault against this confidence. They saw reason as far more limited, certainty as an illusion, and the idea of human progress as being shattered by the devastation of World War I, the death camps and the Holocaust, and the mass slaughter of millions in the most violent century in human history.[17] Many late nineteenth-century thinkers had high hopes for the twentieth century, where the lion would lie down with the lamb and war would be but a distant memory. Well, the lion did lie with the lamb and

---

[12]See Jean-François Lyotard, *The Postmodern Condition: A Report on Knowledge*, trans. Geoff Bennington and Brian Massumi (Minneapolis: University of Minnesota Press, 1984), xxiv-xxv.
[13]"Scientism" includes both the commitment to scientific reasoning and to the idea that science (and not much else) can be counted on for steadily improving the human condition and the world in which we live.
[14]Two prominent Christian thinkers who take this view are James K. A. Smith and Merold Westphal.
[15]See Alister McGrath, *Christian Theology: An Introduction*, 3rd ed. (Oxford: Blackwell, 2001), 91.
[16]There are notable exceptions, such as the Scottish skeptic David Hume.
[17]The perceptive reader will note that many of these awful events were in the twentieth century, after Nietzsche had already died. Nietzsche's name is included here because of his massive influence on postmodern thought.

then ate it, putting to rout the idea of an extended period of peace and prosperity in the twentieth century.

The previous pages make it apparent that postmodernism is a complicated and diverse movement, one that challenges evangelical Christians to carefully rethink their beliefs and traditions. Evangelical Christianity traditionally has been committed to the objectivity of truth, the stability of language, and the idea that the Christian metanarrative is far from oppressive, as well as to a degree of trust in the deliverances of human reason. In this book we seek to carefully understand and respond to the various challenges presented by postmodernism, and to determine whether some Christian beliefs need to be modified or rejected in light of these challenges.

CONCERNING POINT OF VIEW

For many years philosophers, theologians, and historians all believed that their particular disciplines could be approached with a cool and dispassionate neutrality. In other words, through sufficient effort we could be fair and impartial observers and arrive in the end with a firm grasp of objective truths. This idea of the neutral observer arises out of the Enlightenment, the rise of science, and a supreme confidence in the human ability to reason. Some central Enlightenment thinkers thought we humans could relate to reality much as an ideal modern-day baseball umpire interacts with baseball. The umpire knows the rules, he plays no favorites, and he fairly and even-handedly applies the rules to both teams, never showing any hint of favoritism or undue bias.[18] The umpire is thus a sort of scientific observer of all that goes on around him. In theology, some theologians believed that theology itself could be grounded on wholly scientific principles, and that the careful theologian maintained a strict adherence to the proper principles of biblical criticism. And in twentieth-century Western philosophy, a movement known as logical positivism attempted to turn philosophy into a scientific discipline that ruthlessly applied a strict set of rules about what did and did not count as knowledge. Unfortunately, neither liberal theologians nor the positivists succeeded in their efforts to make their discipline truly scientific. The theologically liberal approach is clearly biased against belief

---

[18]It should be noted that the word *bias* is not a bad thing. The bad sort of bias is *arbitrary bias*, where the point of view or angle of seeing is unsupported by evidence of any sort. Throughout this book we will use the word in the decent, wholesome, and nonarbitrary sense (unless otherwise noted).

in miracles, a bias that no decent evangelical scholar can agree with.[19] And positivism, after a brief and glorious fling at the top of the charts (in philosophical circles), died a painful and (some would say) richly deserved death around 1960.[20] American historians, though also priding themselves on their scientific approach to history, fared no better than their counterparts in theology or philosophy. The historian Peter Novick eloquently describes the rise and fall of such an approach in his book *That Noble Dream*.[21]

It is now widely acknowledged by Christian and non-Christian scholars alike that such neutrality is not humanly possible. N. T. Wright,[22] Jay Wood,[23] Alan Padgett,[24] and a number of other fine evangelical scholars readily admit this. Does this mean that we are all caught in a web of our own biases, prejudices, and cultural influences? The answer is no, though it requires both training and discipline to minimize the influence of such factors, though some degree of influence will always be present. As scholars we should identify our assumptions and biases, put them on the table so to speak, and write and think from a point of view that acknowledges all these influences. That is what we intend to do in this book.

OUR WORKING ASSUMPTIONS

So what sorts of assumptions do we have? In what follows we list both our core beliefs and a few facts about ourselves that influence how we look at the world.

Background influences:

1. We are evangelical Christians.

2. We are Protestants.

3. Our training is in philosophy and theology.

---

[19]For more on the shortcomings of the method of theological liberals, see Stewart E. Kelly, "Miracle, Method, and Metaphysics: Philosophy and the Quest for the Historical Jesus," *Trinity Journal* 29, no. 1 (2008): 45-63.

[20]Alvin Plantinga has been one of many philosophers to celebrate the demise of positivism. See his "Advice to Christian Philosophers," *Faith and Philosophy* 1, no. 3 (1984): 253-71.

[21]For a detailed overview of the early years of the historical profession in America see Kelly, *Truth Considered and Applied*, esp. 153-56.

[22]See N. T. Wright, *The New Testament and the People of God* (Minneapolis: Fortress, 1992).

[23]See W. Jay Wood, *Epistemology: Becoming Epistemically Virtuous* (Downers Grove, IL: InterVarsity Press, 1998).

[24]See Alan Padgett, "Advice for Religious Historians: On the Myth of a Purely Historical Jesus," in *The Resurrection*, ed. Stephen T. Davis, Gerald O'Collins, and Daniel Kendall (Oxford: Oxford University Press, 1997).

4. We are both trained in what is known as the analytic tradition (as opposed to the continental tradition).

5. Politically, we are in the conservative to moderate range on most issues.

Core beliefs:

1. We have a modest confidence in human reason.

2. We are committed to the inspiration and inerrancy of Scripture.

3. We are committed to make every effort to treat every view with respect and care.

We offer our conclusions not in the spirit of Descartes (who thought a high level of certainty was possible), but rather as broadly reasonable claims, submitted by fallible and situated knowers. We readily admit we are answerable to the same standards as all other humans: the truths (and Truth) of Scripture, the laws of logic, and the carefully sifted evidence of human experience and human reason. We do not claim that our views are always the only view possible, though we do offer them as what we take to be the best explanation of all things considered.

The list above does not exhaust our various assumptions and biases, though it does give a representative sample. We both also reject the idea that all of our beliefs and values somehow reduce to one or more of the factors that have influenced us. If that were true, then all we would be doing is sharing our own stories with no claim to truth or reasonability. Yes, many factors shape and influence us, but that is a long way from any sort of ideological determinism, where truth claims and claims about rationality merely reduce to our respective social situations. This is an extreme version of the idea of the sociology of knowledge.

OVERVIEW OF THE BOOK

In the upcoming pages we cover a lot of ground, make a number of substantive (and controversial) claims, and seek to understand and evaluate the family of views known as postmodernism from a viewpoint grounded in the truths of the Scriptures and the historic Christian faith. We devote a full chapter to each of the ten main strands of postmodernism, and even in this we are being selective and not dealing with many worthwhile issues. To deal with all the relevant issues in significant detail would require a much longer book, one that would please neither our readers nor our editors. So what we offer is an overview of some key themes of postmodernism. Some of the issues we address are, to put it simply, complicated. At times we seek to simplify, but hopefully never to the point of distortion or caricature.

In chapter two we present a framework for understanding postmodernism. The framework helps to make sense of the background of the Enlightenment, the context in which postmodernism arose, and the various historical events that contributed to the decline of Enlightenment modernism. The wild and crazy 1960s and the social unrest that marked this time period clearly contributed to the breakdown of the older ways and the rise of new (and not always improved) ways of understanding truth, knowledge, language, and the broader world around us. It is fair to say that the world looked very different in 1970 than it did to many academics in the late '50s and early '60s. The Vietnam War, the events in Paris in 1968, the rise of antiwar and free speech movements, and a general disillusionment with traditional authorities all converged to challenge the old ways and to foster new ways of looking at familiar issues.

In chapter three we offer an overview of the worldview spawned by the Enlightenment, namely, modernism. Modernism challenged the authority of the Scriptures, the role of the church, and a view of the universe in which God was at the center of things. Modernism questions the existence of God, seriously doubts the doctrine of original sin, elevates human reason, sees science as the key to future human progress, and generally doubts the miraculous. Traditional Christianity was also challenged by deism,[25] Socinianism,[26] the reduction of Christianity to mere morality,[27] and good old-fashioned humanism.[28] But as the twentieth century unfolded, the central beliefs of modernism began to crumble one by one, only to be replaced a variety of views that can be conveniently grouped under the heading "postmodern."

---

[25]Benjamin Franklin, Thomas Jefferson, and the French philosophe Voltaire all embrace some form of deism.

[26]Socinians question the traditional doctrine of the Trinity and reject the divinity of Jesus. Both Isaac Newton and John Locke show marked sympathies with Socinianism. On Locke, see John Marshall, *John Locke, Toleration, and Early Enlightenment Culture* (Cambridge: Cambridge University Press, 2010).

[27]Many Enlightenment thinkers move in this direction, though the most influential is Immanuel Kant, one of the leading thinkers of the Enlightenment and the Western intellectual tradition.

[28]The Marquis de Condorcet is a prime example here.

In chapter four we discuss Enlightenment thinkers, such as Descartes, who were confident of their ability to be neutral, detached, and scientific observers of the world around them. By focusing and reflecting, we could see the world as it truly is, rising above the influence of our social situation. The first professional American historians proudly proclaimed their ability to produce scientific histories.[29] Many prominent theologians likewise proudly proclaimed that their scientific and scholarly approach to the New Testament ruled out belief in the miraculous, including the belief in the bodily resurrection of Jesus. Traditional Christianity, needless to say, did not fare well in the work of such scholars. Some leading historians such as Charles Beard and Carl Becker rejected the idea that a scholar could be neutral and detached, but the idea of scientific neutrality lasted well into the 1980s in theological circles.[30] Postmodern thinkers, following the lead of Beard, Becker, Thomas Kuhn, Nietzsche, and others, readily admitted that there was no neutral starting point. In evangelical circles the New Testament scholar N. T. Wright has made it clear that he does not strive for the neutrality and detachment of his modernist predecessors. We will argue that the recognition of the idea that humans are embedded (or situated) is simply facing up to what has been true all along. More importantly, we argue that recognition of this preexisting point of view does nothing to undermine the reasonableness of traditional Christianity.

Most thinkers before 1900[31] had confidence that human language had the ability to accurately capture the external reality to which it referred. In this sense language was seen as the mirror (or faithful copy) of nature. Under the influence of Ferdinand de Saussure, Roland Barthes, Jacques Derrida, and others, language was no longer seen as having the ability to mirror reality. It was now seen as an arbitrary and unstable (changing over time) human invention that did not generally refer to anything outside itself. In the United States the assault on the traditional mirroring function of language was carried out by the philosopher Richard Rorty. Though Rorty did

---

[29]The role model for these historians, working in the 1880s, is the great German historian Leopold von Ranke, who was thought to promote the idea that the writing of history was a straightforward and scientific matter.

[30]For example, John Meier and E. P. Sanders, both brilliant and well-respected theologians, clearly still thought such an approach was possible in their written works in the '80s and later. See John P. Meier, *A Marginal Jew: Rethinking the Historical Jesus*, vol. 1, *The Roots of the Problem and Person* (New York: Doubleday, 1991); and E. P. Sanders, *Jesus and Judaism* (Philadelphia: Fortress, 1985).

[31]Nietzsche is a notable exception here.

not doubt the existence of the external world, he did doubt the ability of humans to genuinely know anything about that world. In chapter five, we conclude with a critique of this view of language.

In John 18:38, Pilate famously asks, "What is truth?" Such questions have long been at the heart of the philosophical enterprise and also at the center of orthodox Christianity. To commit oneself to the good news of the gospel is to commit oneself to the truth of the message. If Jesus truly died and rose again it is good news indeed, but if he did not we are most of all to be pitied (see 1 Cor 15:14-19). In chapter six we focus on the nature of truth and whether it is better described as something discovered or something created or constructed. Much hinges on this issue if traditional Christianity is to be taken seriously, and we seek to determine to what extent, if any, truth is merely a human creation. Traditional Christianity has always affirmed that God speaks truthfully in and through the Scriptures, and that these truths transcend (rise above) our various and sundry positions in life. Some evangelicals argue, correctly we think, that to tell the good news of the gospel is to speak objective truth to a lost and dying world.[32] As such, traditional Christianity is a broad and overarching story (a metanarrative) of the human condition and the work of the one true God.

Descartes, who sought to use autonomous human reason[33] in his efforts to find an absolutely certain starting point for philosophy, is often identified as the first truly modern philosopher. Skepticism, a view that seriously questioned the human ability to acquire genuine knowledge, was the enemy, and Descartes searched high and low for a firm foundation in response to the skeptics. He doubted everything it was possible to doubt, eventually arriving at what he took to be an absolutely certain truth.[34] He discovered that he could not doubt that he was doubting, hence his famous phrase, "I think, therefore I am," by which, roughly speaking, he means that if I am thinking, then I must exist. This he declared to be indubitably true, that is, incapable of being doubted. Philosophers ever since have wondered what the word *I* refers to here. Descartes's answer would be "the self," the person or subject

---

[32]See D. A. Carson, *The Gagging of God: Christianity Confronts Pluralism* (Grand Rapids: Zondervan, 1996), 507.

[33]By "autonomous" here we mean consciously independent of the Christian tradition, relying solely on unaided human reason.

[34]Ironically, not very many philosophers since Descartes, Christian or otherwise, have agreed with Descartes's starting point.

who is doing the thinking. Okay, but how does he know that there is a self in the first place, or at least a self that stays the same over time? The short answer is that he doesn't; he pretty much assumes a particular understanding of the human self (what makes us who we are) over time. The question then arises whether we should think of the self as remaining constant over time—that I am the same person from one day to the next—or whether it is constantly in flux. For example, Hume questions whether Descartes's view of the human self holds up under scrutiny, and Buddhist thought in general holds a differing conception of the self. Most postmodern thinkers have tended to side with Hume and against Descartes on this matter. Thus in chapter seven we examine various understandings of the self, including postmodern developments.

The 1600s in Europe gave rise to the remarkable rise of modern science, led by eminent scientists such as Francis Bacon and Isaac Newton. Both leading scientists and leading philosophers (such as Descartes and Locke) firmly believed that humans could use objective (or science-like) methods to guarantee the individual genuine knowledge of the world around us. So, the idea goes, if someone seeking knowledge follows the rules of science properly, then they have an excellent chance of acquiring bias-free, objective knowledge. Of course, this method assumes that the observer is *ahistorical*, meaning they are not trapped within their own cultural situation and influences, but instead are able to rise above the various influences to achieve truly certain knowledge. Postmodern thinkers are not impressed. They seriously question both the idea that the observer is not situated or embedded in their social context,[35] and that the rules of knowledge seeking are either as obvious or as easy to grasp as was thought in the Enlightenment. In chapter eight we thus investigate the postmodern critique of what we will call methodological objectivity, and we seek to determine how much validity there is in the criticism. We also seek to defend a version of scientific realism against postmoderns who tend to advocate some form of antirealism.

As noted above, well into the twentieth century many American history texts had relatively little to say about the rather shabby treatment of various minorities in American history. So the idea that African Americans, women,

---

[35]The social context would include everything that influences the individual, ranging from family to school to neighborhood to subculture to the media and beyond.

Latinos, Jews, Native Americans, and others had been systematically mistreated received little attention and less discussion. But the writing of
American history began to shift its focus in the 1960s and 1970s, and the
growing awareness of social and cultural history gave rise to an increased
sensitivity to these difficult aspects of our past.[36] In fact, in postmodern con-
ceptions of history it came to be considered more accurate to write of the
oppression of all these groups, and to admit that the previous texts in
American history distorted the past by not recognizing the existence and
degree of oppression of these groups. In chapter nine we investigate both
these claims as well as the more radical idea that all history writing is
somehow oppressive.

In chapter ten we focus on Lyotard's well-known claim "Simplifying to
the extreme, I define postmodern as incredulity towards metanarratives."[37]
There are a number of important issues here, of which we examine only two
or three. The first issue deals with what exactly a metanarrative is, which not
surprisingly includes the issue of what a narrative is. A second issue deals
with what exactly Lyotard's claim means. Does he have all worldviews in
mind (including Christianity), or does he just have a few specific views in
mind that do not include Christianity?

In chapter eleven we tackle issues surrounding the concept of truth. To
say that the idea of truth is a complicated matter is an understatement of
colossal proportions.[38] There are numerous views among philosophers regarding the nature of truth, and we examine a few of the leading contenders.
We will argue that one of the many understandings of truth is more reasonable than the others.

Finally, in chapter twelve we take a look at the Enlightenment understanding of human reason and how that understanding influenced the
course of subsequent thought. We also examine the postmodern rejection
of Enlightenment reason and whether postmodern views of human reason
are any closer to the truth than the various Enlightenment views. And

---

[36]For an excellent introduction to these issues and much more, see Joyce Appleby, Lynn Hunt, and
  Margaret Jacob, *Telling the Truth about History* (New York: Norton, 1994).
[37]Lyotard, *Postmodern Condition*, xxiv.
[38]There are a number of helpful introductions to the various theories of truth, but readers should
  be forewarned that virtually all of them are tough sledding. This is not because they write poorly
  or don't grasp the issues, but because there are some very difficult issues tied up with the idea
  of truth. One of the best such books is by Richard Kirkham. See his *Theories of Truth: A Critical
  Introduction* (Cambridge, MA: MIT Press, 1995).

though we agree with the postmoderns that the Enlightenment view of reason has significant flaws, we also see postmodern views as not doing justice to the concept of reason properly understood. We defend a view of knowledge known as modest foundationalism.

In chapters thirteen and fourteen we conclude the book by focusing on the central claims of traditional Christianity as embodied in the good news of the gospel and by summarizing what we have done in the book and the many issues that remain to be more fully addressed in the future. Those hoping to find either a sustained critique of all that postmoderns believe or a welcome embrace of all postmodernism suggests will be sorely disappointed. We hope to fairly present and examine postmodernism, to evaluate it in the light of biblical Christianity, and to challenge the reader to carefully and humbly draw their own conclusions about what we present.

Suggested Readings

Copan, Paul. *True for You, but Not for Me: Overcoming Objections to Christian Faith*. Grand Rapids: Bethany House, 2009. A very readable approach to the idea of truth by a leading evangelical philosopher.

Grenz, Stanley J. *A Primer on Postmodernism*. Grand Rapids: Eerdmans, 1996. An introductory book by a leading evangelical who is sympathetic to some major postmodern claims.

Groothuis, Douglas. *Truth Decay: Defending Christianity Against the Challenges of Postmodernism*. Downers Grove, IL: InterVarsity Press, 2000. One of the better introductions to postmodernism by an evangelical philosopher.

White, Heath. *Postmodernism 101: A First Course for the Curious Christian*. Grand Rapids: Brazos, 2006. A brief and highly readable introduction to postmodernism.

2

CRITERIA FOR EVALUATING
POSTMODERNISM

HOW SHALL WE EVALUATE POSTMODERNISM?

If we wish to be in a good position to properly evaluate postmodernism, we have a number of challenges ahead of us. First, we need to have some idea of what it is, as it makes no sense to critique a view when you don't know what that view is![1] Second, if we adopt criteria that are ultimately relativistic (tied to some particular or local standard) rather than objective in nature, then we have no hope of succeeding. For example, if truth is relative to each country, then Japan, Nigeria, China, the United States, and the Netherlands would all have their own version of truth. So the version of postmodernism we seek to evaluate might be, on this approach, true in China and Japan, but false in the other three countries. Furthermore, we can imagine each country having different subcultures with their own standard of truth. So there would not be just one standard of truth in China, but rather one for Shandong province, one for Jiangsu, and so on for each of the twenty-two provinces in China. A third point is that we should, if possible, adopt a framework that is not hostile to postmodernism as such. This would be to stack the deck against a favorable reading of postmodernism. For the annual North Dakota Chicken Casserole Contest (an imaginary contest) you don't invite three vegetarians to be the judges. Similarly, for the annual Great Polka Music

---

[1]In the Supreme Court case Jacobellis v. Ohio, Justice Potter Stewart famously commented, "I don't know what it is, but I know it when I see it." It is difficult to make illegal what you can't define!

Festival you don't ask three heavy metal devotees to be the judges, unless they somehow like both heavy metal and polka music (a rare but possible combination). So we need to do the best we can to choose criteria that give postmodernism a fair and balanced hearing.

If Richard Rorty and Friedrich Nietzsche are correct, then the traditional philosophical pursuit of knowledge is pretty much pointless. Rorty thinks we need to replace the (outmoded) concept of truth with something more therapeutic in nature, something that will help us cope with the demands and difficulties of human existence (as regularly portrayed in soap operas and country-western music). We will have more to say about Rorty later, though for now it is enough to say we're not sure that Rorty's view would be of any great help in evaluating postmodernism. In a similar vein, Nietzsche often seems to believe that a view is best when it is life affirming, rather than if it is "true," whatever that might mean (and the standards for what is life affirming are particular to Nietzsche's own outlook on life). We will adopt criteria that possess a measure of objectivity for the following reasons: (1) many postmodern thinkers are comfortable with a modest commitment to objectivity and truth;[2] (2) such a standard is consistent with the beliefs of traditional Christianity; and (3) any set of nonobjective standards we might adopt would be hopelessly arbitrary.

One matter that consistently complicates attempts to fairly understand postmodern thinkers is that they at times make rather outlandish claims, claims that seem to say that there is no truth, or no facts, or no objective truth, or the like. Foucault himself once wrote, "I am well aware that I have never written anything but fictions."[3] This claim, taken literally at face value, does not inspire hope. But the central questions here are (1) what is the context of this quote? and (2) does this mean he denies the existence of (objective) truth? We will argue that Foucault is best understood as *not* being a relativist, but rather a thinker who rejects certain traditional versions of truth. The next line from Foucault, immediately after the one just mentioned, is "I do not mean to say,

---

[2]We will argue that the assertion that they are all relativists with respect to truth is clearly false. Nietzsche, Foucault, and others clearly make a number of claims that require some degree of objectivity if we are to take them seriously. See Pauline Rosenau for a sensible take on all this; Pauline Marie Rosenau, *Post-modernism and the Social Sciences* (Princeton, NJ: Princeton University Press, 1991).

[3]Michel Foucault, *Power/Knowledge: Selected Interviews and Other Writings, 1972–1977*, ed. Colin Gordon (New York: Pantheon, 1980), 151.

however, that truth is therefore absent."[4] So whatever else Foucault might mean here, it seems doubtful that he is rejecting any and all ideas of truth.[5]

THE HASKELL PRINCIPLE

There is a very fine book on the history of the history profession in the United States written by Peter Novick, a highly esteemed historian who taught at the University of Chicago for many years. Novick's book, *That Noble Dream*, is an eloquent six-hundred-page-plus overview and analysis of the history profession in the United States. His book focuses on the rise, reign, and demise of the idea of history as an objective ("scientific") profession. He concludes by lamenting the loss of this objectivity and is unsure what historians should replace it with. But a careful reading of Novick's generally impressive and learned work clearly indicates that Novick himself does not really reject the idea of objectivity. Thomas Haskell persuasively argues in his *Objectivity Is Not Neutrality* that Novick is very much mistaken. First, he makes a strong case that Novick doesn't properly understand what objectivity amounts to. And second, he demonstrates that Novick's entire book presupposes the very idea of objectivity he is attacking.

Novick thinks that the "objective historian's role is that of a neutral, or disinterested, judge; it must never degenerate into that of an advocate or, even worse, propagandist."[6] The fairly obvious problem is that human beings are not capable of this sort of impartial neutrality, and never have been. Humans lack the ability to totally set aside all the factors that color and shape how they look at the world: gender, class, education, family background, genetics, peer influences, the role of media in one's life, ethnicity, and so on. In this sense, as Thomas Nagel has famously argued, there is no view from nowhere.[7] Novick correctly argues that such neutrality is beyond human capabilities, a view echoed by the evangelical New Testament scholar N. T. Wright, who notes that the idea of writing value-free, neutral history is a dream.[8] Novick though, unlike Haskell and Wright, seems to think the

---

[4]Ibid.

[5]A little bit of context goes a long way in determining the meaning of a particular quote.

[6]Peter Novick, *That Noble Dream: "The Objectivity Question" and the American Historical Profession* (Cambridge: Cambridge University Press, 1988), 2.

[7]See Thomas Nagel, *The View from Nowhere* (New York: Oxford University Press, 1986).

[8]See N. T. Wright, *The New Testament and the People of God* (Minneapolis: Fortress, 1992), 82. Wright's view is also the consensus view among evangelical scholars.

traditional historical enterprise is in deep trouble if his notion of objectivity is undermined. Novick himself rejects the idea of objectivity because he thinks it requires human neutrality and that is an ideal not attainable by flesh-and-blood humans.

But Novick is very much mistaken, because the idea of objectivity does not require the commitment to neutrality and impartiality that Novick believes it does. If it did, then any historian who ever wrote passionately in defense of some particular view would automatically be dismissed for their lack of objectivity. Haskell points out that some of the best historical work in recent years has been anything but dispassionate. He mentions the work of Eugene Genovese, a historian of note, who wrote passionately about slavery in the American South but still easily "passes my test of objectivity with plenty of room to spare."[9] Suppose two historians wrote identical articles on a controversial topic. And further suppose that one of them wrote with a burning passion, while the other wrote with relative detachment and little emotional involvement. On Novick's criterion, though the two articles were identical, one would be worthy of praise for writing "objectively," while the other would clearly be guilty of violating the norm of objectivity by writing with passion. This, of course, is nonsense. The same article should receive the same level of praise and/or condemnation. Haskell himself notes that if "objectivity could be reduced simply to neutrality, I would not bother to defend it."[10]

So what exactly does Haskell think that objectivity amounts to? He writes that it requires

> that vital minimum of ascetic self-discipline that enables a person to do such things as abandon wishful thinking, assimilate bad news, discard pleasing interpretations that cannot pass elementary tests of logic, and, most important of all, suspend or bracket one's own perceptions long enough to enter sympathetically into the alien and possibly repugnant perspectives of rival thinkers.[11]

Haskell is getting at the notion of not assuming as true what one wants to be true, including information that may be contrary to one's own original ideas, and allowing other thinkers to receive a fair and even-handed hearing as one would hope they would receive themselves. The upshot here is that

---

[9] Thomas L. Haskell, *Objectivity Is Not Neutrality: Explanatory Schemes in History* (Baltimore: Johns Hopkins University Press, 2000), 148.
[10] Ibid.
[11] Ibid.

objectivity does not equal neutrality, but rather a fair and even-handed portrayal of works that (may) disagree with one's own.

Ironically, Haskell makes evident that Novick's book itself "passes all my tests for objectivity with flying colors."[12] He is, for example, committed to believing in the reality of the past, though in his book he ties this belief to his understanding of objectivity.[13] As Haskell rightly notes, it is not at all clear what would be left of the traditional idea of history-writing if the past is not viewed as real (having objective existence). The fact that Novick spends more than six hundred pages describing this past in detail suggests he probably doesn't really question the objective existence of the past. Novick also criticizes the historian Hayden White for his skeptical (and possibly relativist) views on a number of historical matters. If objectivity is dead and gone, why should we worry about White or even care whether he is a relativist or not? Novick also takes great pains throughout his book to present a number of controversies fairly, and such efforts and the commitment that underlies them are also part and parcel of a commitment to objectivity. For all these reasons it is more than clear that Novick himself is both committed to a degree of objectivity and to its importance for properly writing history.

So with the above in mind, we suggest that the following should be adopted as a helpful tool for evaluating postmodernism (though its application is much broader than that): the Haskell principle. *We should understand thinkers both by what they explicitly claim and by what they presuppose in making such claims.* This makes for a broader and more charitable interpretation, one that better does justice to the thoughts and thinkers being examined. Haskell's own interpretation thus correctly understands Novick to be committed to an ideal that he consistently criticizes. Furthermore, this gives Novick more credit than he would receive if we took his often-stated rejection of objectivity at face value. So Novick looks better, our understanding is broadened and enriched, and everyone is happy.

The question arises, how exactly will the Haskell principle help us better evaluate postmodernism? The answer is that it will encourage a broader (and fairer) reading and interpretation of each postmodern thinker, and at the same time serve as an example of the principle of charity. So when

---

[12]Ibid., 147.
[13]Novick, *That Noble Dream*, 1.

Nietzsche, Foucault, or Derrida make some (seemingly outrageous) claim that suggests there is no objective truth, or that truth is as you like it, we won't jump to the conclusion that they are all relativists and dismiss them accordingly.[14] Nietzsche does have different ideas about truth, Foucault does at times read like a relativist, and Derrida (given his general lack of clarity) can be understood to hold almost any view imaginable. But the substantive commitments in their general writings show them not to be simple-minded relativists, or even relativists at all. Now the Haskell principle may not rescue some thinkers, such as Bruno Latour[15] and Steve Woolgar, who seem very much determined to be as consistently relativistic as possible.

TOWARD A FRAMEWORK FOR UNDERSTANDING POSTMODERNISM

Here we want to briefly present seven considerations that need to be taken seriously if postmodernism is to be given a fair hearing. Two of the considerations offer recommendations for dealing with postmodernism, while the other five are substantive claims:

Two recommendations:

1. We must apply the principle of charity. See above for a brief overview of what this involves. It goes without saying that some of the postmodern views under discussion cry out for a charitable interpretation.

2. We need to understand postmodernism as a diverse movement. Christianity is not a monolithic movement. There are Protestants, Catholics, and Orthodox divisions, and each of these large umbrella movements has numerous subdivisions, especially the Protestants, who subdivide faster than cockroaches can multiply. Baptists, Congregationalists, Lutherans, Methodists, Pentecostals, Presbyterians, and numerous other groups dot the Protestant landscape. In a similar fashion, postmodernism is also not a unified or monolithic view, but rather a family of views gathered under a large umbrella. A few examples are in order here. First, some postmoderns are primarily destructive or negative in their approach, while others are more constructive/affirmative. Second, some postmoderns do push the envelope toward relativism with

---

[14]The dismissal being based (properly so) on the understanding that relativism concerning truth is incompatible with the truths of traditional Christianity.

[15]For an eye-opening take on Latour's intellectual shenanigans, see Alan Sokal, "Professor Latour's Philosophical Mystifications," Alan Sokal personal page, New York University, accessed November 29, 2014, www.physics.nyu.edu/sokal/le_monde_english.html.

respect to truth, while most do not, affirming one or more substantial claims to be "true" in some meaningful sense. And third, postmoderns do not all work out of the continental philosophical tradition, as many are trained in and work within the analytic tradition.

Five substantive claims:

1. We work with a cautious optimism regarding truth and knowledge. We have confidence in human reason, but it is a modest degree of confidence. We believe that a middle course can be steered between two extreme positions:

A. That no genuine knowledge is possible.

and

B. That we can be supremely confident in all that we view as clear and distinct.

Most modern Anglo-American philosophers agree with the postmoderns that Descartes's classical foundationalism has serious problems and merits our rejection. Descartes was supremely confident of his ability to access and know the external world. Modern philosophers are generally less confident, and postmodern philosophers are even less confident than most moderns. The challenge for the postmodern here is to avoid some version of relativism, where "true" simply means something like "true for me" or "true according to my community" or "true according to my culture." If that is all truth amounts to then we are left with what might be called descriptive sociology, where culture A believes *x*, culture B believes not-*x*, culture C believes *y*, and there is no way to judge between differing or competing views. I have my story (about what is true and the like), you have yours, and all God's children have stories. Here no metanarrative is true, only local stories are. The fact that Richard Rorty, eminent philosopher and fashionable postmodern, began his career teaching philosophy and ended teaching comparative literature illustrates the point here. The challenge to the reader and to all evangelicals is to ably defend a view that avoids *both* the Cartesian extreme on the one hand and the relativistic comparative literature extreme on the other.

2. Humans are radically situated. Again, Descartes is the bad guy here. He, like most of his fellow Enlightenment moderns, believed that humans can approach reality from a neutral, detached, scientific viewpoint. Though he endeavored to be neutral, one Descartes scholar writes that his "views on knowledge were conditioned by the time in which he lived, which had witnessed a gradual erosion of beliefs held for centuries."[16] Descartes believed that his method for gaining knowledge not only avoided the errors of methods then current but also provided a certain guarantee for acquiring knowledge.

Such an observer was one without presuppositions, assumptions, biases of any sort, and so on—totally objective and coolly dispassionate. Such a view is problematic to say the least, and is fairly widely rejected both by postmoderns and by evangelical scholars.[17] Postmoderns, on the other hand, believe humans are radically situated or enmeshed in a web of social and psychological influences. They see our position in time, society, and culture as radically shaping how we look at the world and understand it. Not many Americans grow up to be Hindu, while many in India do. Americans are drawn toward football as their favorite sport, while soccer is easily the most popular sport in the majority of other countries in the world. Europeans tend to think more highly of women's rights than do some Middle Easterners. Finally, in honor of my family's recently deceased favorite rodent, Zoe the guinea pig, guinea pigs are seen as good pets in North America, though apparently some in South America view them as a culinary possibility. All this is to take seriously what is often called the *sociology of knowledge*, and to admit the obvious—that culture and/or society plays a massive role in how we see ourselves, our society, our fellow humans, God, and the broader world around us. Some postmoderns write as if these influences actually determine (or cause) our particular beliefs and values, while many evangelicals are more likely to acknowledge merely the powerful influence of such factors.

Sociologists have identified a number of factors that play a prominent role in the socialization and development of human beings. To mention just a few: the family, race, social class, school environment, school curriculum, peers, mass media, and national and local culture.[18] Each of these elements plays an important role in the shaping and development of our personality, our character, our values and beliefs, our attitudes toward others and the world around us, and so forth. One helpful way of understanding postmodernism

---

[16]John Cottingham, "René Descartes," in *A Companion to Epistemology*, ed. Jonathan Dancy, Ernest Sosa, and Matthias Steup, 2nd ed. (Malden, MA: Blackwell, 2009), 307.

[17]See Wright, *New Testament and the People of God*, part 2, for the best overview of the issues here.

[18]For one of the leading sociology texts on this matter, see John J. Macionis, *Sociology*, 11th ed. (Boston: Prentice-Hall, 2007), esp. 121-23, and following.

is to see it as a worldview that gives full and serious attention to this process of socialization. It is true that some will get carried away and see socialization as virtually swallowing up the individual and eliminating free will. But one can grant the massive combined influence of all the above factors and still be committed to free will and human responsibility. To put it simply, the above factors all influence us, but we alone choose. We can lead a thoughtful and reflective life where we become aware of the various factors involved in socialization, but on any given occasion we can act in accordance with the most powerful influences *or* we can act contrary to them. Our belief in free will and responsibility and our knowledge of socialization lead us to affirm that both are true, and there is nothing inherent in postmodernism that requires us to say that we are entirely the product of socialization. The Scriptures consistently hold humans accountable for their actions, and we know of no good reason why we shouldn't enthusiastically agree on this matter.

3. Human history is dominated by the reality of past oppression. We acknowledge that human history is characterized by people's inhumanity to other people, and that along the way many groups have been targeted as inferior and treated with disrespect. We also affirm that Western civilization has produced many worthwhile accomplishments, in medicine, in science, in industry, in living conditions, and in many other regards

4. The privileged status of science is to be doubted. During the Enlightenment (ca. 1660–1789) the scientific paradigm provided the basic model for the pursuit of medical, technological, and other kind of knowledge. Science was viewed as both progressive and heroic,[19] and essentially replaced the church as the final authority on many matters of importance. By diligently seeking after truth, "the universities were able to become, in a sense, the heirs of the churches."[20] We share some of the postmodern concerns about science and question whether it merits the privileged status often granted it in Western culture.

5. Pluralism and tolerance are important realities. One can make a decent case that much of the twentieth century has revolved around one group of

---

[19]See Joyce Appleby, Lynn Hunt, and Margaret Jacob, *Telling the Truth About History* (New York: Norton, 1994), chap. 1.

[20]Mark Noll, "Scientific History in America: A Centennial Observation from a Christian Point of View," *Fides et Historia* 14, no. 1 (1981): 21.

people being intolerant toward one or more other groups. The slaughter of World War I, the massacre of Armenians by the Turks, the massive casualties during the Mexican Revolution, the slaughter of the Chinese by the Japanese in Nanking and elsewhere, the devastation of World War II and the Holocaust, Stalin and the purges, Idi Amin, Pol Pot, Rwanda, Bosnia, and the list goes on. One can make a decent case that the twentieth century was the century of intolerance par excellence. Even the immensely popular Harry Potter books revolve around ideas of pure blood, mixed blood, and racial/ethnic purity. Part of the emotional power of the stories is how well they resonate in a world all too familiar with death camps and the Nazi search for the final solution.

We believe these two recommendations and five substantive claims will enable us to give postmodernism a fair and measured hearing. We do not assume that just because a particular belief is distinctively "postmodern" that we should then automatically accept or reject it in accordance with the beliefs and values we hold.

SUMMARY

1. There is a general need for standards by which to evaluate post-modernism.

2. Both the view known as classical foundationalism and views that are relativistic with respect to truth are not good candidates in this regard.

3. Peter Novick's book *That Noble Dream* is a sustained critique of the idea of objectivity (or objective truth). His claim that objectivity should be rejected is not well supported by his reasoning, as Thomas Haskell makes clear.

4. From Haskell's book we adopted the Haskell principle—the idea that authors should be judged *both* by what they claim and by what assumptions they make. This principle helps us understand postmodernism in as broad (and charitable) a manner as possible.

5. Given that postmodernism is both a diverse and unfamiliar view, we need to make every effort to present it as sympathetically as possible.

6. The recognition of seven factors help us move toward the goal of a sympathetic reading:

    A. We should adopt the principle of charity (see chap. 1).

B. Rather than understanding postmodernism to be a unified and homogeneous view, we need to see it as diverse in nature and broad in its emphases. It may well be best understood as a family of views with certain common points of emphasis.

C. We should see postmodernism as a generally skeptical outlook on knowledge and truth.

D. Humans should not be understood as detached and neutral observers, but rather as radically situated (or embedded), which hugely influences how we look at the world.

E. We need to understand and appreciate the concerns of postmodernism with the reality of significant oppression in the past.

F. There is a need to question science and its privileged status, and to recognize that many important questions in life cannot be answered by science.

G. It is imperative that we see postmodernism as promoting both plurality (more than one reasonable way to look at the world) and tolerance, where "different" does not automatically mean "bad."

SUGGESTED READINGS

Dew, James K., and Mark W. Foreman. *How Do We Know? An Introduction to Epistemology*. Downers Grove, IL: IVP Academic, 2014. A highly readable introduction to the central issues in the theory of knowledge.

Kelly, Stewart E. *Truth Considered and Applied: Examining Postmodernism, History, and Christian Faith*. Nashville: B&H Academic, 2011. Examines in detail the central claims of postmodernism from an evangelical perspective. Having some background knowledge is helpful.

Rosenau, Pauline. *Post-modernism and the Social Sciences*. Princeton, NJ: Princeton University Press, 1991. An excellent examination of postmodernism as it influences the social sciences. Not for beginners.

White, Heath. *Postmodernism 101*. Grand Rapids: Brazos, 2006. A brief and well-written introduction to some key postmodern issues.

3

THE DEMISE OF
ENLIGHTENMENT MODERNISM

The broad movement known as postmodernism did not originate in a vacuum. Rather, it began as unease and dissatisfaction with Enlightenment modernism steadily increased. By the 1960s it was very clear that modernism was disintegrating and that it was time for something new and improved to take its place. This chapter briefly examines five core modernist beliefs and why some of these beliefs came to be questioned and/or rejected. These are not the only reasons modernism was rejected, but combined they help us make sense of modernism's demise.[1]

FIVE CORE BELIEFS OF MODERNISM

First, modernist thought had a high level of confidence in human reason and in the human ability to know reality with certainty. In various ways Descartes (1595–1650), Locke (1632–1704), Newton (1642–1727), and the French philosophes (of whom Voltaire [1694–1778] is the best known) embraced what Alister McGrath has called the omnicompetence of human reason.[2] We will review below the reasons why so many have rejected this view of reason.

---

[1]Lawrence Cahoone lists six specific planks of Enlightenment modernism: (1) a technological attempt to master nature, (2) democracy, (3) the supremacy of the nation-state, (4) modern science, (5) secularism, and (6) humanism. Lawrence E. Cahoone, *The Dilemma of Modernity: Philosophy, Culture, and Anti-culture* (Albany: State University of New York Press, 1987), 1. We discuss the last three of the six he mentions.

[2]See Alister McGrath, *Christian Theology: An Introduction*, 3rd ed. (Oxford: Blackwell, 2001), 91.

Second, many central Enlightenment thinkers were committed to the widespread progress they thought science made possible. Science made the Industrial Revolution possible and contributed to major medical advances; and following Descartes's lead,[3] many came to believe that science made belief in the God of Christianity unnecessary.

Third, many important Enlightenment figures, following the lead of John Locke, rejected the doctrine of original sin as repugnant to human reason. In the fifth century, Augustine, followed in the sixteenth century by Luther, Calvin, and many Protestant Reformers, argued that Adam's sin resulted in all subsequent humans being born guilty before God and with a sinful nature. Locke and many of his contemporaries saw humans as generally decent creatures who, with proper education and cultivation, were fully capable of leading a morally praiseworthy life without dependence on God or the Holy Spirit. The horrors of the twentieth century strongly suggest that this optimistic view of human nature, sometimes known as meliorism, is unjustified and hint that the biblical view of humans as fundamentally sinful is much better supported by the historical record.

Fourth, the majority of Enlightenment intellectuals saw European culture as the pinnacle of modern civilization. Following on their rejection of original sin, they (conveniently) saw themselves as rational, educated, cultured, decent, and scientifically advanced. Combined with the growing wealth and material prosperity of European countries, these factors gave them much of which to be proud. By the 1960s, if not earlier, many had come to realize that the idea of European moral superiority had little foothold in reality. Critics noted that European culture had excluded women, oppressed African Americans and people of color, and exploited millions in the many colonies that nineteenth-century Europeans thought themselves entitled to.[4]

And fifth, though many Enlightenment figures either rejected or radically modified traditional Christianity, Christian faith was still an important part of European culture throughout most of the nineteenth century. So it is worth noting that four of the most influential European thinkers in the late nineteenth and early twentieth centuries were *not* big fans of traditional

---

[3]Descartes himself believed that God existed, because he believed his reason supported such a belief. This approach opens the door to those who think that reason does no such thing, that is, that belief in God is contrary to human reason.

[4]The Belgian Congo (especially between 1880 and 1905) and India are two of many examples.

Christianity. Karl Marx (1818–1883), Charles Darwin (1809–1882), Friedrich Nietzsche (1844–1900), and Sigmund Freud (1856–1939) all thought Christianity was for the morally weak (Nietzsche) or the psychologically unhealthy (Freud), was a tool of oppression (Marx), or was scientifically unsupported (Darwin). Though we are not persuaded by the various critiques of Christianity they offer, there is little doubt that their writings combined to undermine traditional/popular Christian belief in Europe from the late 1800s onward.

THE LOSS OF CONFIDENCE IN HUMAN REASON

These thinkers represent the more secular branch of the European Enlightenment, and their work clearly shows that many Enlightenment thinkers rejected traditional Christianity. In the twentieth century, many postmodern thinkers would reject both these four thinkers and the Christianity they rejected. Traditional Christianity saw human reason as both supporting belief in God and affirming the truthfulness of the Bible as God's revelation to humanity.

Descartes, Spinoza, Locke, and others moved the basis of authority from God's revelation in Scripture to an autonomous human reason. Descartes, though he believed in God, ultimately did so because his reasoning led him in that direction. Descartes's method, with its reliance on human reasoning unhitched from the authority of God's revelation, opened the door to reason, leading Enlightenment thinkers away from God.[5] If human reason is the final authority, then if it leads us to question and/or reject the trustworthiness of Scripture, traditional Christianity is in big trouble.[6]

The development of intellectual trends in England in the 1600s illustrates the general point here. In the early to mid-1600s England was dominated by orthodox Christian thinkers such as William Perkins (1558–1602) and John Owen (1616–1683). By the 1690s the two leading intellectuals in England, John Locke (1632–1704) and Isaac Newton (1642–1727), both publicly professed orthodox Christianity. But both their writings and their private correspondence indicate something different altogether. For both Locke and Newton denied the doctrine of the Trinity—more particularly, they denied

---

[5]Descartes (and Locke) would vigorously contest the idea that reason could be competently used to point toward atheism or even agnosticism.

[6]Spinoza, one of the first to publicly question the truthfulness of Scripture, is a prime example here of reason run amok.

the divinity of Jesus, adopting a particular heresy broadly known as Socinian-ism.[7] Socinians, following their founder Faustus Socinus (1539–1604), reduced Christianity to belief in God the Father, being morally good, going to church, and loving one's neighbor. They thought reason and Scripture did not support the Trinity, the doctrine of original sin, or the immortality of the human soul.

Descartes's knowledge project was extremely ambitious—to anchor human knowledge in beliefs that were absolutely certain. This certain foun-dation would ground less certain beliefs. Such an approach to knowledge is often called foundationalism, in that just as the foundations of a building or house supports the remainder of the structure, so our certain beliefs provide sure support for the remainder of our beliefs. Descartes's version of founda-tionalism, often called classical foundationalism, was enormously influential in philosophy for hundreds of years.

But classical foundationalism is no longer the consensus view, though it still has some capable advocates today. The Christian philosopher Alvin Plantinga has noted that classical foundationalism sets a standard for knowledge that no knowledge claim can meet.[8] Worse yet, classical foun-dationalism fails to reach absolute certainty itself. So by the very standard classical foundationalism sets for itself, it colossally fails! Any view that vio-lates its own central standard is worthy of our rejection.

The noted philosopher Alvin Goldman, who specializes in the theory of knowledge, writes that Descartes's classical foundationalism has long since been discredited, "as everybody in the field knows."[9] There are more modest versions of foundationalism that seek to anchor our beliefs to bedrock be-liefs that are (highly) probable.[10] This view has many capable defenders

---

[7]Whether Locke endorsed all the tenets of Socinianism is unclear and debated. What is clear is that he rejected the divinity of Jesus. He saw Jesus as God's Messiah (specially anointed by God) but *not* as the preexistent second member of the Trinity. The best work on Locke here is John Marshall, *John Locke: Resistance, Religion and Responsibility* (Cambridge: Cambridge University Press, 2010). Locke's *Reasonableness of Christianity* carefully avoids explicitly rejecting the divin-ity of Jesus, for this was an offense still punishable by death, as Thomas Aikenhead found out a few years later (when he was hanged for denying the Trinity).

[8]See Alvin Plantinga, *Warrant: The Current Debate* (New York: Oxford University Press, 1993).

[9]Alvin Goldman, *Knowledge in a Social World* (New York: Oxford University Press, 1999), 27. Goldman clearly has a degree of confidence in human reason, but not to the point where he would endorse Descartes's view.

[10]See the works of Michael DePaul, Richard Foley, and Richard Fumerton mentioned in this chapter's suggested readings.

today, though it is a view that begins with the idea that Descartes's version has significant challenges and is thus now not the best option available. This view, known as modest foundationalism, sees our foundation as fallible, meaning there is always a possibility of being mistaken. Postmodern thinkers happily reject both forms of foundationalism and any other view that requires a degree of confidence in human reason.

It may be important in life to set lofty goals for oneself, but in philosophy this often results in failure and disillusionment. In the late 1800s there was a dramatic increase in the number of professional historians in the United States. These historians, massively influenced by Descartes and the search for certainty, promoted history as a science resting on certain foundations. Needless to say this view of history had a relatively short life. Though it survived into the early 1900s (and in some ways into the 1960s), very few professional historians now claim history is a science or that it rests on infallible foundations. Mark Noll and many others have persuasively demonstrated that though genuine historical knowledge is possible, history is a long way from the goal of certainty promoted by Descartes and the European Enlightenment.[11]

One final (historical) note is worth mentioning here. During Descartes's adulthood a long and brutal war rocked Europe: the Thirty Years' War (1618–1648). Hundreds of thousands were killed, Catholics killing Protestants and Protestants killing Catholics, all (supposedly) to the glory of God. Many came to believe that if serious religious beliefs led to such large-scale slaughter and savagery, then so much the worse for serious religious beliefs. Such wars encouraged a more tolerant attitude toward others, and such tolerance broadly undermined the kind of certainty Descartes and his minions thought possible.[12]

THE COLLAPSE OF SCIENTIFIC PROGRESS

At the heart of the Enlightenment was a commitment to science and the significant human progress it made possible. The (increasingly popular)

---

[11]See Mark Noll, "Traditional Christianity and the Possibility of Historical Knowledge," *Christian Scholar's Review* 19, no. 4 (1990): 388-406. For a detailed examination of whether historical knowledge is genuinely possible, see Stewart E. Kelly, *Truth Considered and Applied: Examining Postmodernism, History, and Christian Faith* (Nashville: B&H Academic, 2011), esp. 153-255.

[12]This broad point is indebted to Chad Meister and James Stump, *Christian Thought: A Historical Introduction* (New York: Routledge, 2010), 391-94.

belief was that science should be seen "as the measure of all human truth."[13] Some have referred to the Enlightenment conception of science as the heroic model of science, as science and scientific geniuses were made into cultural heroes/icons.[14] This heroic model "equated science with reason: disinterested, impartial, and if followed closely, a guarantee of progress in this world."[15] So science provides us an excellent model for human knowledge while also promoting advances that would serve to bring progress to modern humanity. Newton, Francis Bacon (1561–1626), Robert Boyle (1627–1691), William Harvey (1578–1657), and countless other brilliant practitioners of the scientific method were thus seen as helping modern society move forward toward the goals of science and leave behind traditional authorities such as the Christian church, both Protestant and Catholic.

But the heroic model of science ran into trouble along the way. First, science was not quite as scientific as originally thought. Discoveries by Werner Heisenberg (1901–1976), a German physicist who helped develop our understanding of how subatomic particles behave, and others showed that a measure of uncertainty comes with scientific knowledge. More importantly, the military technology of the twentieth century amply demonstrated that science, while making both medical and technological advances a reality, also helped make possible the mind-numbing slaughter of World War I, the "war to end all wars." Many devotees of reason, science, and progress were horrified by the staggering casualties and sheer brutality of World War I (1914–1918). The American Civil War (1861–1865), the deadliest war in American history, killed some six hundred thousand soldiers. By comparison, World War I concluded with some seventeen million casualties: ten million soldiers and seven million civilians. So the ballpark estimate of total deaths is about twenty-eight times the total of the American Civil War. These are breathtaking numbers. In just two extended battles, Verdun (February–December 1916) and the Somme (July–November 1916), some six hundred thousand were killed in each battle! As philosopher Lawrence Cahoone has said, "The 1914–1918 war, previously unthinkable in the scope of its destruction, permanently changed the climate of optimism and progress

---

[13]See Joyce Appleby, Lynn Hunt, and Margaret Jacob, *Telling the Truth About History* (New York: Norton, 1994), 15.

[14]Ibid.

[15]Ibid. Others have referred to this view of science as scientism.

that had still been pervasive among intellectuals and in popular culture."[16] In 1900 many believed that the twentieth century would be a period of extended peace, where the lion would lie down with the lamb. Well—the lion ate the lamb.

Science had been admired for many reasons as the nineteenth century gave way to the twentieth. It had contributed to medical, technological, industrial, and many other sorts of advances. In the twentieth century alone it would make possible all of the following: antibiotics, air conditioning, the electrification of cities, the polio vaccine, devices to bring music into the home, and a large number of material comforts and forms of entertainment. But the common view of science came under question in August of 1945 when the United States dropped atomic bombs on the Japanese cities of Hiroshima and Nagasaki. The bomb, instantly killed some sixty to eighty thousand people and another seventy thousand over the next five years due to radiation poisoning. At ground zero the temperature was higher than ten thousand degrees Fahrenheit. The two atomic bombs made it evident that nuclear technology had the ability to destroy civilization as we know it. And ordinary people became increasingly anxious "about the uses to which the new technology might actually be put."[17]

The Enlightenment promoted the ideal of progress, both for individuals and society as a whole. The twentieth century did not show this moral optimism to be justified. The two great wars and the carnage of the twentieth century made clear that no such optimism was justified.

ORIGINAL SIN AND THE FAILURE OF MELIORISM

One of the hallmarks of Enlightenment culture had been the rejection of the doctrine of original sin—the belief that Adam's sin nature was passed on to all future humans and that we are born guilty before God.[18] Both Locke, a professing Christian, and the Marquis de Condorcet (1743–1794), one of the leading French philosophes, reject the doctrine of original sin in their

---

[16]Lawrence E. Cahoone, *The Dilemma of Modernity: Philosophy, Culture, and Anti-culture* (Albany: State University of New York Press, 1988), 3.

[17]Ibid., 161.

[18]Romans 5 is a key passage for understanding the relation between Adam's sin and the sinfulness of all humans after him, though some in the Arminian/Wesleyan traditions affirm that all are born sinful (due to Adam's sin being passed down) but deny that we are born guilty, given that we have not yet sinned. It should also be noted briefly that we authors both affirm that Adam and Eve were genuine human beings who existed at a particular point in the past.

writings. Locke agrees that humans lost their immortality through Adam's sin, but denies that newborns are guilty before God and denies they inherit Adam's sinful nature. He joins with the Socinians in rejecting Augustine's understanding of original sin, finding it contrary to God's goodness and justice as clearly revealed in the Scriptures. Locke joins with the Socinians in emphasizing the human ability to do good and that this ability had not been damaged by the effects of Adam's sin passed down to us.[19]

The fairly optimistic view of humans endorsed by Locke and the philosophes has not fared well in the twentieth century. Views of human nature need to be able to explain human behavior in general, and it is difficult to see how an optimistic (even rosy) view of human nature can explain the twentieth century. To mention but a few examples (all from the twentieth century), there were:

- King Leopold (of Belgium) and the Congo; between two and five million slaughtered, from the mid-1880s until the early 1900s.

- World War I; deaths around seventeen million.

- The slaughter of the Armenians (by the Turks) (1915–1918); at least five hundred thousand dead.

- World War II (1939–1945); sixty to seventy million deaths is on the conservative side.

- Stalin, the purges, and the gulags;[20] twenty million deaths is a rough estimate.

- Communist China under Mao (1949–1975); somewhere between thirty-five and forty million deaths.

The total number of victims from these episodes in history boggles the imagination. But it gets worse! The above list, though it includes many of the worst examples from the twentieth century, is also *a partial list*.[21] There are dozens of events where three hundred thousand people or more were killed that are not included on the above list.

Andrew Carnegie (1835–1919) was one of the most successful businessmen in world history. Rising from poverty, he amassed a fortune that in modern

---

[19]See Marshall, *Resistance, Religion, and Responsibility*, for more on Locke's theology.
[20]The gulags were hard labor camps spread throughout the Soviet Union.
[21]For all the gruesome details, see Matthew White "Source List and Detailed Death Tolls for the Primary Megadeaths of the Twentieth Century," Necrometrics, last updated February 2011, http://necrometrics.com/20c5m.htm.

dollars would be around $300 billion dollars (some five times the current wealth of Bill Gates). Toward the end of his life he envisioned a twentieth century where world peace was the norm and war was a rare aberration. Toward that end he established the Carnegie Endowment for International Peace in 1910. Located in Washington, DC, and other major world cities, the goal of this organization is expressed as follows:

> The Carnegie Endowment for International Peace is a unique global network of policy research centers in Russia, China, Europe, the Middle East, and the United States. Our mission, dating back more than a century, is to advance the cause of peace through analysis and development of fresh policy ideas and direct engagement and collaboration with decision makers in government, business, and civil society. Working together, our centers bring the inestimable benefit of multiple national viewpoints to bilateral, regional, and global issues.[22]

With this in mind, Carnegie funded the Peace Palace in The Hague (in the Netherlands), which was completed in August 1913, less than one year before World War I. Carnegie's Peace Institute's construction was widely hailed as a significant step toward long-term international peace.[23] As the first international peace conference was getting underway in 1914, Europe was in the process of mobilizing the millions of soldiers and pieces of artillery to engage in a slaughter and carnage none could have ever imagined.

So what view of human nature is supported by the many slaughters of the twentieth century? This is a broad and messy topic, but it is fair to say that an optimistic view of human nature is *not* one of the leading options. The traditional Christian view is that humans are fundamentally selfish beings whose default mode is to put themselves first, and others (and God) second. Such a view of human nature can be found in the writings of William Golding and C. S. Lewis. Golding's *Lord of the Flies* (1955) is a brutally realistic depiction of what happens to humans when there are no laws to constrain them.[24] Many of Lewis's works present a similarly unflattering view of

---

[22]From the website of the Carnegie Endowment for International Peace, accessed July 11, 2015, http://carnegieendowment.org/about/.

[23]See Peter Krass, *Carnegie* (Hoboken, NJ: John Wiley & Sons, 2002), 457-71.

[24]The original idea that humans would act savagely without laws to constrain them originates with the British philosopher Thomas Hobbes (1588-1679). The film *The Purge* (2013) explores a similar theme.

humans. We are the (morally) bent creatures, who though dignified and valuable, are nonetheless deeply flawed.[25]

In 1919 a young Swiss theologian, Karl Barth (1886–1968), published a commentary on the book of Romans.[26] The book was a massive indictment of the prevailing (in theological circles) optimistic view of humanity found in Adolf von Harnack (1851–1930) and liberal German Protestantism. Harnack had reduced Christianity to two basic ideas: the fatherhood of God and the brotherhood of man. He, and many of his fellow German theologians, had also naively signed the Manifesto of the Ninety-Three, a document that supported, even celebrated, the German entrance into the war of wars. This combination of optimism about the human condition and rabid German nationalism convinced the young Barth that a return to a view of human nature grounded in the Bible was desperately needed.

As the mass slaughter of the twentieth century demonstrated, modern meliorism was a faulty conception of human nature.

THE DEMISE OF EUROPEAN EXCEPTIONALISM

The "Enlightenment" is really shorthand for the "European Enlightenment." Almost all of the leading Enlightenment thinkers thought it obvious that the Europe of the seventeenth century and following was the pinnacle of human civilization. To paraphrase a popular slogan in a beer commercial: "It doesn't get any better than this." This passionate commitment to European superiority can be called European moral exceptionalism. A commitment to European exceptionalism was still alive and well at the dawn of the twentieth century. But by the late twentieth century it lay tattered in ruins.[27] There are many complex and interrelated reasons for the demise of European exceptionalism; here we will briefly mention three.

Europe, Africa, and the Berlin Conference. King Leopold II of Belgium invited Henry Morton Stanley to join him in his mission to colonize Africa.[28]

---

[25]See Lewis's space trilogy, *Out of the Silent Planet, Perelandra*, and *That Hideous Strength*.

[26]Karl Barth, *The Epistle to the Romans*, trans. Edwyn C. Hoskyns, 6th ed. (Oxford: Oxford University Press, 1968).

[27]For an early indictment of the European Enlightenment and all it stood for, see T. S. Eliot's long poem *The Waste Land* (1921), a scathing indictment of all Europeans held dear. *The Waste Land* is not easy reading, but a careful study of it is worth the effort. No one doubts the brilliant contributions made to science and technology in Europe. The doubts are much more of a moral nature.

[28]Adam Hochschild, *King Leopold's Ghost: A Story of Greed, Terror, and Heroism in Colonial Africa* (Boston: Houghton Mifflin, 1999), 58-63.

Leopold saw the opportunity not only for personal glory but also an opportunity to harness the considerable economic resources found in Africa. Gold, timber, cheap labor, and a number of other valuable commodities beckoned to the enterprising Europeans. By the early 1880s Belgium, France, Germany, England, Portugal, and others were salivating over the economic opportunities in Africa. Leopold convinced France and Germany that common trade in Africa "was in the best interests of all three countries."[29] As tensions heightened, a need was seen for a conference to settle differences and draw up a plan for the division of Africa. It goes without saying that African leaders were neither consulted nor invited to the conference, held in Berlin the winter of 1884–1885. The aim of the conference, as Otto von Bismarck made plain in a speech on November 15, was "to promote the civilization of the African natives by opening the interior of the continent to commerce."[30] The noble European conferees agreed to promote and spread the three Cs: commerce, Christianity, and civilization, ultimately for the good of the African peoples themselves! Leopold would go on to amass a huge personal fortune, and to condone the mass slaughter of the people in Congo, with estimates of deaths ranging from two to five million, or more.[31] After the extent of Leopold's brutality came to light, Belgium's congress removed him from power.

In a world where individual rights and human dignity are fairly widely recognized (with many notable exceptions), the racial arrogance implicit in the Berlin Conference and the slaughter endorsed by Leopold together undermine any European claims to the moral or intellectual high ground.

Colonialism. The time period from 1875 to 1914 has been called the Age of Empire. During that time period, Great Britain, France, Germany, Italy, the Netherlands, Belgium, the United States, and Japan combined to divide up much of the world outside Europe and the Americas. By 1914 virtually all of Africa belonged entirely to the British, French, German, Belgian, Portuguese, and Spanish empires. What was also striking was the various superpowers all saw themselves as morally superior to the people they were subjugating, with many believing that the subjugation was actually for the

---

[29]Ibid.

[30]Thomas Pakenham, *The Scramble for Africa: White Man's Conquest of the Dark Continent from 1876 to 1912* (New York: Perennial, 1991), 241.

[31]See ibid. for more. Also see Hochschild, *King Leopold's Ghost*, for a chilling and horrific account of Leopold's brutality in the Congo.

good of those subjugated! Thus the world as we knew it was partitioned "among a handful of states, . . . [and] was the most spectacular expression of that growing division of the globe into the strong and the weak, the 'advanced' and the 'backward.'"[32] This desire to spread one's political and economic influence was hardly peculiar to Europe. The United States "rescued" Cuba from the Spanish (1898) and killed thousands of Filipinos (1899–1902) to thwart their desire for independence; in short, American meddling in foreign countries was infused with the same racist attitudes that dominated the European division of Africa at the Berlin congress. William Howard Taft, later president of the United States and chief justice of the Supreme Court, assured President McKinley "that 'our little brown brothers' would need 'fifty or one hundred years' of close supervision to 'develop anything resembling Anglo-Saxon political principles and skills.'"[33] Taft's racism was shared by Teddy Roosevelt and the great majority of Americans of the day.

So both the Berlin Conference and the desire for increased colonies, along with the underlying racism, combine to show that Europe in the late 1800s was nothing to write home about. By limiting democratic principles and autonomous rule to civilized white people just like us, Europe significantly undermined any genuine claim to superiority of any meaningful sort.

The problem of war. We have already looked at the staggering number of casualties in the wars and conflicts of the twentieth century. Next we will simply briefly revisit the main point: great and (morally) advanced civilizations do not engage in mass slaughter of their fellow humans. It is as simple as that.

So we now have offered three reasons, good reasons, for rejecting European exceptionalism. Though there are many other relevant issues, we believe these three reasons are sufficient for our purposes here.

THE DEMISE OF RELIGION/CHRISTIANITY

During this time, the work of several philosophers and practitioners challenged the dominance and assumed relevance of Christianity. We mention just a few, briefly: Darwin's work became widely known by the 1870s, and it was seen by many as making belief in the God of Christianity unnecessary.

---

[32]Eric Hobsbawm, *The Age of Europe* (New York: Vintage, 1987), 59.
[33]Stuart Creighton Miller, *"Benevolent Assimilation": The American Conquest of the Philippines, 1899–1903* (New Haven, CT: Yale University Press, 1982), 134.

Marx saw the Christian faith as a tool of oppression that should be eliminated if humans were to create a better world. Nietzsche argued that belief in God was no longer necessary or relevant in the modern era. Freud believed that healthy adults had no need to lean on God and promoted a naturalistic world without him. Finally, Jean-Paul Sartre (1905–1980) thought it obvious that the horrors of World War I meant that God did not exist. Now, he believed, we live in a world in which we are alone and life lacks objective meaning.

In their collective work, we see both the collapse of traditional values and some of the major reasons for the steady decline in traditional religious belief in Europe. We also see that there are few if any good reasons to believe that European moral exceptionalism is true. So we now have considered yet another aspect of the demise of Enlightenment modernism in the late nineteenth and early twentieth centuries. The combination of the decline of traditional Christianity and the mass slaughter of the twentieth century created space for a new outlook to come to the forefront, and that new outlook was postmodernism.

SUMMARY

1. There are five reasons why Enlightenment modernism fell out of favor:
    A. A loss of confidence in human reason, especially the approach adopted by Descartes.
        i. The demise of classical foundationalism.
        ii. The unattainability of certainty in knowledge.
    B. The demise of the heroic model of science.
        i. Science is not capable of disinterested and impartial objectivity (as was often advertised).
        ii. Science made mass military slaughter possible.
        iii. Hiroshima and Nagasaki caused us to rethink the relationship between science, technology, and human values.
    C. The demise of meliorism.
        i. The mass slaughter of the twentieth century radically undermined faith in human goodness.
        ii. Carnegie's Peace Initiative failed.

      iii. A more realistic view of human nature can be found in the work of William Golding and C. S. Lewis.

      iv. Karl Barth's critique of Harnack and Protestant German liberalism challenged the melioristic tendencies in German theology.

   D. The demise of European exceptionalism.

      i. The Berlin Conference of 1884–1885 and its underlying arrogance and racism.

      ii. The unapologetic colonialism of the European countries.

      iii. The horror of World War I.

   E. The intellectual assault on traditional Christianity.

      i. Darwin made belief in God seem unnecessary.

      ii. Marx saw Christianity as a tool of oppression.

      iii. Nietzsche saw God as no longer relevant for modern humanity.

      iv. Freud viewed religion as a crutch for the psychologically needy and unhealthy.

      v. Sartre thought that the extent of human suffering made it obvious that God did not exist.

2. These five reasons combined to demolish what was left of Enlightenment modernism.

SUGGESTED READINGS

Appleby, Joyce, Lynn Hunt, and Margaret Jacob. *Telling the Truth About History.* New York: Norton, 1994. An excellent and reader-friendly introduction to the heroic model of science.

Barth, Karl. *The Epistle to the Romans.* Translated by Edwyn C. Hoskyns. 6th ed. New York: Oxford University Press, 1968. Barth's famous critique of German Protestant liberalism.

Benson, Bruce Ellis. *Graven Ideologies: Nietzsche, Derrida and Marion on Modern Idolatry.* Downers Grove, IL: InterVarsity Press, 2002. A generally readable introduction to Nietzsche and to other important postmodern figures.

Clark, Maudemarie. *Nietzsche on Truth and Philosophy.* Cambridge: Cambridge University Press, 1991. A brilliant and thorough introduction to a difficult philosopher. Some philosophical background is helpful, though Clark's style makes Nietzsche as accessible as possible.

DePaul, Michael, ed. *Resurrecting Old-Fashioned Foundationalism*. Lanham, MD: Rowman & Littlefield, 2001.

Elster, Jon. *An Introduction to Karl Marx*. Cambridge: Cambridge University Press, 2005. A sympathetic but critical introduction to Marx's thought. Well written, though philosophically dense at times.

Foley, Richard. *The Theory of Epistemic Rationality*. Cambridge, MA: Harvard University Press, 1987. A challenging work by a leading epistemologist arguing in support of one version of modest foundationalism.

Fumerton, Richard. *Epistemology*. London: Wiley-Blackwell, 2006.

Gay, Peter. *Freud: A Life for Our Time*. New York: Norton, 2006. A brilliant and sustained introduction to the life and thought of Freud. Though Gay, a respected historian, is much too sympathetic to Freud and his thought, it is a worthy introduction.

Golding, William. *Lord of the Flies*. London: A & A, 2013. A classic literary work that forcefully challenges the Enlightenment idea that humans are basically good (or even half decent). Well worth reading.

Kelly, Stewart E. *Truth Considered and Applied*. Nashville: B&H Academic, 2011. Contains an extended critique of Enlightenment modernism.

Pakenham, Thomas. *The Scramble for Africa: White Man's Conquest of the Dark Continent from 1876 to 1912*. New York: Perennial, 1991. A detailed introduction to the European division of Africa.

Plantinga, Alvin. *Warrant: The Current Debate*. New York: Oxford University Press, 2000. A brilliant analysis of the nature of knowledge by a leading Christian philosopher. Not for beginners.

4

THE OBSERVER AS SITUATED

INTRODUCTION: THREE BROAD OPTIONS

Both philosophers and nonphilosophers have long been interested in why people believe what they believe, and how much of a role one's environment plays in shaping and influencing particular beliefs we have. The study of these influencing factors is sometimes referred to as the sociology of knowledge. We are interested in the reasons for belief, whether the belief is reasonable, whether the belief is true, and so forth. Supposing that we can separate human reason from our emotions, desires, beliefs, and the like, there seem to be only three options in replying to the issue of how our beliefs relate to reason.

The first option is that we believe what we believe apart from (or above) the influence/shaping of various social and cultural factors (family, peers, culture, the media, education, and so forth). This is the idea that humans possess the ability to be purely rational, and to set aside any emotional or social factors that might get in the way.[1] Descartes and a number of Enlightenment thinkers endorse this possibility, and we shall call it the purely rational view. This view dominated throughout the Enlightenment and well into the twentieth century, even up into the 1960s.

The second option is the idea that, though reason may play a role, what we believe is influenced, perhaps heavily, by a wide range of social and cultural factors. We will label this the modestly rational view. Blaise Pascal,

---

[1]This is an ideal (goal). It is granted that no human is fully capable of attaining this. Descartes claims that we can free ourselves from all preconceived opinions, a lofty claim indeed.

Abraham Kuyper, and countless contemporary thinkers endorse this view. This view does not rule out human reason playing a role in what we believe, but merely specifies that it is not the only factor involved.

Finally, there is the view advocated by a number of (radical) postmodern thinkers that sees all our beliefs as not just being influenced or shaped by social and cultural factors, but as being caused (or determined) by these various nonrational factors. Let us call this view the purely nonrational view.[2] On this view the environment broadly understood is the cause of the individual's belief, and not just an influence. Here the individual is (for whatever reasons) unable to rise above their environment but simply believes what these various factors cause them to believe. On this view beliefs, including religious and political beliefs, are relative to the environment we live in (and have lived in). So here if someone says, "I believe in the Easter Bunny," they are not really claiming that the Easter Bunny factually exists, but only that such a belief is *true for them*[3] individually (or their particular culture). If this view is correct, and a decent number of postmoderns lean in this direction, then the traditional idea of truth is severely compromised, where "true" always meant "true for everyone," or "objectively true," and never merely "true for me." The fact that each belief is environmentally determined[4] entails that the truth of each belief is relative to the individual's society/environment. Such beliefs could be true, but only because the particular society in question happened to cause the individual to believe a true belief.

The important question now is, which one of the three views best holds up to careful examination? Should we look behind Door Number One (for the purely rational view), Door Number Two (for the purely nonrational view), or Door Number Three (for the modestly rational view)? Let's briefly examine each of the three to see how they fare. There is relatively little consensus nowadays as to which of the three is the best option, though we believe that a fairly strong case can be made for one of the three.

---

[2]*Nonrational* should not be confused with *irrational*. *Irrational* is clearly a negative word, meaning "contrary to reason," while *nonrational* simply means "outside the realm of reason," and does not automatically have the negative overtones that *irrational* has.

[3]We both readily admit that the very idea of "true for me" makes us squirm a bit. We will offer arguments along the way to support our being uncomfortable with such claims.

[4]That is, fully shaped by the realities surrounding us.

THE PURELY RATIONAL (ENLIGHTENMENT) VIEW

Suppose someone claimed it was true that everything that everyone believed was entirely on the basis of good reasons, such that no one ever believed anything other than for good reasons. So, for example, people who believe that God exists, that material objects exist, that $2 + 2 = 4$, that Columbus sailed west in 1492, that platypuses are difficult to categorize, that Frisians were hardy folk, and that Jim Brown was the best NFL running back of all time do so believe entirely on the basis of carefully considered and rational factors. This would be a pure fantasy. Such a claim is not only false but also ludicrous. Humans have many beliefs for which they can offer good reasons, but certainly not all of them. One reason is that humans have a finite and limited perspective on reality—we only see things from one angle.[5] And there is very much we do not understand about reality. Another important factor is that the consideration of reasons is not the only reason we believe what we do. There are many other factors that shape and influence our beliefs. A number of these factors revolve around what can be called socialization, where socialization is understood to mean the "lifelong social experience by which people develop their human potential and learn culture."[6] It amounts to everything in our life experience that influences us. This covers a lot of territory, and that is understating matters. An enormous number of factors influence us, some of them significantly, others less so. Though part of what and who we are is the result of biology/genetics, a sizable portion is not.

Okay, so what is the point of knowing something about socialization in a book on postmodernism? Well, for starters, the two are connected. Postmoderns think many of our most important beliefs and values are largely (if not entirely) the product or result of these various social factors.

Studies of the Enlightenment tend to emphasize the influence of the thought of Descartes. For Descartes, the knowing subject is quite different from the view of the knowing subject found in many branches of postmodernism. First, Descartes believes that what makes us who we are—our "self"—remains constant over time.[7] Postmoderns, following Nietzsche,

---

[5]The movie *Vantage Point* (2008) clearly explores this idea in detail.

[6]John J. Macionis, *Sociology*, 11th ed. (Boston: Prentice-Hall, 2007), 118.

[7]It should be noted here that many Christian thinkers would more or less agree with Descartes on this matter. Though Descartes's goals for knowledge are too lofty, many of his other beliefs merit serious consideration.

Hume, and others, generally believe that there is no such enduring self, but only a bundle or collection of characteristics that change over time. Second, through the use of human reason, humans are able to access what they are thinking (the content of their mind, so to speak). Reason can thus be seen as the gatekeeper to the mind, and it gives us the ability to identify what is in the mind, to sort and categorize what we find, and to discard that which we don't find pleasing. The philosopher Robert Solomon writes that "there is no question but that Descartes, 'the father of modern philosophy,' was also the founder of the modern [Enlightenment] philosophical obsession with the self as the locus and arbiter of knowledge."[8] Descartes and other moderns clearly think that the basic self (common human nature) is the same for everyone in the world. So if others carefully follow Descartes's method for acquiring knowledge, they too will be successful, as Descartes before them was. This enduring self, through the careful and meticulous use of reason and the proper method, can be confident in the pursuit and acquisition of knowledge. Descartes believes we can be certain of all the contents of our minds. We can be certain, he claims, both that we exist ("I think, therefore, I am") and that we are thinking at any given moment.[9] Also, note here that for Descartes human reason can successfully be disentangled from our emotions, passions, desires, and the like. So a stable and enduring self, making use of what might be called pure reason (as opposed to reason entangled with emotions and the like), and relying on a sure-fire method, makes objective human knowledge possible.[10] As a rationalist, Descartes has supreme confidence in human reason, but he is skeptical of the use of our five senses in seeking knowledge. He urges that "we must systematically disregard the confused deliverances [results] of the senses, and rely instead on the 'clear and distinct' concepts of pure mathematics, which God has implanted in our souls."[11]

So how exactly does Descartes think human knowledge is possible? We first "must begin by giving up all our beliefs about the external world, since

---

[8]Robert Solomon, *Continental Philosophy Since 1750: The Rise and Fall of the Self* (New York: Oxford University Press, 1988), 5.

[9]See Michael Della Rocca, "René Descartes," in *A Companion to Early Modern Philosophy*, ed. Stephen Nadler (Malden, MA: Blackwell, 2008), 74.

[10]There are other key issues that Descartes addresses, such as the existence of God and how God helps guarantee the reliability of our senses and the existence of other minds.

[11]John Cottingham, "René Descartes," in *A Companion to Epistemology*, ed. Jonathan Dancy and Ernest Sosa (Oxford: Blackwell, 1992), 90.

each is susceptible to doubt, and accept beliefs only if they meet foundational requirements."[12] The requirements mentioned here are that our beliefs be absolutely certain, with no possibility of error at all. We do this, Descartes confidently claims, by relying on our reason to identify beliefs that are both *clear and distinct*. So with a stable self, a powerful and pure human reason, and a reliable method, we are well on our way to acquiring genuinely certain knowledge.[13] Many later postmodern thinkers will come to question much, if not all, of Descartes's approach, not to mention his general confidence in human reason.

Now jump ahead some 250 years to the late 1800s. The location is the United States and the context is the rise of academic history as a profession. Prior to the 1860s there were very few academic historians in the United States. That rapidly changed in the last twenty-five years of the 1800s. These professional historians, many of them trained in Germany, where history was already a well-established discipline, sought to get their discipline in America off to a good start. Given their German training, they looked to Germany and their leading historians as models or paradigms for how to be good historians. One of the leading German historians, Leopold von Ranke (1795–1886), was especially admired. He taught that history should be practiced as a science. How does this work in practice? First, the historian acts as a neutral and impartial observer. Second, they use fair and objective methods. And finally, the application of the first two steps results in historical knowledge and a high level of certainty, one that might even impress Descartes. The eminent British historian J. B. Bury wrote that "history is a science, no less and no more."[14] The American historian George Burton Adams wrote that "the actual result has been a science of investigation, and a method of training the future historian, which if it is not too much to say, have taken complete possession of the world of historical scholarship."[15]

So the first American (professional) historians saw themselves as scientists, and believed that the practice of history could closely imitate the

---

[12]Hilary Kornblith, "In Defense of a Naturalized Epistemology," in *The Blackwell Guide to Epistemology*, ed. John Greco and Ernest Sosa (Malden, MA: Blackwell, 1999), 159.

[13]Most postmodern thinkers doubt the human self is enduring and stable. Nietzsche is one such example. See chap. 7 for more on the self.

[14]J. B. Bury, *An Inaugural Lecture, Delivered in the Divinity School, Cambridge, on January 26, 1903* (Cambridge: Cambridge University Press, 1903), 7.

[15]George Burton Adams, "History and the Philosophy of History," *The American Historical Review* 14, no. 2 (1909): 223.

cautious and respected practice of the sciences. The historian merely had to collect and classify facts, "to ascertain as nearly as possible and to record exactly what happened."[16] In the 1970s, I (Stewart) was taught in high school to write history papers in what might be called the third-person omniscient mode. Using the words *I* or *my* were strictly forbidden, as was anything that even hinted of human subjectivity. The historian, professional or amateur, was to use "the distant (not laughing) voice of the omniscient narrator, familiar from the realist novels of the nineteenth century and modeled on the voice of the scientists in their laboratory reports."[17] This all-knowing narrator "stood above superstition and prejudice to survey calmly and dispassionately the scenes of the past and tell a truth that would be acceptable to any other researcher who had seen the same evidence and applied the same rules."[18]

This emphasis on the objective, scientific observer/researcher, relying just on the facts, dominated American history (and also other disciplines) well into the 1960s. Then things came unglued. A number of significant events turned the world upside down, and also indirectly served to challenge the dominant approach to doing history and other disciplines. Some of these events undermined the existing status quo, while others played an active role in the final demise of modernism. Twelve major events[19] can be listed as follows:

1. The free speech movement at California at Berkeley in the early 1960s. This movement challenged many of the beliefs of mainstream American culture.

2. The assassination of President Kennedy in November of 1963. This tragic event can be viewed as ending the sense of innocence that accompanied American society in the 1950s.

3. The growing civil rights movement. This challenged widespread American beliefs about the treatment of blacks.

---

[16]Richard Hofstadter *The Progressive Historians: Turner, Beard, Parrington* (Chicago: University of Chicago Press, 1970), 38.

[17]Joyce Appleby, Lynn Hunt, and Margaret Jacob, *Telling the Truth About History* (New York: Norton, 1994), 73.

[18]Ibid. Much of this paragraph is based on Stewart E. Kelly, *Truth Considered and Applied: Examining Postmodernism, History, and Christian Faith* (Nashville: B&H Academic, 2011), 161.

[19]Even listing twelve events is being highly selective. The list is taken from Kelly, *Truth Considered and Applied*, 37-39.

4. Racially related riots in Los Angeles, Newark, and many other American cities. These riots served to undermine the social stability of American culture.

5. The Vietnam War and the student protest movement, along with a general loss of trust in the American government (culminating with the Watergate scandal in the early 1970s). The war protests made evident that it was no longer taken for granted that the United States always made morally justified military decisions.

6. The growing awareness (by some political candidates) concerning establishment values (Robert Kennedy is a prime example here). There was a drift toward what the historian Arthur Schlesinger called an "imperial presidency."[20] Kennedy was the first major presidential candidate to publicly come out against the war.

7. An increased awareness of other cultures, especially Majority World cultures. Western values, it was recognized, were not the only way to live.

8. An increased sense of the evils of colonialism and imperialism. Colonialism and imperialism, and the underlying attitude of moral superiority, were no longer seen as acceptable.

9. Increased doubts about the function of language and the role of traditional metanarratives. It was no longer obvious that language captured reality in a manner as simple as we once thought.

10. The rise of the New Left and a politically active counterculture. The Left made it clear that the traditional political options of conservative and moderate were no longer adequate choices.

11. The devastating year of 1968: the Tet offensive, Martin Luther King Jr.'s assassination, Robert Kennedy's assassination, and the disastrous Democratic National Convention. Mick Jagger of the Rolling Stones, shocked by all the upheaval of 1968, wrote in "Gimme Shelter" that anarchy was "just a shot away."

12. The beginning of the women's movement. There was an increasing realization that women had not been treated as equals in American society.

---

[20]See Arthur M. Schlesinger Jr., *The Imperial Presidency* (New York: Mariner, 2004).

It became increasingly obvious that not everyone looked at the world exactly the way we did, and that there was no good reason to automatically think that our way of looking at things was right (or "true") just because it was our way. "Clear and distinct" was now better understood as "clear and distinct from a particular point of view." In short, our way (or the "American" way) of looking at things was no more objective or scientific than the viewpoint of someone in a foreign country. We had working assumptions (or presuppositions), they had such assumptions, and no one looked at the world "straight," that is, from a totally unbiased and objective point of view. Rather, as humans we all look at the world through a lens that is colored by our individual personality, our upbringing, our national and local subcultures, the media, our education, and a host of other factors. Humans are extraordinarily complex creatures, and figuring out why we believe what we believe is no simple matter. Think how often we make simple decisions based on fairly insignificant whims. For example, I am wearing a green polo shirt today because my favorite blue shirt was dirty, the green one was within easy reach, and I simply felt like wearing the green one as opposed to a number of other shirts that I did not choose today. Now this is a rather ordinary or mundane matter, but we should not automatically assume that more important matters involving our religious and political beliefs, for example, are settled by an appeal to reasons more impressive than the ones behind my choice of shirt today.

One final example should be sufficient here. Professional historians generally do not claim anymore to write history exactly as it was. For openers, the research and writing of history is massively selective. We choose to read certain books, articles, and archives, but choose not to consult others. This is a choice, hopefully a defensible one, but it is not a scientific or purely objective choice. And after we read all we have chosen to read, we don't write a book that incorporates all of our research material, but rather we selectively focus on a number of key issues that are central to our task, but ignore others that we value less or simply don't have time to cover in this particular scholarly work. As the eminent New Testament scholar N. T. Wright says, "To make any statements about the past, human beings have to engage in a massive programme of selection."[21] And all this selection,

---

[21]N. T. Wright, *The New Testament and the People of God* (Minneapolis: Fortress, 1992), 83.

Wright notes, "involves a major element of interpretation. We are trying to make sense of the world in which we live. If we do not we are being bath-sponges, not humans."[22] So doing history involves selection, it involves interpretation, and it involves our own beliefs about what is most important and most reasonable. This does not mean that all interpretations are equally reasonable, but it does allow for the possibility that on some fairly important matters[23] reasonable people may disagree. So for all these reasons, most modern scholars reject the purely rational view. That leaves us with two remaining possibilities: the modestly rational view and the purely non-rational view. There is much at stake here, for if the purely nonrational view is the most reasonable of the three, it becomes unclear in what sense we can still (reasonably) say that Christianity is true or that Jesus is the Way, the Truth, and the Life (see John 14:6). We would simply mean "Christianity is true for me (or us)," or that "Jesus is Lord for me," though he might not be that for anyone else. Truth would be entirely subjective, and the idea that the Christian gospel, the good news of what God has done through Jesus, would no longer be good news for everyone, but only for those who see it as "true." Below we summarize four reasons for rejecting the purely rational view.

1. The purely rational view is humanly unattainable. All humans are influenced by a wide variety of factors, are unable to be completely neutral and impartial on crucial matters, and cannot fully separate reason from the emotions, desires, and other nonrational aspects of our minds.

2. The reality and pervasiveness of socialization undermines the purely rational view. Where we live, when we live, and what environment we have grown up in are all powerful shaping influences on what we believe. It's naive to think we are able to rise above all these factors, while people who disagree and live in different cultures are all unable to do the same.[24]

3. Our claims to knowledge are not claims to absolute certainty of the sort that Descartes mistakenly put forth. They are all *defeasible* claims. To

---

[22]Ibid.

[23]On historical matters, at least. Note we are not saying that reasonable people can believe differently on all matters, which would be a much stronger claim.

[24]For an instructive example of how much the environment shapes how we speak (dialect), go online and take the *New York Times* dialect quiz. It makes obvious what we already know—that both the language we speak and how we speak it are massively influenced by our environment (nytimes.com/interactive/2013/12/20/sunday-review/dialect-quiz-map.html).

be defeasible is to be capable of being defeated or overturned if better arguments come along. They are thus not claims of 100 percent certainty of the sort Descartes prized. If someone says "*x* is true" and *x* has a 99 percent chance of being true, that is a very impressive claim, one that is most probably true. So for a claim or a belief to be defeasible is not a bad thing, just a bit more modest (and realistic) than the sort of claims Descartes and other Enlightenment thinkers made.[25] And recognizing many claims as defeasible is to be truer to the human condition and our finite minds and capacities.

4. We do not need Descartes (or his method) to achieve knowledge. Furthermore, as evangelical Christians, we have the Scriptures as the inspired and inerrant Word of God. As such, the Scriptures are true.[26] Over the centuries Christians have not claimed that the Scriptures were merely the result or byproduct of first-century-AD Palestinian culture. If this were true, then the Scriptures would have nothing to say to us who live in the twenty-first century. Whatever value the Scriptures had would be locked into that culture and that time period. But the Scriptures, being the Word of the one true Creator God, are true and relevant for all humans in all times. With Descartes's own method in mind, the truth of Scripture transcends any and every social setting, and it offers hope to sinners past, present, and future. Now it must be made clear that the Scriptures were written in a particular time and place and culture, and that the nature of the times can be seen in the Scriptures. For example, Paul and John both write addressing themselves to particular problems going on in the first century. But none of this precludes or rules out either the truth or the relevance of the Scriptures for the modern human condition. We, just like our fellow humans in the first century, are sinners in need of a Savior, a Savior that a gracious God has provided for all who believe.

For all these reasons, then, we are more than justified in rejecting the purely rational view as a viable account of human reason. That leaves us with two remaining options: the purely nonrational view and the modestly rational view.

---

[25]Though Descartes may be too confident about reason, David Hume has little trust in reason at all.
[26]With suitable allowances for the various genres of Scripture. Poetic language is not literally true, but historical claims (e.g., "He is risen") and claims intended to be taken literally are.

THE PURELY NONRATIONAL VIEW

Virtually all postmodern thinkers categorically reject the purely rational view as a naive pipe dream with no firm footing in reality. And most of the modestly rational folk agree with them. But many of these same postmoderns also reject the modestly rational view in favor of a much more radical view, the purely nonrational view. This view celebrates the triumph of our situatedness, the idea that all the things that influence us actually determine or dictate what we believe on any important matter, religious, political, and otherwise.[27] They believe we are simply unable to rise above or transcend all these powerful influences. Our beliefs and values are the result of all these socializing influences. So on this view the idea of a belief or claim being rational makes no sense, as "reasons" reduce to various social influences working together.

Let's briefly summarize why advocates of this view reject the purely rational view. First, they might begin by taking notice of the various factors that influence us, what might be called the *agents of socialization*. These agents include family, peers, culture (national and local), education, and the media. Each of these factors significantly influences us. Postmoderns are impressed by the degree and extent of these factors, and argue that it is reasonable to believe that, ultimately, these factors combine to cause us to do what we do and believe what we believe. Second, postmoderns also agree with the philosopher Thomas Nagel that there is no view from nowhere. As Nagel claims, "Since we are who we are, we can't get outside of ourselves completely." To be fully impartial we would have to be able to do this, but we simply can't. A third reason for rejecting the purely rational view is based on the work of Thomas Kuhn, who wrote a controversial work on the nature of science, *The Structure of Scientific Revolutions*, first published in 1962. Kuhn attacked the idea that science and scientific discovery were as straightforward and "objective" as they were traditionally believed to be. He argues, fairly persuasively, that social factors and personal commitments also play a role in how science proceeds from one view to another. He does not deny there are objective elements in modern science, but claims only that the objective and the social are both genuine factors.[28]

---

[27]The Greek philosopher Protagoras clearly thought all human beliefs were relative to the culture in which they lived. Sometimes the word *historicism* is used to designate the view that everything we humans believe is *entirely* the result of our social circumstances and environment.

[28]Many postmoderns read into Kuhn more than is there, though Kuhn is not as careful as he should be at times. In later works, Kuhn makes clear that science still retains an objective component.

The theologian John Franke notes that the sort of neutrality that Descartes so greatly prized is both overrated (as a worthy goal) and unattainable.[29] Franke believes we should acknowledge our presuppositions and various influences, and then work from that acknowledged standpoint.

Other prominent evangelicals agree with Franke in rejecting the purely rational view. D. A. Carson, Wright, and Kevin Vanhoozer all concur that complete objectivity is not a human possibility. Carson writes that "all our understanding is interpretive, and . . . the interpretive communities in which we find ourselves are extremely influential."[30] Wright believes that the postmodern critique of Enlightenment rationalism (and its commitment to pure reason) is "a necessary judgment on the arrogance of modernity, and it is essentially a judgment from within."[31] Vanhoozer agrees with postmoderns when he says that "we should be suspicious of any textual interpretations that make claim to the sort of apodeictic [absolute] certainty that Descartes longed after."[32] We can't achieve such certainty, as we see the world "through finite and fallible interpretive frameworks."[33] So here we have three leading evangelical theologians who join with the postmoderns in rejecting the purely rational view. Another reason such thinkers might reject Descartes and company is that some postmoderns see most (if not all) claims as disguised power claims. The historians Bonnie Smith[34] and Keith Jenkins believe along these lines. Smith sees traditional history writing as oppressive of women, while Jenkins rather cynically claims that "in the end history is theory and theory is ideological and ideology just is material interest."[35] This is a breathtaking assertion! A paraphrase of this claim might read as follows: History is dominated by a view of how history should be done (the theory), theory is dominated by particular worldviews,

---

[29]See John Franke, *The Character of Theology: An Introduction to Its Nature, Task, and Purpose* (Grand Rapids: Baker Academic, 2005), 7. It is not just that it is unattainable, but that the goal is way beyond our best efforts.

[30]D. A. Carson, *The Gagging of God: Christianity Confronts Pluralism* (Grand Rapids: Zondervan, 1996), 129.

[31]N. T. Wright, "The Resurrection and the Postmodern Dilemma," *Sewanee Theological Review* 41, no. 2 (1998): 144.

[32]Kevin Vanhoozer, *Is There a Meaning in This Text? The Bible, the Reader, and the Morality of Literary Knowledge* (Grand Rapids: Zondervan, 1998), 458.

[33]Ibid.

[34]See Bonnie Smith, "Whose Truth, Whose History?," *Journal of the History of Ideas* 56, no. 4 (1995): 661-68.

[35]Keith Jenkins, *Re-thinking History* (London: Routledge, 2007), 23-24.

and worldviews are dominated by questions of personal and/or material gain or profit. One immediately wonders whether Professor Jenkins intends this sweeping claim to apply to his own writings, or whether he wants to exempt his view from what applies to everyone else? In either case, his main claim here is in trouble.

There clearly is much history written by passionate and committed scholars, but the question remains whether such commitments rule out the possibility of objectivity (as Peter Novick believes[36]). As I (Stewart) argue in *Truth Considered and Applied*, "Situatedness does not entail radical subjectivity. . . . Radical subjectivity (no degree of objectivity possible) would follow only if different worldviews entailed an inability to critically compare two such views."[37] The agents of socialization and our broader culture definitely shape how we look at the world, but they don't create the world itself: it is already there.[38] Postmoderns need to come to grips with the sheer givenness of the world; it predates our awareness of it, and it limits how many different ways we can reasonably describe it.

Given good reasons for rejecting the purely rational view, are there also good reasons for rejecting the purely nonrational view? We think so. So here are the top eight reasons we have our doubts about the purely nonrational view.

1. God has graciously revealed himself in Scripture and in creation. As Carson argues, if God is a personal and active God, then "there are some massive implications for our understanding of truth and communication."[39] The Reformers, especially John Calvin, developed the doctrine of divine accommodation, according to which God chooses to communicate to us through human language and through the testimony of the Holy Spirit.[40] Though there is much we cannot know about God, we can definitely know that he is, that he loves us, and that he has sent his Son to die on our behalf. Those are significant truths, ones anchored both in Scripture and in the history of first-century-AD Palestine.

---

[36]See Peter Novick, *That Noble Dream: "The Objectivity Question" and the American Historical Profession* (Cambridge: Cambridge University Press, 1988).

[37]Kelly, *Truth Considered and Applied*, 76.

[38]See John Searle, *The Construction of Social Reality* (New York: Free Press, 1995), esp. chap. 7.

[39]Carson, *Gagging of God*, 130.

[40]John Calvin, *Institutes of the Christian Religion*, trans. Henry Beveridge (Peabody, MA: Hendrickson, 2007), 1.13. See William Bouwsma, *John Calvin: A Sixteenth Century Portrait* (New York: Oxford University Press, 1988), 132-33.

2. Though social context is undoubtedly important for understanding who we are and why we believe what we do, it is possible to overstate the importance of environmental influences. Too much emphasis on social context "threatens to reduce truth to mere social history."[41] When ordinary people say, "It really happened," they typically do not mean "My particular social context made me say that!" They mean that if you had been at a particular place and time you, too, would have witnessed the event in question. So yes to the importance of the sociology of knowledge, but no to all attempts to reduce all truths to that context.

3. There is a correspondance between our statements and reality. Anthony Thiselton makes this point:

> For a great many speech-acts there is a vital and non-negotiable element, which consists of the "fit" between what is said and events in the extra-linguistic world. [42]

4. If postmoderns attempt to defend a commitment to the purely non-rational view, they run into major problems in a hurry. Remember that the supporter of the purely nonrational view is committed to the idea that all our beliefs are dictated by the environment. But as Plantinga convincingly argues, if she says something like the following:

(EC)[43]—One's environment causes one to believe everything they believe

then that would include EC itself! For it, too, would be a belief caused by the environment of the person claiming it. So if EC is true, then whether any particular claim is true depends not on how the world is (objective factors), but rather on one's particular environment. And one could live in an environment where that environment causes one to believe that EC is false. So if EC is true, then its truth depends on the particular environment of the speaker. And if it depends on the particular environment of the speaker, then it will often be false! Having grown up in an environment where truth is seen as genuinely existing, a supporter of EC can only say to me, "Well, my environment caused me to think it's true." To which I would reply, "So

---

[41] Anthony Thiselton, *Interpreting God and the Postmodern Self* (Grand Rapids: Eerdmans, 1995), xi.

[42] Anthony Thiselton, *New Horizons in Hermeneutics: The Theory and Practice of Transforming Biblical Reading* (Grand Rapids: Zondervan, 1992), chap. 15.

[43] For "Environmental Causation."

what;[44] my environment causes me to think differently and to reject your view. So there." One can admit their own situatedness, their own cultural baggage, and so forth. But none of this does away with the idea that certain events really did happen and certain objects really are out there. We see reality through a lens, but we do "see" reality.[45]

5. One can make a good case that postmodernism is at heart a moral critique of some of the central beliefs and values of the Enlightenment and the Western world. And there is no good reason why evangelical Christians cannot join in this critique of the past (and present) treatment of African Americans, women, Jews, the disabled, and many other people groups.[46] But if all of our claims reduce to our social situation, then so do our moral critiques of Enlightenment modernism. So the claim

(B) African Americans were mistreated

doesn't really mean that they were objectively mistreated, but only that one's overall social situation caused them to *think and claim* they were mistreated. These are two very different sorts of claims. Being caused to think a belief is true and the belief itself being true are two (very) different things. The former might require some sort of intervention in the human brain, while the latter usually requires some sort of external reality to genuinely exist. People who are delusional might think everything is orange or that the Cubs have won the World Series every year since 1908, but neither belief would be true.

The historical fact of oppression in no way threatens traditional Christianity. More impressively, traditional Christianity can provide an objective moral standard for making a claim about oppression, it can offer genuine hope to past and present victims of oppression (Jesus can free them from the bondage of sin and the temptation of a bitter and unforgiving spirit), and it even offers the perpetrators of oppression a challenge to repent.[47] Scripture is full of examples of individuals and countries who have suffered oppression, and also of the hope for redemption promised

---

[44]Common response for people from New Jersey. My environment made me write this.
[45]See Appleby, Hunt, and Jacob, *Telling the Truth About History*, 269. For an excellent philosophical treatment of some of these issues, see Searle, *Construction of Social Reality*.
[46]See Mark Noll, Alvin Plantinga, and others on this point.
[47]The well-documented story of the British slave trader John Newton (1725–1807), is a case in point here. After his conversion Newton penned "Amazing Grace."

in the man Christ Jesus. In Ephesians 1 Paul speaks of Jesus as our Redeemer, while in 1 Timothy 1 he presents Jesus as our hope. At the end of the day, what the oppressed and the oppressor need more than anything else is the genuine hope of a Redeemer. Christianity offers that hope. Hebrews 10:23 says, "Let us hold unswervingly to the hope we profess, for he who promised is faithful."

6. Accepted belief does not equal true belief. If one overemphasizes the idea of situatedness, we lose the traditional idea of making truth claims For we are no longer claiming that *x* is true, but *only* that our current situation caused us to believe *x*. This involves a shift from making claims about the world (what we might call objective claims) to claims about our inner mental life (and these are subjective or inner mental claims). As Alvin Goldman points out, for some postmoderns truth simply equals accepted belief.[48] So if there is a sufficient consensus or agreement concerning a particular belief, then we may regard it as true. So

truth = commonly accepted belief.

But even a little thinking about this claim shows it is not true. The majority of people used to believe that the earth was flat, that bleeding the sick made them better, that mental illness was (always) demonic in nature, and that most professional baseball players never used steroids in the '90s. These were all accepted beliefs, but none of them is true. Rather, they are false beliefs. Our beliefs subdivide into true and false, and whether they are widely accepted has no necessary connection with whether they are true.

Richard Rorty, Stephen Shapin, and other prominent thinkers have suggested giving up the traditional idea of truth. Rorty's idea of truth as what your peers will let you get away with is fairly close to Shapin's idea that truth simply is accepted belief.[49] Just think what a whole class of students could do on a math exam if they successfully lobbied (through YouTube, for example) the world, with the majority agreeing with them that 2 + 2 really is 5. The math teacher would be outvoted, so to speak, and 2 + 2 would be 5![50]

---

[48]Alvin Goldman, *Knowledge in a Social World* (New York: Oxford University Press, 1999), 8-9.

[49]For a thoughtful and provocative analysis of Rorty on truth, see Plantinga, "Postmodernism and Pluralism," in *Warranted Christian Belief* (New York: Oxford University Press, 2000). For a discussion of Shapin's view, see Goldman, *Knowledge in a Social World*, 7-8.

[50]The point here hinges on the idea that 2 + 2 ≠ 5, and that basing one's answer on the current

Students would no longer need to know the truth of a matter, but only what the majority believed on a given matter. Truth would move from the discipline of philosophy (where it has long been a central issue) to sociology. Of course on Shapin's view, suppose that the community of professional philosophers believe that truth ≠ accepted belief. On Shapin's own view, then, it would be false that

truth = accepted belief.

So Shapin's own conception of truth hinges on what the broader community/society believes, rather than on the way the world is or has been. As Goldman and Charles Taylor[51] have argued, to believe something is to consider it as true, and to believe that belief and truth can be totally divorced leads to the sort of nonsense that Rorty and Shapin promote.

7. Keep in mind that much of postmodernism focuses on past acts of oppression toward various groups and individuals. So we are justified in claiming that women, African Americans, Latinos, Jews, and many other groups have been genuinely wronged. But what happens to these claims about oppression if truth is no longer about what "really happened" (which Rorty clearly thinks is a rather useless idea), but only what is commonly accepted? Suppose both Rorty and Stanley Fish are correct that there are no external moral criteria (other than the various communities to which we belong). What then justifies our claims about past (or ongoing) oppression? It cannot be an appeal to objective standards or criteria, for Rorty and Fish have thrown them overboard. Rorty ridicules such approaches, though he is clearly comfortable with his own critique of bad practices. Why is what is good for the goose also not good for the gander? We see no way for Rorty to be able to privilege (give special or authoritative status to) his own critique while simultaneously undermining the basis for other critiques. If there are any genuine external criteria, then Rorty's view is simply mistaken. If there are not, then Rorty has no basis for criticizing anyone. As much as he would like it, he simply cannot have it both ways.

8. Objective truth cannot be dispensed with. No one doubts that the various influences on the reader of a text hugely influence how the inter-

---

popular consensus is nonsense.

[51]See Charles Taylor, "Rorty in the Epistemological Tradition," in *Reading Rorty: Critical Responses to Philosophy and the Mirror of Nature and Beyond*, ed. Alan R. Malachowskip (London: Blackwell, 1991), 258.

preter reads and understands a particular text. But texts have a certain objectivity to them that is nonnegotiable—they cannot be reasonably read to mean whatever the individual interpreter(s) think they mean. In Fish's case, the result is that interpretation is relativized to the interpreter, with no outside or external mooring or reality check. But texts often have meanings that simply cannot be reduced to the reader's various influences.[52] As Carson argues, even in the famous story of the six blind men and the elephant (where each of the six takes reality to be the limited part of the elephant's body where they are situated), there are objectively real elements present.[53] First, if any of the six listened to the other six while they were on the elephant they would quickly determine that there is more to reality than their own perception. Second, *how* did the narrator of the story know it was an elephant in the first place? If none of them knows about the other five parts of the elephant (and its five interpreters), then how would they ever figure out there *really was* an elephant? It sure seems like a sighted person needs to be brought into the discussion to declare, "Yes, it is an elephant." Even with the six blind men, if it is not first true that there *are* six blind men, then the story never gets off the ground. How meaningful is it for six genuinely existing human beings to tell us that reality is what our very limited perceptions take it to be (depending where we are on the elephant)? For the story to work we need to acknowledge the reality of the six storytellers![54]

We can acknowledge that humans are limited and finite creatures and still humbly claim that genuine knowledge is possible. We can admit our cultural influences, that our grasp of truth is often partial, and still remain committed to the idea that there is an objective reality external to our knowing minds.[55] Historians, for example, have a shared commitment to objective knowledge. This "forces people to examine rigorously the relation between what they bring to their subject and what they find."[56] Both

---

[52]See Carson, *Gagging of God*, 122-23.

[53]See ibid. 122-25.

[54]There are other required and objective elements needed here. They really are telling a story; telling a story typically requires someone to hear the story; and so forth.

[55]See Appleby, Hunt, and Jacob, *Telling Truth About History*, 269. Also, see Kelly, *Truth Considered and Applied*; Mark A. Noll, "Traditional Christianity and the Possibility of Historical Knowledge," in *Christian Scholar's Review* 19 (June 1990): 388-406; and C. Behan McCullagh, *The Logic of History: Putting Postmodernism in Perspective* (New York: Routledge, 2003).

[56]Appleby, Hunt, and Jacob, *Telling Truth About History*, 269.

external reality and the past are knowable. Historians differ about the causes of the American Civil War, but no competent historian doubts that it happened. If you had been in Gettysburg, Pennsylvania, in 1863 you would have seen flesh-and-blood soldiers firing bullets at each other, thousands of bodies falling, and many other things. That humans are finite, promotes humility and limits how certain we are of our interpretation, but it hardly makes knowledge in general impossible. Objective truth is literally indispensable.

Professional philosophers (as well as those in other disciplines) often complain that someone who has written about their views has not fully and/or properly understood what they are claiming.[57] They argue that the interpreter has not been faithful to what was written/said previously. Rorty himself is one prime example.[58] But the complaint that others have misrepresented your view *only* makes sense if there is a certain objective givenness (e.g., "*this* is what I wrote, and this is what it means"). So Rorty's own complaints about others misrepresenting him assumes what he otherwise denies!

We see that the purely nonrational view is beset by serious difficulties, difficulties significant enough to warrant its rejection. Given we have so far rejected both the purely rational view and the purely nonrational view, our remaining hope is the modestly rational view. To it we now turn.

THE MODESTLY RATIONAL VIEW

The modestly rational view[59] is widely held by a large number of Christian scholars today. For example, Alvin Plantinga, N. T. Wright, D. A. Carson, Mark Noll, Alan Padgett, and many other noted Christian thinkers can rightly be viewed as belonging in this camp. Below are listed five reasons for seriously considering the modestly rational view. They are

---

[57]Even Derrida, in his impassioned defense of Paul de Man, claims de Man's writings and actions have not been properly understood. See Alan Spitzer, *Historical Truth and Lies About the Past: Reflections on Dewey Dreyfus, de Man, and Reagan* (Chapel Hill: University of North Carolina Press, 1996).

[58]The philosopher Simon Blackburn has noted how difficult it is to pin Rorty down as to what he is actually saying.

[59]The words *modestly rational* intentionally have a dual meaning. On the one hand, the view lacks the confidence in human reason that Descartes and other Enlightenment figures had. On the other hand, the view can be said to be "modest" in that it acknowledges the noetic effects of sin. For a definition of "the noetic effects of sin," see number 3 in the numbered list here.

1. The failure of the two other views. Both the purely rational view and the purely nonrational view are beset by serious problems. Cartesian certainty is humanly unattainable while the purely nonrational view is self-defeating.

2. Human finitude. Humans are finite creatures; that is, we can't know everything and our intellectual capabilities are limited. This line of reasoning is nicely developed by the philosopher William Alston in his work on the problem of evil.[60]

3. The noetic effects of sin. This means that Adam's fall not only affects our wills (which became self-seeking rather than God-seeking) but also our minds (noetic comes from the Greek word for mind), which are now partly clouded by the effects of sin.

4. The sociology of knowledge. The modestly rational view gives the sociology of knowledge its due, but without overstating its importance, as the purely nonrational view does.

5. Probability as an adequate guide for daily life. We do not need to achieve certainty to make wise and informed daily decisions.

These Christian thinkers recognize the importance of identifying our assumptions, and also are quick to point out that the assumptions of many prominent non-Christian thinkers are often not only different from Christian assumptions but also in fact hostile to traditional Christianity. For example, many modern historians believe that miracles do not happen (and never have).[61] Not only do they not happen, but they cannot happen. They are ruled out from the very start. So if the four Gospels are full of miracle stories, which must be false, they cannot be reliable historically.

As human beings affected by the fall of Adam and limited in our intellectual abilities, we don't understand the world the way God does. We don't know everything, we are heavily influenced by our environment, our reasoning skills are tarnished by the fall, and we have the further limit of having physical bodies, which limit how many perspectives we have on reality. All of these factors affect how we read and understand texts, in-

---

[60]See William P. Alston, "The Inductive Argument from Evil and the Human Cognitive Condition," *Philosophical Perspectives* 5 (1991): 29-67.

[61]For an excellent recent book on miracles, see Craig Keener, *Miracles: The Credibility of the New Testament Accounts*, 2 vols. (Grand Rapids: Baker Academic, 2011).

cluding the Bible. Some postmoderns suggest that our attempts to understand texts is interpretation all the way down, meaning that everything we
say about the text is the result of all these factors that influence us, and
virtually none of it is actually (objectively) true. Suppose it is true that all
interpretations are simply the inevitable result of many environmental
factors influencing us. So what if we have three interpreters: Juan from
Argentina, Ernst from the Netherlands, and Xiaojing from China. They all
read the same text (the Bible, for example), and they then offer three competing interpretations of the meaning of the text. If no degree of objectivity
is possible, and all interpretation is controlled by environmental factors
outside our control, then our three interpreters have nothing meaningful
to say to each other. They aren't really saying "My interpretation is (objectively) true," they are merely stating "This is my interpretation," with no
claim being made about truth or objectivity. So if the text in question was
John 8:58-59, "'Very truly I tell you,' Jesus answered, 'before Abraham was
born, I am!' At this, they picked up stones to stone him, but Jesus hid
himself, slipping away from the temple grounds." Suppose our three interpreters understand these verses as follows:

1. Juan claims the verses are ultimately about the insecurities of Jesus.

2. Ernst claims the verse is about the history of bees in the Netherlands.

3. Xiaojing claims that Jesus is making a claim to be more than human;
   that he is claiming divinity for himself (which also explains the outrage
   of his listeners in verse 59).

If all three claims are a matter of interpretation all the way down, then we
have three different claims[62] and no way to judge which is most faithful to
the meaning of the text itself. Juan has his interpretation, Ernst has his, and
Xiaojing has hers, and since they are all merely the result of the various
factors influencing each of them, no one of the three is any more likely to be
"true" than any other. All three claims are merely *descriptive*: they describe
what the three people believe, but they are not normative or prescriptive in
any sense in that they don't tell us what we *ought* to believe. If they were, they
would be claiming both that this *is* what the passage means and that there
are good reasons you ought to understand it this way too. Another way of

---

[62]Similar environments here could produce claims that overlap in content.

looking at what they are saying is "If you had been influenced by all the same factors I had, then you would have ended up with the same interpretation I did." So this batch of environmental causes (let's call them E) results in/ causes this particular interpretation (call it I). Notice that no claims about truth, or what the text "really" means, or what the text "objectively" means, ever enter into the conversation.

These brief examples show that there are good reasons to think some claims are true and some false, irrespective of the various influences on the people making the claims. As Carson writes, "I agree that all our understanding is interpretive, and that the interpretive communities in which we find ourselves are extremely influential. But this does not mean, on the one hand that we cannot articulate objective truth, and on the other that our interpretive communities bind us utterly."[63] Carson is claiming that outside influences and objective truth are not enemies, and can peacefully coexist. And though our fellow scholars ("interpretive communities") heavily influence us, we have the tools and ability to disagree with them when we see the evidence as supporting such disagreement. Of the three claims above, there are very good reasons to claim that Xiaojing's interpretation is both more plausible than the other two and is, in fact, the correct interpretation.[64]

The writing of history today is a good example of the three views discussed above. Some historians believe that the writing of history can be a fairly scientific and objective matter, where outside influences and individual temperament are kept to a minimum. A well-known example here is the British historian G. R. Elton (1921–1994). Elton, in his characteristically straightforward style, writes that the study of history "amounts to the search for truth."[65] Elton clearly thinks that the history scholar has the ability either to avoid having assumptions or at least to be able to rise above all of them. He views such assumptions as only getting in the way of pursuing history properly. He writes, "What I have called ideological theory threatens the work of the historian by subjecting him to predetermined explanatory schemes and thus forcing him to tailor his evidence so that it fits the so-called paradigm imposed from the outside."[66] Elton thinks we

---

[63]Carson, *Gagging of God*, 129.
[64]See Craig Keener, *The Gospel of John*, 2 vols. (Grand Rapids: Baker Academic, 2010).
[65]G. R. Elton, *The Practice of History*, 2nd ed. (New York: T. Y. Crowell, 1991), 46.
[66]G. R. Elton, *Return to Essentials: Some Reflections on the Present State of Historical Study* (Cambridge: Cambridge University Press, 2002), 27.

need to understand the past on its own terms, "from the inside" so to speak. This means being able to set aside whatever current beliefs and/or values we might have that would be foreign to the time period being studied. That Elton believes such a thing is possible indicates just how confident he is of objectively presenting the past entirely as it was. Many historians agree with Elton that a degree of objectivity is possible (and desirable), but would part ways with him about the extent of that objectivity. More than a few historians have noted that Elton's own political views (which are best described as conservative) often seem to find their way into his books. The historian John Tosh notes that "Elton was sometimes accused of seeing everything in Tudor England [1485–1603] as if it related to bureaucratic administration."[67]

For many historians, to see a past event as being *probable* is to give it high praise. There are some past events that we are certain happened (that Henry VIII existed, that he was married multiple times, etc.), but good and interesting history needs to take these certain events, integrate them with events that are probable, and weave them together into a coherent story/narrative that does a decent job of explaining the events and time period under consideration. There are not enough certain past events to make putting a general narrative together an easy thing. Historians need to use their creativity and imagination in putting all the pieces of the puzzle (and some pieces are usually missing) together into one coherent narrative. There can be different interpretations of the same time period, and it is possible in theory for both accounts to be reasonable. How is this possible? It's not possible because there is no such thing as truth or a genuine historical past, but it is possible because of our limited knowledge, our selective use of sources, our general limits as human beings, and the idea that there is (often) a sizable gap between the information provided by the sources we have and what actually happened. Furthermore, there is a degree of leeway in what is the best way for filling in this knowledge gap. Reasonable historians can disagree on some matters of interpretation, just as evangelical New Testament scholars do not always understand a particular text the same way, though both scholars may be committed to the inerrancy of Scripture and to using the same methods in trying to figure out what a passage means. Evangelicals with shared commitments and values may find

---

[67]John Tosh, *The Pursuit of History*, 4th ed. (Harlow, UK: Pearson, 2006), 192.

some interpretive matters intractable, that is, not easily settled by any straightforward method. Differing temperaments, different questions asked, and differing documents consulted can all result in somewhat different outcomes. This does not mean that there is no way to try and figure out which interpretation is more reasonable, but only that human factors enter into the process of interpretation and that such results may be probable, though still lack the level of certainty we can attain in, say, mathematics and similar disciplines. Sometimes the most plausible interpretation of a particular event only emerges over time as new information comes to light and new interpretive skills are honed and refined.

SUMMARY

1. The Purely Rational View
   A. Descartes is the prime example.
   B. Leopold von Ranke was the first professional historian in the United States, in the 1880s.
   C. Detached, neutral objectivity is the goal.
   D. The belief in total objectivity fell on hard times in the 1960s, when everything not nailed down hit the fan.
   E. Four weaknesses of this view
      i. The goal of certainty is humanly unattainable.
      ii. The reality of significant socialization undermines our ability to be completely neutral.
      iii. Knowledge claims are fallible.
      iv. Our bedrock foundation in life is not properly acquired beliefs, but the inspired and inerrant Scripture.

2. The Purely Nonrational View
   A. Four factors suggest this view as worthy of our consideration:
      i. It recognizes the agents of socialization.
      ii. There is no purely impartial or objective view; there is no "view from nowhere."
      iii. Truth claims are viewed as disguised power claims.
      iv. Thomas Kuhn showed the history of science fell far short of the rational ideals it often promoted.

B. Eight criticisms of the purely nonrational view

    i. God has revealed himself in Scripture and creation.

    ii. The influence of the environment is overstated.

    iii. Texts have a nonnegotiable (or fixed) element.

    iv. Stating that the purely nonrational view is true is self-contradictory.

    v. The moral critique central to many postmoderns simply reduces to social and environmental factors, and it is clearly put forward as a truth claim.

    vi. It is false that accepted belief equals true belief. Truth is more than merely being accepted.

    vii. Rorty, Fish, and others criticize various beliefs and actions, but have no objective standard/criteria for making such claims.

    viii. It is not possible to dispense with objective truth. If there were no truth, then it would be true that there is no truth.

3. Five Reasons to Consider the Modestly Rational View

A. The two other views fail. Both the purely rational view and the purely nonrational view are beset by serious problems. Cartesian certainty is humanly unattainable while the purely nonrational view is self-defeating.

B. Humans are very much finite creatures; that is, we don't know much, and our intellectual capabilities are limited. This line of reasoning is nicely developed by the philosopher William Alston in his work on the problem of evil.[68]

C. Adam's fall introduced the noetic effects of sin, meaning that sin does not only affect our wills (which became self-seeking rather than God-seeking) but also our minds, which are now partly clouded by the effects of sin.

D. The modestly rational view gives the sociology of knowledge its due, but without overstating its importance as the purely nonrational view does.

---

[68]See Alston, "The Inductive Argument from Evil."

E. Probability is an adequate guide for daily life. We do not need to achieve certainty to make wise and informed daily decisions.

Suggested Readings

Carson, D. A. *The Gagging of God: Christianity Confronts Pluralism.* Grand Rapids: Zondervan, 1996. A major work by a leading evangelical scholar.

Descartes, René. *Meditations on First Philosophy: With Selections from the Objections and Replies.* Edited by John Cottingham and Bernard Williams. Cambridge: Cambridge University Press, 1996.

Israel, Jonathan. *Radical Enlightenment: Philosophy and the Making of Modernity, 1650–1750.* New York: Oxford University Press, 2002. A brilliant and controversial overview of the Enlightenment.

Kelly, Stewart E. *Truth Considered and Applied: Examining Postmodernism, History, and Christian Faith.* Nashville: B&H Academic, 2011.

Nagel, Thomas. *The View from Nowhere.* New York: Oxford University Press, 1986. A classic (and readable) book addressing the idea that humans always look at reality from a particular point of view.

Searle, John, and Richard Rorty. "Rorty v. Searle, at Last: A Debate." *Logos* 2, no. 3 (1999): 20-67. Two philosophical heavyweights square off here. Searle's view seems much more compatible with traditional Christianity than Rorty's does.

Smith, James K. A. *Who's Afraid of Postmodernism? Taking Derrida, Lyotard, and Foucault to Church.* The Church and Postmodern Culture. Grand Rapids: Baker Academic, 2006. An articulate and well-argued defense of some key postmodern ideas. Smith works out of what can be called the continental philosophical tradition.

Thiselton, Anthony. *New Horizons in Hermeneutics.* Grand Rapids: Zondervan, 1997. A careful and detailed work on major issues concerning the interpretation of texts (including the Bible). Thiselton is a prominent British evangelical.

Wright, N. T. *The New Testament and the People of God.* Minneapolis: Fortress, 1992. A brilliant work by a leading British evangelical. Addresses in detail the issue of individual perspective.

5

PHILOSOPHY OF LANGUAGE

At the heart of postmodern thinking is a particular view of language, what it is, and how it makes genuine communication possible. Postmodern views of language typically reject some of the more traditional philosophical understandings of language, and then offer a radical alternative to these traditional ways of thinking. In this chapter we will briefly look at some of these traditional approaches to language, evaluate them with postmodernism in mind, and then seek both to understand and carefully critique the view of language put forth by leading postmodern thinkers,[1] especially the view put forward by Jacques Derrida, widely recognized as one of the four or five most influential postmodern thinkers.[2]

The views of language that developed in the nineteenth and twentieth centuries generally reflected the optimism of Enlightenment thinking both in that humans could have genuine knowledge and that language could adequately express this confidence. The British philosopher John Stuart Mill (1806–1873) adopted a view of language that has often been referred to as the Fido-Fido theory of language. On his view what made the sentence "Fido is the name of my dog" meaningful is that the word *Fido* referred to a genuinely existing dog who belonged to him. So the real-life, flesh-and-blood Fido becomes the referent (that to which the word *Fido* refers) for the word *Fido* in the above sentence. This all seems pretty straightforward and thus

---

[1]The postmodern view examined here is both sophisticated and nuanced. The amount of detail reflects a sustained attempt to take Derrida's view of language seriously.

[2]The five most influential would probably include Friedrich Nietzsche, Ferdinand de Saussure, Michel Foucault, Jacques Derrida, and Richard Rorty.

seems to work rather well. And in addition to my dog, Fido, suppose a student asks me what the meaning of the following words is:

1. Computer

2. Book

3. Coke

I reply by pointing to my desktop computer, one of the books in my office, and the bright red can of Coke on my desk. The student now grasps what I mean by each of these three words. This is a very neat and tidy view of language—for every word that is meaningful there is (at least) one object in the real world to which it refers. Words and the objects to which they refer exist in a one-to-one relationship. The Fido-Fido theory of meaning is thus named because of the obviously close relationship between a word and its referent. Now the question is whether the Fido-Fido theory is a plausible view of language. And upon a little reflection, the answer no becomes readily apparent. Suppose we are interested in knowing the meaning of the following words:

1. Stewart Kelly

2. Rory

3. Blue

4. Happiness

5. And

6. Wow

Examples one and two are easily handled on the Fido theory—the words *Stewart Kelly* refer to me, the particular human being who is presently typing these words. So far so good.[3] And *Rory* refers to my family's male orange tabby, who is presently draped over some piece of furniture at home.[4] So we are two for two so far in pointing out what particular words mean. But now consider examples three through six. These are not handled so easily. What exactly does the word *blue* refer to? There are many blue objects, and there are also many different shades of blue on the color spectrum. Does there exist in the real world the idea/concept of what all blue objects have in

---

[3]We will ignore for now the real possibility that there are other human beings named Stewart Kelly.
[4]No doubt there are many other Rorys in the world, not to mention Rory Kellys.

common, namely, *blueness*? Plato and others thought that blueness existed independently of whether there were any blue objects in the world. This is both a complicated and controversial matter, though it is far from clear whether blueness exists in the same sense as Stewart Kelly and Rory the cat do. Along similar lines, *happiness* might be seen as what all happy creatures have in common. But it is far from clear that happiness exists as an abstract and independently existing entity. Besides abstract entities such as *blueness* and *happiness*, it is far from clear what we should do with words such as *and* and *wow*. *And* is a meaningful word and is a conjunction. What exactly would it refer to in the real world to make it meaningful? Fans of Plato might suggest something along the lines of *andness* (roughly the universal idea of this particular conjunction), but it is not clear what it would mean for such an entity to exist on its own. And the exclamation *wow* simply drives home the already apparent point that Mill's theory struggles to explain what makes exclamations and conjunctions meaningful. Indeed, if all words were proper names (Stewart Kelly and Rory) then Mill would be in business. But alas, this is not the case, and many have questioned whether the Fido-Fido theory can adequately account for the richness and diversity of human language.

Finally, consider the following example:

James Bond does not exist.

This is clearly a meaningful statement in English, though it is not clear the Fido-Fido theory can handle it. Remember that Mill sees meaningful statements as ones that refer to objects in the real world. But James Bond does not really exist, so on Mill's view the words *James Bond* refer to absolutely nothing and are therefore meaningless. Yet the sentence is clearly a meaningful one (as it is not nonsense), and, equally importantly, it is a true sentence. It should be contrasted with sentences such as

Inga binga boo

which is not even meaningful, though Mill's view does not enable us to distinguish nonsense from the true sentence involving Mr. Bond. For these and other reasons many philosophers and linguists decided that Mill's Fido-Fido theory was not the best explanation of what makes language meaningful.[5] The big question now is whether there is a better alternative waiting

---

[5]For a much more detailed discussion of the strengths and weaknesses of Mill's view of language,

in the wings. A number of leading European philosophers and linguists in the twentieth century think there is.

SAUSSURE AND STRUCTURALISM

Early in the twentieth century more traditional views of language began to be seriously questioned. At the forefront of these challenges was the Swiss linguist Ferdinand de Saussure (1857–1913).[6] Saussure had significant doubts that the best way to understand language was by the reference of key words to objects in the real world. Through his study of language and how it works Saussure came to have doubts about Mill's theory and about the whole idea of extratextual reference, where words get their meaning by referring to objects beyond the text and are anchored in the real/external world. Suppose that rather than centering on the idea of reference to objects in the world, language needs to be understood in a fundamentally different manner. Suppose we think of language more as a game, say like chess, where the rules of chess govern what any piece can and cannot do. Saussure and later structuralists think the view of nicely packaged language where we have the idea of a particular dog, where we use the word *Fido* to refer to that particular dog, and Fido exists in the real world is fundamentally wrong-headed. Let's begin by thinking about the word *dog*. Dogs, Saussure would argue, are part of what might be called a language system or game. To truly know what a dog is we also need to know what an animal is, what a mammal is, and the particular type/breed of dog to which Fido belongs, in this case a Shetland sheepdog.[7] Along similar lines, Fido is not a cat, a weasel, a reptile, or an insect. So Fido is an animal, a mammal, a dog, and a Shetland sheepdog. Furthermore, he is not an insect or reptile, nor is he a different kind of animal. All this is relevant for beginning to properly understand exactly what a dog is, and the word *dog*, Saussure believes, is defined in relation to all these other relevant concepts. As such *dog* is defined *internally* and relationally, in that it is defined by appealing to *other* concepts/words (and not by reference to anything external) and in light of its relationship to

---

see Michael Devitt and Kim Sterelny, *Language and Reality: An Introduction to the Philosophy of Language*, 2nd ed. (Cambridge, MA: MIT Press, 1999), esp. chaps. 2–6.

[6]Saussure is particularly important both because he critiques traditional views of language and because he paves the way for important postmodern thinkers.

[7]Much of the present details are indebted to Heath White, *Postmodernism 101* (Grand Rapids: Brazos, 2006), 90-91.

other concepts, rather than referentially to some object outside of language and in the world.

Saussure also notes that it didn't have to be this way. For example, we don't have to divide animals into mammals and nonmammals. We could just as easily have divided them according to size, with elephants, hippopotamuses, giraffes, and lowland gorillas in the big group, and chipmunks, rats, rabbits, and cats in the small group. And we could add one or two groups for the midsize models: bigger dogs, beavers, otters, wombats, and baboons. The point of all this is that there is nothing sacred either in the traditional divisions of animals or in the words we choose to apply to them. In some important senses, then, human language is arbitrary. Saussure and later structuralists also noticed that the dividing scheme we use to categorize animals is *socially constructed*—it is entirely the creation of human beings, and we can clearly imagine dividing things up differently. So both concepts and categories are human creations and in that sense arbitrary.

Consider the word *man*, for example. Historically it has been used to refer both to human beings in general and to human males in particular. And many of us older folks were taught to write with predominantly male pronouns. Whenever we had in mind a generic human being (any human being), we would use the pronoun *he* to refer to that person, though presumably the odds were fifty-fifty that such a person was female. Nowadays, it is considered more decent and considerate to, say, alternate between male and female pronouns, and to believe that women are the full equals of men. It was no accident that the common pattern of using the pronoun *he* reflected the widespread cultural belief that women were inferior to men in certain important ways (mentally, physically, socially, etc.). When the Founding Fathers wrote, "We hold these truths to be self-evident, that all *men* are created equal . . . ," it was no accident that at that time women were neither allowed to vote nor (in many instances) own property. This brief example shows that words can and do have ethical and political overtones, and as such are not morally neutral terms.

So if words and concepts are not to be defined by reference to objects outside of language, how then should we understand their meaning? Saussure's answer is that each word is defined by the sum total of its relation to all the other words being used. Each word is thus understood relationally and *intertextually* rather than referentially and extratextually. Words are defined by *their role in the system of words in which they are enmeshed*. Think of language as a web-like system where each word is understood in relation to the other words and to the web as a whole. As Saussure writes, "Each linguistic term derives its value from its opposition to all the other terms."[8] Some views of language may see linguistic meaning as involving both referential issues (what objects key terms refer to) and relational ones (how each word relates to the other words present), but Saussure and later structuralists make the more radical claim that the full meaning is decided *entirely* by relational issues, not referential ones. Thus "meaning is determined wholly by the role of a term within a language."[9] So we understand the meaning of the word *brown* by its relation to all other color terms, and not by its relation to brown objects in the world.[10] This view of language is therefore decidedly holistic, with each and every word "defined not simply by its relation to a few other words but by its place in the entire structure. Make the least change in that structure and the term's meaning changes."[11]

On the Fido-Fido theory of language both words and meaning are generally stable, in that we continue to use the same words (whenever we have a particular object in mind) to mean the same thing, and to pick out the particular idea of a dog. The introduction of one new term into a language "changes all terms. And there is no question of the new term 'bringing a meaning with it.' We cannot coin a term, giving it a meaning, and simply add it with its meaning to the language. We cannot borrow a foreign word with its meaning; once borrowed, its old meaning is irrelevant."[12] As Saussure writes, the meaning of a word "exists only through its relation with, and opposition to, words associated with it, just like any other genuine sign."[13] The upshot of Saussure's view is that a language is an autonomous system, "to be

---

[8]Ferdinand de Saussure, *Course in General Linguistics*, ed. Charles Bally and Albert Sechehaye, trans. Wade Baskin (New York: McGraw-Hill, 1966), 88.

[9]Devitt and Sterelny, *Language and Reality*, 262.

[10]See Jonathan Culler, *Saussure* (London: Fontana, 1976), 25.

[11]Devitt and Sterelny, *Language and Reality*, 263.

[12]Ibid.

[13]Saussure, *Course in General Linguistics*, 22. For Saussure, human language is much more arbitrary than we ever imagined. Consider the word *dog* and also the idea of a dog. Saussure refers to the former as the "sign" and the idea of a dog as a "signifier." Everyone agrees we could have used a different word (instead of *dog*) to refer to that creature. Thus the word is in some sense arbitrary. But he also thinks the concept of "dog" is arbitrary, as there are no good or compelling reasons to focus on the five or six characteristics we think are essential to "dogs." There is much more to Saussure's view, but the striking feature here is how utterly arbitrary language is.

explained entirely in its own terms *without any reference to anything outside its structure.*[14] It is both "self-defining" and "self-contained."[15] Saussure's view of language thus has no genuine role for the idea of external reference to play, and is governed, much like chess, by a set of rules that apply to language but to nothing beyond language. Structuralists after Saussure followed him in their attempt to determine what language structures apply to each language and to the social conditions that give rise to language. Structuralists thus promoted the idea that structuralism was objective and scientific every bit as much as chemistry and biology. The focus of the structuralist is not on particular linguistic acts (e.g., one person talking to another), but the broad system of language that lays down the rules which make particular language acts possible and meaningful.

Finally, prior to Saussure linguistics was very much interested in the historical development of languages. For example, that a particular word (W) comes from the Latin and Greek, that it used to mean such and such but now has broadened in meaning and also means thus and thus. Such a historically informed approach to language is obvious to anyone who has consulted the mammoth *Oxford English Dictionary* (often known as the *OED*), which seeks to present the known historical background and word origin for virtually every word in this very big dictionary.[16] Such historical approaches are often referred to as diachronic—they are interested in how certain words and their meanings have developed over time. By contrast, however, Saussure and the later structuralists advocated an approach that is essentially ahistorical, that is, historical development is irrelevant to the meaning of a word. Rather, his approach is synchronic (occurring at a given or particular time). What matters is how a word relates to others words in the language system here and now. What it might have meant last year or in Shakespeare's England is completely irrelevant for its present meaning, which is determined by the whole language system in which it is but one small part. One central idea in structuralist interpretation is to "study the structure of all the elements in the [particular] work taken as a whole; these elements become the clue or 'code' that points to the deeper meaning-structure behind the

---

[14]Devitt and Sterelny, *Language and Reality*, 264 (emphasis added).

[15]Saussure, *Course in General Linguistics*, 26.

[16]One recent edition of the *OED* is twenty volumes long and contains some 22 thousand pages and 59 million words!

writer's surface words."[17] Structuralists believe that human language structures have basic similarities with other structures and that this structure is ultimately grounded in the way the human brain works, making the broad structures the same across different cultures and different languages. When one considers that meanings are determined by their current place/role in a particular language system, one can quickly see how the idea of meanings being stable (unchanging) over time evaporates into thin air. What a word meant in 1903, 1953, or 2003 is completely irrelevant to what the word means in, say, August of 2015 as I write.

To say that structuralism came under attack would be a significant understatement. For both philosophical and political reasons it came to be replaced by an even more radical view of language and meaning, one pioneered by the French thinker Jacques Derrida (1930–2004) that began to emerge in the wake of the massive political protests in Paris in 1968.[18] Grant Osborne, D. A. Carson, John Searle, Anthony Thiselton, and others have been sharply critical of structuralism, and here we will only briefly present four of the criticisms of it.[19]

First, the idea that historical development does not matter for current word meaning is simply untenable. Words and their meanings do not arise out of nothing, but rather in a particular social and cultural environment, an environment that is decidedly historical.

Second, many scholars see the concept of intentionality (what a person is seeking or intending to do) as crucial for understanding both written and spoken language. When one person talks to another they are typically attempting/intending to convey or communicate some sort of message to the other person. They may be saying how they feel, asking a question, answering a question, commenting on the weather, or a host of other possibilities. And if we don't fully understand what someone has just said, we may well ask, "What do you mean by that?" Then our conversation partner may reword or rephrase in an attempt to make clearer what they intended to communicate the first time.

---

[17]Grant Osborne, *The Hermeneutical Spiral: A Comprehensive Introduction to Biblical Interpretation* (Downers Grove, IL: InterVarsity Press, 1991), 372.

[18]For the general importance of 1968 for French thought and culture, see Kristin Ross, *May '68 and Its Afterlives* (Chicago: University of Chicago Press, 2002).

[19]For more detailed criticisms, see the cited works of Searle, Osborne, Carson, Wolterstorff, and others.

Third, focusing on structure may fail to grasp key differences in meaning. Consider the following two examples:

(A) John is easy to please.

and

(B) John is eager to please.

As John Searle rightly argues, these two sentences look as if they have the same grammatical structure, as each "is a sequence of noun-copula-adjective-infinitive verb." Yet in spite of this surface similarity, "the grammar of the two is quite different. In the first sentence, though it is not apparent from the surface word order, 'John' functions as the direct object of the verb to please; the sentence means: it is easy for someone to please John."[20] But in the second sentence "John" "functions as the subject of the verb to please; the sentence means: John is eager that he please someone."[21] Searle notes that there "is no easy or natural way to account for these facts within structuralist assumptions."[22] They have the same structure, but very different meanings, a distinction that structuralism cannot adequately account for.

Fourth, for both structuralists and later critics of structuralism such as Noam Chomsky (1928–), language is defined by its grammatical structure and this grammatical structure is grounded in the workings of the human brain. But both Searle and many of Chomsky's students argue that one of the key factors in shaping grammatical (or syntactical) structure is semantics, where semantics can be understood to be the study of meaning. Searle argues that "saying something and meaning it is essentially a matter of saying it with the intention to produce certain effects on the hearer. . . . Any attempt to account for the meaning of sentences must take into account their role in communication, in the performance of speech acts, because an essential part of the meaning of any sentence is its potential for being used to perform a speech act."[23] Suppose someone makes the fairly simple claim

The flower is red.

---

[20]John Searle, "Chomsky's Revolution in Linguistics," in *On Noam Chomsky: Critical Essays*, ed. Gilbert Harman (New York: Doubleday, 1974), 5.
[21]Ibid.
[22]Ibid.
[23]Ibid., 35-36.

What is involved in making this claim? Searle argues that the statement involves performing an action (saying the above sentence) "with the intention of producing in the hearer the belief that the speaker is committed [intellectually speaking] to the existence of a certain state of affairs [a particular way the world is], as determined by the semantic [meaning-oriented] rules attaching to the sentence."[24] So a very simple claim involves the speaker doing something, intending for the hearer to understand them, and believing that the external world contains a red flower. So a simple claim is already a very rich one in that it involves a number of important concepts: speech acts, intending or intentionality, and the idea of reference that Saussure and other structuralists wanted to do away with.

For these and a host of other reasons detailed by Searle, Osborne, Carson, and various literary theorists, the structuralist account of language is no longer the latest and greatest view on language. In France and other countries structuralism has been superseded by even more radical views of language, dominated by the work of Jacques Derrida and what has come to be called poststructuralism or deconstruction. Deconstruction, according to one dictionary, can be defined as "a method of critical analysis of . . . language that emphasizes the internal workings of language and conceptual systems, the relational quality of meaning, and the assumptions implicit in forms of expression."[25]

Before we examine Derrida's view, it is helpful to briefly make mention of two influential movements that also influenced theories of language, namely, New Criticism and the work of the (later) Ludwig Wittgenstein.

Up until the 1930s the author was seen as having a key role in properly understanding a text; the intentions of the author were relevant for understanding what the author has produced in a particular text. Then in the 1930s and 1940s arose a very different approach to understanding texts, an approach often called New Criticism. William Wimsatt and Monroe Beardsley[26] published a number of influential essays in which they claimed that the idea of authorial intent is irrelevant for understanding a particular text, emphasizing much more the text itself than any possible contribution

---

[24]Ibid., 36.

[25]Archie Hobson, *The Oxford Dictionary of Difficult Words* (New York: Oxford University Press, 2004), 115.

[26]William K. Wimsatt and Monroe C. Beardsley, "The Intentional Fallacy," *Sewanee Review* 54 (1946): 468-88.

the author may or may not have made to the meaning of the text. This New Criticism dominated until 1960 or so, and is still influential today.

Ludwig Wittgenstein (1889–1951) is one of the most influential thinkers of the twentieth century. His early work is brilliant and original, though not relevant for the current discussion. The work he did in the last twenty years of his life, what is usually referred to as the later Wittgenstein, is what concerns us here. In a posthumously published work known as the *Philosophical Investigations* (1953), Wittgenstein argues at length that the ordinary and everyday use of language does more to obscure reality than it does to make it plain. We need to properly understand how language works before we are in any position to even consider pursuing philosophical issues and problems. He writes that "philosophy is a battle against the bewitchment of our intelligence by means of language."[27] What we think of as genuine philosophical problems are merely the symptoms or consequences of the misuse of language. In this sense, Wittgenstein's approach can be seen as therapeutic: paying careful attention to language helps us better see there really was no genuine philosophical problem after all. Wittgenstein sees language use as governed by a set of rules that in many ways compares to games we play. As such, we don't really understand the game (language) unless we first become familiar with the rules.

DERRIDA, DECONSTRUCTION, AND THE DEFERMENT OF MEANING

Derrida is one of the most influential thinkers of the past fifty years. The problem is that it is not always clear exactly what Derrida is claiming, and some have had their doubts whether Derrida himself really knew what he saying! Traditional views of language were committed to language being objectively meaningful, to many sentences being true, and to there being a difference between literal and metaphorical meaning.[28] Derrida's view of language seriously challenges all of these commitments and much, much more.[29] Given that Derrida's main claims are notoriously difficult to pin down, what follows is a brief and general overview of the broad outlines of Derrida's approach, summarized in six central claims.[30] So, Derrida in a nutshell:

---

[27]Ludwig Wittgenstein, *Philosophical Investigations*, trans. G. E. M. Anscombe (Oxford: Blackwell, 1953), no. 109.

[28]This is indebted to Devitt and Sterelny, *Language and Reality*, 260.

[29]Derrida's views on language are captured in his *Of Grammatology*, trans. Gayatri Chakravorty Spivak (Baltimore: Johns Hopkins University Press, 1976).

[30]For some sympathetic approaches to Derrida, see the work of James K. A. Smith, *Who's Afraid of*

1. Traditional Western philosophy (stretching back through Descartes to Plato) has been committed both to the possibility of knowing things and to there being such a thing as objective truth, where what is true is independent of what any humans might think about it.[31]

2. This Western tradition, Derrida argues, has worked with (or assumed) a view of language that is simple and transparent, and seen language as having the capability to mirror or reflect this objectively real world, which we can capture with language.[32]

3. This view of language is radically flawed, and as such doing philosophy while working with this mistaken view of language is a futile and doomed enterprise.

4. Derrida proposes that we understand language differently, that we deconstruct it—take it apart piece by piece to reveal what is truly going on beneath the surface. He argues that a good deal of what is going on beneath the surface is not neutral, objective writing about some particular topic, but rather a clearly political/ethical commentary on who and what is good and who and what is not.

5. In this sense deconstruction is a tool for *delegitimization*, that is, to identify, challenge, and (perhaps) overthrow the political authority structures of the world we live in, a world that he sees as historically oppressive and exclusionary and thus in need of change. Deconstruction is thus a tool of liberation.

6. At its heart then, Derrida's deconstruction is a politically motivated attack on the injustice of the traditional West and a call for language and discourse to promote and reflect this fundamental commitment to justice. Derrida (and many other postmoderns) is clearly comfortable emphasizing politics and justice more than he emphasizes truth. Whether he can justify putting politics before truth is a worthwhile question.

Postmodernism? Taking Derrida, Lyotard, and Foucault to Church, The Church and Postmodern Culture (Grand Rapids: Baker Academic, 2006); Merold Westphal, *Postmodern Philosophy and Christian Thought* (Bloomington: Indiana University Press, 1999); and Jonathan Culler, *On Deconstruction: Theory and Criticism After Structuralism* (Ithaca, NY: Cornell University Press, 2008).

[31]It is accurate to understand Derrida as a skeptic of sorts.

[32]As Derrida puts it, "A text remains, moreover, forever imperceptible." See Jacques Derrida, *Dissemination*, trans. Barbara Johnson (Chicago: University of Chicago Press, 1983), 63.

In what follows we will briefly seek to unpack these six claims, and then seek to determine their various strengths and weaknesses.

Claims 1-3. Derrida is undoubtedly correct that traditional Western philosophy is committed to the possibility of humans having genuine knowledge of the world and to the idea of objective truth apart from both humans and their use of language. He emphatically rejects both of these commitments, and in so doing he ends up "rejecting most of the fundamental pillars of modern Western civilization."[33] Traditionally, language has been seen as capable of accurately capturing metaphysical truth about the world, and as such it is understood as a device "for putting thoughts ('meanings') into words so as to communicate them from author to reader, and by that view of interpretation which takes as its goal the recovery of those thoughts from the words."[34] Derrida labels this philosophical commitment belief in *presence.* Derrida understands this presence to have two major components.

First, self-presence: to be self-present (or present in all the fullness of what something is) is for something to exist on its own prior to being presented/expressed in language. In some definite sense a dog is not fully a dog independent of its being presented and expressed in language.[35] In other words, part of what makes a dog a dog is its relation to all nondogs (of which there are many!). To use the word *dog* apart from all of its relations (of which there is an infinite number) is to present only a part (or *trace*, as Derrida calls it) of the idea of a dog. To mistake the word *dog* (or any other word) for a full-blooded and complete concept is to misunderstand how language works and how it has influenced (in this case, infected) traditional Western metaphysics. In this important sense Derrida argues that the full meaning of any and every concept can never be captured by human language. Each word is related to everything that is different from it (the sum total of all its relations to other words), and this idea of *difference* cannot be adequately captured by language. Traditional Western

---

[33]Lawrence Cahoone, introduction to *From Modernism to Postmodernism: An Anthology*, ed. Lawrence Cahoone (Oxford: Blackwell, 1996), 2.

[34]Nicholas Wolterstorff, *Divine Discourse: Philosophical Reflections on the Claim That God Speaks* (Cambridge: Cambridge University Press, 1995), 156.

[35]Derrida believes that all thought is mediated (filtered) through language, but language always fails to fully express these thoughts. Derrida asks, "How could a piece of knowledge or language be properly clear or obscure?" See Jacques Derrida, *Margins of Philosophy*, trans. Alan Bass (Chicago: University of Chicago Press, 1985), 252.

philosophy, following Plato and Descartes, has mistakenly assumed that the full meaning of any concept is present in language. Derrida's goal is to demonstrate this fundamental mistake and replace it with a much more modest (and playful) view of language. This is a big part of what deconstruction is all about—undermining the authority and tradition of Western philosophy. Meaning, Derrida affirms, occurs only when language is used. "It does not exist anterior [prior] to signification."[36] This is part of the context for Derrida's often-repeated (and often misunderstood) claim that "there is nothing outside of the text." We can now see that he means that there are no meanings prior to or apart from language, and even then language only captures traces of the real thing.

Second, presence to consciousness: Here Derrida is making a claim about human knowledge. Remember that Plato, Descartes, and the Western tradition thought that certain human knowledge was possible. But knowledge of what? Knowledge of concepts and their existence in the external (objectively real) world.[37] But, Derrida asks, how is this possible? If concepts lack genuine self-presence, then they certainly lack availability (through human consciousness) for humans to know them. And since they do lack self-presence, they are hardly fully available to human thought/consciousness.[38] Derrida argues that neither objects (what we are thinking about) or the subject (self) doing the thinking are fully present. Rather than having a fully present (and enduring) self thinking about a fully present object, and thus knowing it, we have the hint or trace of a self/subject thinking about the trace of an object/concept. This is certainly not knowledge according to the Western tradition! Both meaning and the human self are the products of human language,[39] and even that in a very minimal way. We thus construct the world in that we make meanings and we construct ourselves.

Claims 4-5. So what exactly does Derrida's idea of deconstruction involve? There is much that could be said here, but we shall limit ourselves to a few comments.

---

[36] Ibid., 157.
[37] For Descartes what is immediately known is in our mind, but that is a topic for another day.
[38] The argument runs something like the following:

    1. Presence to consciousness requires self-presence.

    2. Self-presence does not occur.

    3. ∴ Presence to consciousness is not possible.

[39] As Wolterstorff puts it, "Meaning is a creature of language." Wolterstorff, *Divine Discourse*, 161.

The purpose of deconstruction is (at least) twofold.

First, deconstruction seeks to undermine and delegitimate the Western philosophical tradition and its commitment to metaphysics. Besides being philosophically flawed, Derrida (and many other poststructuralists) sees traditional writing as both exclusionary and oppressive. What does he mean by this? Throughout Western history particular groups of people have treated other ("different") groups of people with hatred and disrespect. In the history of the United States alone, it is relatively simple to quickly bring to mind a long list of people groups who have been, for various reasons, excluded from positions of power and from mainstream society, including (among others), African Americans, Jews, Native Americans, Latinos, and gays and lesbians. Derrida, himself a Jew of Algerian descent, often felt the sting of discrimination growing up. Following a political path that is clearly left leaning,[40] Derrida's program of deconstruction clearly seeks to undermine the privilege and authority that goes with writing, and the writing of history in particular. Traditional writing, Derrida believes, privileges particular hierarchies (systems) of authority and tends to exclude all who are regarded as radically other (different). History shows us that to be considered different is to be excluded, both in theory and in practice, and deconstruction seeks to overturn this entire Western tradition.

Second, given the reality of there being no self-presence, the idea of a text having a particular, fixed, or stable meaning quickly unravels. Texts are rather polyvalent—they have multiple meanings. Each interpretive community is free to read and understand a text on its own terms. Thus different communities will tend to produce different meanings. Realizing that all language is (at best) metaphor, one finds language is characterized by radical absence (no literal meaning) and a lack of rigid guidelines for determining the meaning(s) of a text.[41] Deconstruction is presented as a tool for decentering, for moving the focus from a literally minded reading of texts that are seen as referential and meaningful to a reading that opens up numerous possible

---

[40]Though many of Derrida's political views are broadly sympathetic to Marxist thought, his views are broad and diffuse enough to resist simple labeling on such matters. He does make clear more than once that he is opposed to de facto Marxism (Marxism in actual practice) or communism. See Simon Glendinning, *Derrida: A Very Short Introduction* (New York: Oxford University Press, 2011), 84.

[41]See Osborne, *Hermeneutical Spiral*, 375-76.

meanings. In this sense, as Grant Osborne says, summarizing Derrida, "Closure [recovering a certain specific meaning] is impossible because when we unlock the door to the signs [the words used], we find the room empty: there is no central or original meaning. Rather, a text is 'open' or free to be reproduced in the reader's experience."[42]

Claim 6. Derrida's commitment to justice is notoriously complex, even by Derridean standards. It will suffice to say that he sees traditional Western thought as secretly smuggling into language the reality of power, exclusion, and oppression. Deconstruction is a means to reveal these underlying structures and to open writing and the world to a broader, more pluralistic, and thus more humane understanding of meanings and the language to which they are attached.[43]

EVALUATION OF DERRIDA

There is a massive literature that deals with Derrida and poststructuralism, and what follows is obviously selective in what it focuses on, though hopefully the comments below indicate that a blanket condemnation of Derrida's thought is neither justified nor fair. What can we learn from Derrida on these matters?

Strengths. Derrida is correct that human language is significantly metaphorical in nature. As Osborne writes, "Any valid hermeneutic must deal with the metaphorical and rhetorical dimensions of language. The process of deriving a core of meaning in a text is every bit as complex (though not so impossible) as Derrida asserts."[44] The Bible is a rich repository of many literary types, and though literal meanings are often to be found, so are many other types of language and literature.

Derrida is also correct that many readers understand texts in a literal sense, even though he sees the text as shot through with metaphors. The key issue here is whether a thoroughly metaphorical understanding of language is defensible, and the great majority of evangelical scholars think Derrida is mistaken on this point. When someone says, "She is in over her head on this

---

[42]Ibid., 382.

[43]Despite his serious doubts about the confident pursuit of certain knowledge by Plato, Descartes, and others, Derrida seems committed to the idea (moral standard) that justice is not susceptible to deconstruction. See Jacques Derrida, "Force of Law: The Mysterious Foundation of Authority," in *Acts of Religion*, trans. G. Amidjar (London: Routledge, 2002), 228-98.

[44]Ibid., 384.

one," we are not referring to her lack of height or to some physical object that is higher than her head. We are affirming that she is in a situation that she may well not have the resources or capabilities to handle easily or well. On the other hand, when we say, "The dog is outside; please let him in," this is a literally intended sentence with no metaphor involved. Finally, even when we use a metaphor such as "It is raining cats and dogs," everyone knows there are no cats or dogs falling from the sky, but there is a literal core here, namely, it is raining hard. Generally speaking, for metaphors to be meaningful they must have some factual/literal connection with the real world.

It is perfectly appropriate to deconstruct some texts in a Derrida-inspired manner. As Nicholas Wolterstorff writes, "There are a few texts, and passages in a fair number of texts, which call for exactly Derrida's style of interpretation."[45] Texts that are heavily metaphorical and/or poetic and texts that clearly have a deeper/hidden level of meaning both lend themselves, when appropriate, to a Derridean analysis. Two examples that come to mind are T. S. Eliot's epic poem *The Waste Land* and George Orwell's *Animal Farm*. *The Waste Land* is poetic, dense, obscure (often intentionally), and cries out for nonstandard analyses. *Animal Farm*, on the other hand, is a thinly disguised barnyard attack on Joseph Stalin and the evils of Soviet-style socialism, a critique that would be extended and further developed in Orwell's *1984*.

Derrida is correct that (at least) many of the concepts we use in language, as Peter Sedgwick says, "are inherently context-related, yet at the same time governed by absolute conditions that make the ultimate determination of meaning irreducible to any particular context."[46] We often need to know quite a bit of context before we can be relatively confident that we are in a good position to grasp the intended meaning. But even here those with some sympathies to Derrida, while agreeing we are often unable to decide on one particular (or "correct") interpretation of a text, can, as Umberto Eco says, "agree on the fact that certain interpretations are not contextually legitimated."[47] Thus according to D. A. Carson, Eco believes that interpreters "can largely agree on what interpretations cannot be accepted as 'the privileged one.'"[48]

---

[45]Wolterstorff, *Divine Discourse*, 169.
[46]Peter Sedgwick, *Descartes to Derrida: An Introduction to European Philosophy* (Malden, MA: Blackwell, 2001), 213.
[47]Umberto Eco, *The Limits of Interpretation* (Bloomington: Indiana University Press, 1994), 41.
[48]Carson, *Gagging of God*, 77.

Derrida is correct in seeing that metaphysics is to be found everywhere. What this means is that there is no absolutely neutral, objective starting point that somehow avoids a commitment both to metaphysics and to what Derrida calls the metaphysics of presence. Whether this commitment to metaphysics is part and parcel of what needs to be rejected is another matter though, a matter on which Derrida's thinking is not always crystal clear. More than once Derrida recognizes that it is impossible to fully escape having metaphysical beliefs.

Weaknesses. Derrida's view of language has many serious weaknesses. Though we argued above that there are various strengths to Derrida's approach, the weaknesses are striking in two important senses: (1) how many there are and (2) how serious many of the problems are. A human prone to headaches, arthritis, stiff knees, and mediocre hearing can live a happy and fulfilling life because none of the health problems are life-threatening or serious enough to compromise the joy of living each and every day. Suppose, on the other hand, that a person has stage four brain cancer, congestive heart failure, failing kidneys, cirrhosis of the liver, Crohn's disease, type 2 diabetes, Parkinson's disease, gout, serious dental issues, and two disintegrating cervical disks! To say such a person has "a few medical problems" would be the understatement of the year. Though we find much that is praiseworthy and/or insightful in postmodernism, Derrida's view of language is seriously compromised by the sheer quantity and quality of the problems it faces. There are more serious problems than can be addressed in an introductory book such as this; here we limit ourselves to the following problems.

Derrida clearly is not a big fan of authorial intent, and he is mistaken in ruling it out. Carson, N. T. Wright, Kevin Vanhoozer, Osborne, Wolterstorff, David Dockery, Searle, Moisés Silva, and Michael Devitt and Kim Sterelny are all committed to the importance of authorial intent. Though authorial intent is not the only factor that helps make objective meaning possible, it is one of them.

As Wolterstorff and many others make clear, Derrida misses the point that much of our everyday communication (through writing, speech, and other modes) is highly effective. If Derrida were right about the pervasiveness of metaphors and what he calls the slippage of meaning (the gap between what the text means and whether the reader grasps the fullness of that meaning), then it would border on the miraculous that effective communication ever took place. And those of you who read the previous sentence probably understood what we had in mind when we wrote it. So the Derridean argument can be generalized along the following lines:

1. If language lacks presence and is shot through with metaphor, then genuine communication is not possible.

2. Language does lack presence and is thoroughly metaphorical.

_____

3. ∴ So genuine communication is not possible.

More formally, we respond to Derrida's *modus ponens* argument with a *modus tollens* argument along the following lines:

1. If language lacks presence and is shot through with metaphor, then effective communication is not possible.

2. But such communication is very much possible.

_____

3. ∴ So it is not true that language lacks presence and is shot through with metaphor.[49]

How do we decide between these two competing arguments? Other than flipping a coin (not a reliable method) or randomly guessing (as our students sometime do), we think there is much more evidence in favor of the claim

(E) Effective communication takes place (easily established)

than Derrida's (highly abstract) claim,

(L) Language lacks presence and is shot through with metaphor.

_____

[49]The logical structure for this argument is:
1. If A, then B
2. Not B

_____
3. ∴ Not A

If we were betting people, we would put our money, virtually all of it, on (E). More importantly, the evidence clearly favors (E) over (L).

Derrida wants us to understand texts as lacking any certain or objective meaning. Okay, so what about Derrida's own texts, the texts where he tells us (over and over) that meaning is endlessly deferred and that there is no metaphysics of presence possible? Is what is good for the goose also good for the gander? If Derrida is correct, then the lack of objective textual meaning infects not only the traditional texts of the West but also his own. To cite Shakespeare here, it seems he is "hoist with his own petard."[50] As Wolterstorff incisively notes, "Paradoxical as it may seem, he wants us to apply to his own texts that very mode of interpretation against which he launches a general attack."[51] Derrida has no good reason to think his own texts are exceptional (deserving of different treatment) in this regard. So we are attempting to figure out the meaning of the texts written by the man who says texts have no fixed or determinate meaning. *C'est incroyable,*[52] as Derrida's colleagues in Paris might say. If all texts lack determinate meaning, then so do Derrida's. If none of them do, then what is the problem?[53]

One need not be a Christian philosopher to find much of Derrida's understanding of language objectionable. Devitt and Sterelny, for example, the authors of a well-respected text on the philosophy of language, write that

> the most surprising and objectionable feature of structuralism [and poststructuralism] is that it *omits reference*. It is central to the meaning of "brown" that it refers to brown things. A word's relation to others in the language—*internal* relations—may often be important to its meaning. . . . But a language's relation to the nonlinguistic world—its *external* relations—are always important.[54]

Structuralists and poststructuralists do talk about reference at times, but they always have internal (rather than external) objects in mind. Terence Hawkes, a noted structuralist, goes as far to claim that "the word 'dog' exists and functions within the structure of the English language, without reference to any four-legged barking creature's real existence."[55] This

---

[50]From *Hamlet*. A petard is a bomb, so the idea is to be blown up by one's own bomb.
[51]Wolterstorff, *Divine Discourse*, 153.
[52]Literally (assuming no metaphors here) "that's incredible."
[53]There is a middle ground here (that only some texts lack determinate meaning), but it is not one pursued by Derrida or his followers.
[54]Devitt and Sterelny, *Language and Reality*, 263 (emphasis original).
[55]Terence Hawkes, *Structuralism and Semiotics* (Berkeley: University of California Press, 1977), 17.

rejection of external reference by both structuralists such as Saussure and poststructuralists such as Derrida make such views "fundamentally implausible. For reference has been a central notion in our theory of language. With its rejection must go the rejection also of a place for a notion of truth in linguistics."[56] A further and very serious problem is that such views tend to lead to antirealism. Realism is the idea, accepted by most Christian and many (most) non-Christian philosophers, that "the ordinary furniture of our environment—cats, trees, stones, etc.—exist independently of us and our thoughts on the matter."[57]

Along these lines, both Saussure and Derrida would have serious difficulties accounting for the obvious reality of linguistic translation. If meanings are entirely determined by the various relations internal to a language system, then "how can the elements of one structure [language] be equivalent to the elements of another? What could make one translation—one matching of the elements of one with the elements of another—better than another? (Structuralists tend to accept that translation is often difficult but not impossible.)."[58] For example, Albert Camus's novel *The Stranger* is written in the French (as *L'Étranger*), and there are numerous English translations, beginning with Stuart Gilbert in 1946. So (1) translation is clearly possible, where it would not be if meaning were entirely determined by the specific language and phrases used in the original writing; and (2) some translations are better than others. For example, a thorough knowledge of French will give a translator of Camus a distinct advantage over someone who has but two years of French in high school.

Derrida and many of the poststructuralists believe that political oppression is a morally bad thing. This is straightforward enough. And Derrida himself clearly develops a serious commitment to the idea of justice. But what does Derrida's position require here, philosophically speaking? If one wants to say that x is bad, one clearly needs some sort of criterion or standard for evaluating x. So, for example, here is the standard for x. Let's call it S; x falls far short of S, so we rightly conclude that x is bad in some moral sense. But do Derrida and his fellow deconstructionists have any objective standard

---

[56]Devitt and Sterelny, *Language and Reality*, 266.
[57]Ibid., 12. Devitt and Sterelny, Searle, Plantinga, Alvin Goldman, and Wolterstorff (to name but six prominent thinkers) are all realists. Derrida, Rorty, and Saussure are all antirealists.
[58]Ibid., 267.

for judging acts such as *x*? There is a dilemma here, one we might call Derrida's dilemma: If the answer is no, then he has no grounds for criticizing oppression. If the answer is yes, then he needs to offer good reasons for thinking such standards exist, something he has not done. If standards, like meaning, are internal to systems, then the big bad wicked Oppressor[59] can always respond to Derrida and company that their standards are fine given their own system of language and belief, and that Derrida's standards are foreign to them and thus simply do not apply. Case closed.

Related to the previous criticism, one gets the impression from reading Derrida that his political commitments are poorly supported, philosophically speaking. Rather, as Mark Lilla and others have noted, it seems more accurate to say that *politics* drives Derrida and deconstruction more than philosophy drives politics. This is a matter of putting the cart before the horse. Lilla writes that "politics dictated and philosophy wrote."[60] As Vincent Descombes has remarked, "Taking a political position is and remains the decisive test in France; it is what should reveal the ultimate meaning of philosophy."[61] There is nothing wrong with having political views or with recognizing the importance of politics. What we object to is when the mere presentation of political claims (such as "oppression is bad") is somehow a substitute for serious argumentation, something Derrida often lacks. Politics could be more important than truth, but at the least we need to see an argument to make the case for this possibility. This Derrida simply does not do. Both Searle and Wolterstorff comment on the striking absence (no presence here) of good (or any) arguments offered in support of Derrida's deconstructive agenda. Wolterstorff notes that when it comes to Derrida's wholesale rejection of metaphysics, especially Western metaphysics, "he doesn't argue, but simply declares his rejection."[62] If I stand on the street corner and declare over and over that all metaphysics should be rejected (itself a metaphysical claim!), the reasonability of the claim does not increase

---

[59]Consider that the actions of the Big Bad Wolf would *not* be considered oppressive by the local Wolves Labor Union (Wolves Local 258).

[60]Mark Lilla, "The Politics of Jacques Derrida," *New York Review of Books*, June 25, 1998, 36-41.

[61]Vincent Descombes, *Modern French Philosophy* (Cambridge: Cambridge University Press, 1980), cited in Lilla, "Politics of Jacques Derrida," 36.

[62]Wolterstorff, *Divine Discourse*, 171.

in direct proportion to how often or how fervently I dedicate *mon coeur*[63] to the antimetaphysical cause.

Many structuralists and poststructuralists believe that human language has significant constructive or world-making abilities. What exactly does this mean? Remember that the idea of reference, discussed above, is the central link between language on the one hand and an independently existing reality on the other. In other words, the view about reality known as realism hinges on there being such a reality as reference (words that genuinely refer beyond language and the human mind to an independently existing reality). But Saussure, Derrida, and a whole bunch of French thinkers reject the very notion of reference as vacuous. The only thing words refer to are other words. Whatever idea of reference there is reduces to being internally related to other words and concepts within the same language system. Consider the following quote from Fredric Jameson on the structuralist view of the sign. He writes, "Its concept of the sign forbids any research into the reality beyond it, at the same time that it keeps alive the notions of such a reality by considering the signified [that to which the word or sign seems to refer] as a concept *of* something."[64] Everyone agrees that languages are humanly constructed. Furthermore, it seems clearly true that *theories* about reality are humanly constructed. Neither of these claims is controversial or unsettling. But both structuralists and poststructuralists such as Derrida go beyond these two truths to claim that humans thus (through their linguistic actions) actually bring reality into existence—we create the world! As Hawkes puts it, "Writing . . . can be seen to cause a new reality to come into being."[65] This is antirealism with a vengeance. We move from humans creating language to humans creating theories to humans constructing the world. They are then committed to the idea that the existence of an external reality depends on what *we* do with language—we are minigods in our ability to create. We do experience the world and we do organize our experiences, but *none* of this has any direct bearing on the debate between the realist and the antirealist. Another problem faced by this sort of constructivism concerns facts about the past. John Searle writes,

---

[63]That is, "my heart."

[64]Fredric Jameson, *The Prison-House of Language* (Princeton, NJ: Princeton University Press, 1972), 106 (emphasis original).

[65]Hawkes, *Structuralism and Semiotics*, 149 (emphasis original).

Are we now constructing facts about the past when we make claims about history? One extreme social constructivist . . . , Bruno Latour, accepts this conclusion with somewhat comical results. Recent research shows that the ancient Egyptian pharaoh Ramses II probably died of tuberculosis. But according to Latour, this is impossible because the tuberculosis bacillus was only discovered by Robert Koch in 1882. "Before Koch, the bacillus had no real existence." To say that Ramses II died of tuberculosis is as absurd as saying that he died of machine-gun fire.[66]

Constructivism about the world and about the past are radical ideas, ones that are neither philosophically supported nor acceptable to traditional Christianity and its commitment to the eternal reality of the triune God.

There is a massive amount of evidence supporting modest conclusions concerning the sociology of knowledge—roughly the idea that our environment, culture, biology, passions, what we read, and countless other factors all influence what we believe and how we look at the world. So far so good. The problem for Derrida and company is that "too much emphasis on social context threatens to reduce truth to mere social history."[67] There are no compelling reasons why we cannot both acknowledge the powerful effect of various influences on what we believe and also claim there is such a thing as objective truth, and, to quote Alvin Plantinga, "It's a good thing, too." As both Searle and Kelly have pointed out,[68] our being situated (or seeing things from a particular perspective) is entirely compatible with there being both objective truth and genuine knowledge of that truth. Searle writes that "actual human efforts to get true representations of reality are influenced by all sorts of factors—cultural, economic, psychological, and so on."[69] But the fact that no view of reality is without presuppositions or the reality of external factors that influence us is not inconsistent with realism. Searle goes on to claim that "this does not seem to be an attack on even the most naïve form of realism. It just says that in order to know reality, you have to know it from a particular point of view."[70] If eight people witness a car accident,

---

[66]John R. Searle, "Why Should You Believe It?," *New York Review of Books*, September 24, 2009, 88-92.

[67]Anthony Thiselton, *Interpreting God and the Postmodern Self: On Meaning, Manipulation, and Promise* (Grand Rapids: Eerdmans, 1995), xi.

[68]See Searle, *Construction of Social Reality*, and Kelly, *Truth Considered and Applied*.

[69]Searle, *Construction of Social Reality*, 151.

[70]John Searle, *Mind, Language and Society: Philosophy in the Real World* (New York: Basic Books, 1998), 21.

each from a particular point of view (depending on their location relative to the accident itself), there are eight different perspectives but it hardly follows that there was no objective (here, public) event that really happened. No police officer has ever argued, "All the witnesses viewed the accident from their own perspective, therefore, there was no accident, objectively speaking." The officer would be reprimanded for general idiocy! So there is nothing about the sociology of knowledge that poses any serious threat to our belief in a mind-independent external world, that is, a belief in realism. One last point is in order here. Some may believe that genuine knowledge requires that the knower/perceiver is somehow without any perspective, but such a view is humanly impossible, as N. T. Wright and Thomas Nagel have argued.[71] As Wright puts it, "The great Enlightenment dream of simply recording 'what actually happened' is just that: a dream."[72] The upshot of all this is that we affirm the significance of the sociology of knowledge but also the existence of a mind-independent world and the possibility of having objective knowledge of that world.

One of the main purposes people write books, articles, essays, and the like is because they believe that what they are writing is true. For example, who would write a book that contained statements that the author thought were mostly false?[73] We write x because we believe x, and we believe x because we think x is true. In this important sense there is an important connection among writing, language, and truth. There is also an intimate connection between belief and truth. Suppose someone said to you, "I believe x, y, and z," but I don't think any of the three beliefs are true. This strikes most of us as puzzling, if not ridiculous. To believe is to think something is (at least) probably *true*. Plantinga writes that to be committed to something "is to think it is true, not just true relative to what you or someone believes."[74] Derrida's appeal to deconstruction makes truth a nonissue in that it undermines the very ideas of external reference and to the concept of truth that reference requires.

Finally, evangelical Christians are committed to the inspiration and the authority of Scripture. They see Scripture as the authoritative revelation (propositional and otherwise) of the one true Creator God. Scripture reveals

---

[71]See Thomas Nagel, *The View from Nowhere* (New York: Oxford University Press, 1986), and N. T. Wright, *The New Testament and the People of God* (Minneapolis: Fortress, 1992).

[72]Wright, *New Testament and the People of God*, 82.

[73]Other than a book on various falsehoods.

[74]Alvin Plantinga, "Augustinian Christian Philosophy," *Monist* 75 (1992): 304 (emphasis original).

truth both about God and about what he has done in and through history in the person of Jesus of Nazareth, who is at once fully God and fully human. Scripture both reveals and constrains. If we take it seriously, we simply cannot believe whatever we want about God, Jesus, sin, salvation, and the good news of the gospel. We aren't free to believe, for example, that God is lacking in goodness, knowledge, or power, nor are we free to deny the divinity of Jesus as deists, Socinians, Arians, Unitarians, Mormons, Jehovah's Witnesses, and many other groups have done in human history.[75]

Deconstruction presents major objections to the idea of the Bible as the authoritative revelation of the one true God. On one hand, it treats the Bible as it would any other text. This undermines the uniqueness of Scripture and the idea that Scripture is authoritative. Jesus himself saw Scripture as authoritative; in John 10 in a dispute with the Jews, who themselves recognize the supreme authority of Scripture, Jesus tells them that a particular command is "written in your Law" (Jn 10:34), and that "the Scripture cannot be broken" (Jn 10:35 NASB). As Carson writes, "The truth of Jesus' claims, and from the Evangelist's perspective, of the Christian claims, was substantiated by the Scripture of the Jews themselves. *Law* here [in Jn 10:34] refers to the entire Old Testament canon, of which the law (the Pentateuch) is the most important part."[76] Being a good Jew, Jesus recognizes the authority of Scripture. Craig Keener writes that "both Jesus and the narrator understand even some detailed acts surrounding his passion as fulfilling Scripture (13:18; 17:12; 19:24, 28, 36), and appeal to Scripture as authoritative elsewhere as well (2:17; 7:38; 20:9)."[77] Though the Jews sometimes seem to bend Scripture to their humanly made traditions, Jesus consistently recognizes the authority and binding nature of Scripture. There is much more that is relevant here, and we will content ourselves with four final comments.

First, as Wolterstorff argues, "The claim that God speaks to human beings occurs over and over in the Bible."[78] Any approach to interpretation that either does not allow for this possibility or sees it as possible but false is fundamentally contrary to Scripture and ultimately answerable to its

---

[75]What most, though not all, heresies/cults have in common is some form of the denial of the divinity of Jesus.

[76]D. A. Carson, *The Gospel According to John*, Pillar New Testament Commentary (Grand Rapids: Eerdmans, 1990), 397.

[77]Craig Keener, *The Gospel of John* (Grand Rapids: Baker Academic, 2010), 1:828.

[78]Nicholas Wolterstorff, "Authorial Discourse Interpretation," in *Dictionary for Theological Interpretation of the Bible*, ed. Kevin J. Vanhoozer (Grand Rapids: Baker Academic, 2005), 78.

authority and the God who inspired it. We have argued that deconstruction errs in not allowing for this possibility.

Second, some approaches to interpreting texts, including the Bible, are better than others. We agree with the New Testament scholar R. T. France when he argues for "the priority in biblical interpretation of what has come to be called 'the first horizon,' i.e. of understanding biblical language within its own context before we start exploring its relevance to our own concerns, and of keeping the essential biblical context in view as a control on the way we apply biblical language to current issues."[79] When we approach texts we need to keep the reader, the text, and the author in mind. To remove any one of these three key elements will not allow us to properly understand or apply any particular biblical text.

Third, the New Testament scholar Ben Witherington rightly emphasizes that the Bible makes many truth claims. Biblical texts also have determinate meaning, though sometimes there may be different levels of meaning for one text, but never an infinite number. He also claims that Scripture is grounded extratextually—in events in space and time witnessed by flesh-and-blood human beings. People in Jerusalem in AD 30[80] would have either seen or heard about the entry into Jerusalem of this man named Jesus. And if they had stayed for the next week, they could have seen his crucifixion and also, that next Sunday, his empty tomb. The fact that the second person of the Trinity became incarnate (literally "in the flesh") attests to the importance of history for traditional Christianity.[81]

And fourth, all of this makes clear that the truth claims of Christianity are textually mediated, that is, they come to us *through texts*. As Francis Watson has argued, the Christian faith is thus committed to the idea that "truth is textually mediated. 'Truth' here is not any truth but the truth that the Word through whom all things were made is the Word who in Jesus Christ has become truth. In this truth all other truth is comprehended."[82] In this very important sense, then, what we have in Scripture is not the absence of presence (and meaning) that Derrida would have us believe, but rather

---

[79]R. T. France, "The Church and the Kingdom of God: Some Hermeneutical Issues," in *Biblical Interpretation and the Church: Text and Context*, ed. D. A. Carson (London: Paternoster, 1984), 41.

[80]Or AD 33, depending on the dating of Jesus' ministry, trial, crucifixion, and resurrection.

[81]See Ben Witherington III, *New Testament History: A Narrative Account* (Grand Rapids: Baker Academic, 2003).

[82]Francis Watson, *Text and Truth: Redefining Biblical Theology* (Grand Rapids: Eerdmans, 2009), 1.

the truth-saturated revelation of God in both the words/texts of Scripture and through Jesus the incarnate Word himself. "In the beginning was the Word, and the Word was with God, and the Word was God" (Jn 1:1). May his name be praised.

SUMMARY

1. Mill's view of language, the Fido-Fido theory, claimed that words get their meaning by reference to objects in the external world. Proper names, such as Fido and Shakespeare, were seen as prime examples. The Fido-Fido theory was beset by problems concerning both meaningful statements that are false (the James Bond example) and statements that are nonsense.

2. Saussure rejected the traditional idea of reference and saw meaning as entirely a matter of how words relate to other words in a language. Meaning is thus entirely internal (as opposed to being partly external) in nature.

   A. Saussure emphasized the arbitrary and conventional nature of language.

   B. Saussure also moved linguistics away from studying the historical aspect of word meanings ("it developed in such and such a way") to simply focusing on the word in its present context.

3. The movement known as New Criticism moved the focus away from authorial intent toward the text, and was influential until the late 1950s.

4. Derrida and the poststructuralists said *Pas du tout* (No way) to Saussure and company.

   A. Derrida advocated a new method known as deconstruction, which sought to both undermine and (in some sense) do away with traditional Western metaphysics.

   B. Derrida sees Western metaphysics as built on a faulty view of knowledge and on the ability of language to adequately express truths about the world, and he sees deconstruction as a way of delegitimizing this Western tradition.

   C. Derrida thinks that Western metaphysics is committed to the idea of presence, both self-presence and presence to consciousness, something he emphatically rejects.

D. Rather than meanings being fairly stable (and attached to the idea of external reference), Derrida sees full and stable meanings as a fiction. All we have are traces of genuine meaning.

E. Strengths of Derrida's view

    i. Derrida is correct that much of language is metaphorical.

    ii. He is right that many people understand texts literally even when many metaphors are present.

    iii. Deconstruction is a perfectly appropriate method for some texts.

    iv. Derrida is correct that there is no neutral or objective viewpoint from which humans can view the world.

    v. Derrida is correct that metaphysics is to be found everywhere.

F. Weaknesses of Derrida's view

    i. Authorial intent is crucial for properly understanding texts, something Derrida denies.

    ii. The effectiveness of everyday communication undermines Derrida's commitment to the instability of meanings.

    iii. Should we apply the technique of deconstruction to Derrida's own texts? Either way he answers, his view is in big trouble.

    iv. Every reasonable view of language requires an acknowledgment of the reality and importance of the idea of external reference. Our ability to successfully translate texts also undermines the idea that meanings exist only in terms of the language system in which they are found.

    v. If political oppression is morally wrong (as we readily agree it is), then we need some sort of objective moral standard by which to evaluate such behavior. Derrida allows for no such standard. His predicament can be called Derrida's dilemma.

    vi. Philosophy should underpin political commitments. As Mark Lilla makes clear, for Derrida it is the other way around. Many of Derrida's important claims are simply assertions, with little or no supporting argument offered.

    vii. Derrida's linguistic constructivism results in the rejection of realism. Realism is well supported by science and common sense, and it is nonsense to think we somehow create the world with our language. We humans construct language, and we construct theories *of* the world, but we don't construct the world itself.

viii. We recognize the influence of many factors on human belief (the sociology of knowledge), but we also recognize that realism is true and that we can have objective knowledge of the world. It is a matter of both/and, not either/or.

ix. Humans have many beliefs. We form beliefs because we think they are true. Any adequate view of language needs to recognize the central importance of truth for understanding language. Derrida fails to give truth its proper due here.

x. The Bible is not one text among many, with no stable meanings, and containing no objective truths (as Derrida would have us believe). Rather, it is the authoritative (a bad word, in Derrida's mind) revelation of the one true God, a text that transcends our cultural setting and the languages we speak. Jesus himself is both the incarnate Word and the Truth himself. In him we find language and truth inextricably intertwined.

SUGGESTED READINGS

Derrida, Jacques. *Acts of Religion*. Edited by Gil Anidjar. London: Routledge, 2002.

———. *Dissemination*. Translated by Barbara Johnson. London: Continuum, 1981.

———. *Margins of Philosophy*. Translated by Alan Bass. Chicago: University of Chicago Press, 1985.

———. *Of Grammatology*. Translated by Gayatri Chakravorty Spivak. Baltimore: Johns Hopkins University Press, 1998. A good place to start in understanding Derrida, but tough going at times.

Devitt, Michael, and Kim Sterelny. *Language and Reality: An Introduction to the Philosophy of Language*. 2nd ed. Cambridge, MA: MIT Press, 1999. An excellent introduction to key issues in the philosophy of language. Background knowledge is very much needed here.

Hill, Leslie. *The Cambridge Introduction to Jacques Derrida*. Cambridge: Cambridge University Press, 2007. One of the more readable introductions to Derrida.

Osborne, Grant. *The Hermeneutical Spiral: A Comprehensive Introduction to Biblical Interpretation.* Downers Grove, IL: InterVarsity Press, 1996. A fine introduction to the interpretation of texts by a leading evangelical.

Saussure, Ferdinand de. *Course in General Linguistics.* Edited by Charles Bally and Albert Sechehaye. Translated by Wade Baskin. New York: McGraw-Hill, 1966. One of the first works to seriously challenge traditional understandings of language and texts. Not easy reading.

Searle, John. *The Construction of Social Reality.* New York: Free Press, 1995. A brilliant defense of what might be called common-sense realism and related ideas. Searle believes there really is a world "out there."

Smith, James K. A. *Who's Afraid of Postmodernism? Taking Derrida, Lyotard, and Foucault to Church.* The Church and Postmodern Culture. Grand Rapids: Baker Academic, 2006.

Wolterstorff, Nicholas. *Divine Discourse: Philosophical Reflections on the Claim That God Speaks.* Cambridge: Cambridge University Press, 1995. A major work by a leading Christian philosopher. He tackles Derrida head on. The issues here are not always easy to grasp.

6

TRUTH AND SOCIAL CONSTRUCTION

Traditional philosophy has been committed to the idea that truth exists independently of humans and their use of language. Plato, Augustine, René Descartes, John Locke, Bertrand Russell, and many others have been committed to this basic idea. Under the influence of Friedrich Nietzsche, Michel Foucault, and others, a number of postmodern thinkers have expressed doubts about this traditional commitment. Rather, they argue, truth should be seen as socially constructed, where the truth in question is ultimately the creation of a human community rather than (in some sense) preexisting the efforts of a particular community. Many postmoderns, rather than seeing "truth" as simply an accurate expression of a preexisting reality, instead see what is called "true" as more often than not an attempt to establish and assert power of some sort. In this chapter we will examine the phenomenon known as social constructivism, seek to identify and examine the underlying reasons thinkers adhere to it, and then evaluate it in light of the central truths of Christianity.

Our first question is, why would anyone think all truths are constructed (or created) rather than discovered? Consider the following claim:

> Systems of representation, such as vocabularies and conceptual schemes generally, are human creations, and to that extent arbitrary. It is possible to have any number of different systems of representation for representing the same reality. This thesis is called "conceptual relativity."[1]

---

[1]John Searle, *The Construction of Social Reality* (New York: Free Press, 1995), 151.

A simple example might involve the following: suppose it is raining and you, an English speaker, are talking with a person from France and a person from Germany. So, the following claims are made:

You—"It is raining"

Yvette—"Il pleut"

Hans—"Es regnet"

Here we have three claims, made in three different languages, in an attempt to accurately describe what each is currently experiencing. This is an easy example of conceptual relativity. Do any of our three speakers approach "reality" from a completely neutral/objective point of view? Not at all. They are all massively influenced by cultural, social, and psychological factors that shape both how they perceive "reality" and how they describe (or attempt to describe) it. Each of the three speakers could have developed a different language (than the one they did) and different words to describe what English speakers typically refer to as "rain." English, rather than being a language of twenty-six letters, could have included both twenty-six letters and various pictures/icons as part of the written language. So suppose that two particular things occurred:

1. English speakers adopted a word other than *rain* to refer to precipitation.

2. They included a picture in the word. The picture is of a raindrop, such that the resulting word in English would include both letters and a picture. The imagined result would be: (A) The word adopted is *marn*, and (B) we add the picture of the raindrop, so that we end up with the following: *ma◆rn*

There is nothing about the development of the English language that requires us to choose the word *rain* over the word *ma◆rn*. It is a series of choices, choices that easily could have been different. So both the language we use and the words in that language are literally human constructions, they are *arbitrary* and *conventional*. Just as Americans could have chosen to always drive on the left side of the road, to shake hands with the left rather than the right hand, and to play cards regularly dealing only from the bottom of the deck, so too the word we adopt for precipitation is one of thousands of possibilities.

All of the above makes the widely accepted point that conceptual relativity is true. We are also committed to the idea that realism is true. Realism is simply the idea that the world (or reality) exists independently of our representations of (beliefs about) it.[2] Note that realism is not a claim about human beliefs about reality; rather, it is claim about that reality apart from human beliefs regarding it. It is a claim about what is, what philosophers call an *ontological* claim. To put matters simply, realism is a belief about what exists, while conceptual relativity is a belief about human attempts to describe that reality (in beliefs, language, etc.). While virtually every human language has a word (or words) for what we call rain, the various words all aim to describe what exists *prior to* their attempts to describe it. We don't go outside, say, "It is raining," and then wait for our chosen words to *cause* it to begin raining. That would be cause for bewilderment and possibly a trip to a counselor! We typically only say, "It is raining" after it has already begun to rain. The rain precedes the belief (and the use of language), not the other way around.

So why would anyone deny something as (seemingly) obvious as this? Well, we can think of three possible reasons:

1. Remember what we argued earlier about metanarratives and oppression? Historically, claims about what is true have often been closely connected (correlated) with power and oppression. Christianity, Marxism, and (Enlightenment) humanism were all seen as true at some point in time by large numbers of people. All three views can also be called metanarratives, and all three were accused of being significantly oppressive. Many politically left-leaning people thus have some foundation for seeing the claim "*x* is true" as a prelude to *x* also being oppressive.

2. Humans seek to be free, and to believe that reality *is* a particular way apart from what humans think about it is to unnecessarily limit that freedom.

3. It is undeniable that the way humans form language and beliefs is massively socially constructed, and social construction (or conceptual relativity) leads to the rejection of the belief known as realism.

---

[2]Ibid., 150.

These three reasons can be labeled as follows:

1. The historical oppression argument

2. The emancipatory argument

3. The conceptual relativity argument

If any one of these three arguments is persuasive, then we will need to concede that realism needs to be either modified or even rejected. So what should we think of these three arguments?

EXAMINATION OF THE THREE ARGUMENTS

We have already taken a close look at the historical oppression argument. We argued that though there was a significant grain of truth in it, that is a long way from establishing that all metanarratives are oppressive. Since Christianity is a metanarrative, and Christianity is not oppressive (rather, it is the opposite), then it follows indubitably that not all metanarratives are oppressive.[3] So the historical oppression arguments fails.

The emancipatory argument is a bit strange. We all know what it means to be free from tyranny and oppression. The Revolutionary War was fought, in part, to throw off the oppressive yoke of the dastardly British ("no taxation without representation" and all that). Historically, there are countless examples of one country ruling over and oppressing another. But what exactly is oppressive about the view known as realism? This is a good question. No answers leap to our minds, but after reading some leading postmodern thinkers we can discern some reasons offered here. Realism can be thought to make claims about realities that exist independently of human thought and culture. Some of these realities are moral in nature. For example, most evangelicals are committed to what is known as moral objectivism. This is the idea that certain moral principles exist independently of humans and depend in no way on cultures either for their existence or their truth. Three such moral principles might be the following:

Principle 1—We should consider other humans to be as important as ourselves. This rules out selfish behavior as morally wrong and thus unacceptable.[4]

---

[3]This is not to admit that some metanarratives are oppressive, though it does open the door to that possibility.

[4]It is worth noting that Jesus is not the only one to put forth the Golden Rule. Confucius, writing around 500 BC, puts forth something fairly similar. The Golden Rule is thus not merely the product of Western civilization and "Western" values (whatever that would mean).

Principle 2—We have obligations to the less fortunate. In other words, in some important sense we are our brothers' and sisters' keepers.

Principle 3—Humans should be monogamous and faithful in their relationships. We are not morally free to marry as often as we please or to treat marriage as a mere legal convenience that we are free to follow or not.

If someone grew up in the 1960s, read Abraham Maslow, and was in search of what Maslow called self-actualization, one could easily see how acknowledging any (or all) of these three principles might put a crimp in one's plans. One can make a case that all of the following are true:

1. Humans are fundamentally selfish, and not naturally inclined to consider others to be as important as ourselves.

2. Many believe we are not our brothers' and sisters' keepers. As an article in the *National Review* in the 1980s proclaimed, "We are not the world."

3. Many believe that marital infidelity is not a moral issue, or, at the least, not an important moral issue.

Someone adopting all three of these approaches would be morally at liberty to

1. Live primarily for themselves and not worry about others (who might be struggling just to survive)

2. Put their money toward their own interests, and only give to charity if it makes them feel better than not doing so

3. With marriage in mind, think "vows schmows!" and have as many extramarital relationships as they wish

One can imagine someone wanting to reject moral objectivism so that they would be able to live their life according to their own lights rather than being answerable to a set of moral principles that clearly entail that certain behaviors are morally wrong. But evangelical Christians take the Bible seriously, seeing it as the authoritative and inspired Word of God. And taking the Bible seriously means acknowledging that it is morally authoritative. It does not offer the Ten Suggestions. Rather it both states and implies a number of moral principles that are objectively true whether we humans acknowledge them as such or not. If the Bible is authoritative, as we believe it is, then we are not free to live selfishly, to ignore our obligation to help the less fortunate, and to approach marriage any way that strikes our fancy. The postmoderns are correct here that moral principles constrain or limit our moral choices. As evangelicals we acknowledge the authority of God's Word and bow before it, and seek to make moral choices that honor God and not ourselves. For all these reasons then, we reject the emancipatory argument.

So what about the conceptual relativity argument? If it is true, does it logically require us to reject realism? We argue that conceptual relativity is true, but that its truth does absolutely nothing to shake our confidence in the truth of realism. Let's begin by taking a closer look at conceptual relativity.

The conceptual relativity argument takes very seriously the existence and the importance of what is often called the sociology of knowledge. Simply put, the sociology of knowledge examines the influence of environment and/or culture on the beliefs, values, and actions of those who live in a particular culture. To pick an obvious example, consider the word Americans use to describe a carbonated soft drink. The American South has a strong preference for the word *Coke*, which refers to a kind of drink rather than the particular brand of soft drink Coca-Cola. On the other hand, those in most of the Midwest use the term *pop* to refer to soft drinks. Finally, much of both the East Coast and the West Coast use the word *soda* to refer to soft drinks. So what word we choose for soft drink is heavily influenced by what part of the country we live/lived in. It is important to note that there is (at least) one important sense in which we can say that a particular region (e.g., the South) *causes* the individual to label a soft drink what they in fact call it.

So far this is all pretty unremarkable. But now suppose that important beliefs are also the byproduct of particular cultures/environments. For example, suppose that beliefs about God, morality, and politics were all the products of particular cultures to the same extent that labels for soft drinks were. If this were the case, then it might well be more accurate to understand the claim

God exists

as more of a statement about one's culture/environment than a claim about what exists. It needs to be mentioned that environments do massively influence what we think and believe about God and politics and a host of other important matters. To push this a little further, one who was impressed by the massive influence of the environment on our beliefs, and who recognized that many of our beliefs are socially constructed (showing the influence of both our broader culture and other particular individuals), might be tempted to think that the claim

Realism is true

means nothing more than "my environment caused me to think that realism is true." Rather than viewing the above claim as an *ontological* claim (making a claim that something exists independently of us), we should see the claim as a factual claim about the massive influence environmental and cultural factors have on our beliefs.

Some philosophers, such as Nelson Goodman (a philosopher of considerable note), have noted that "alternative conceptual schemes" (different ways of looking at the world) allow, as John Searle notes, "for different descriptions of the same reality, and that there are no descriptions of reality outside of all conceptual schemes."[5] Goodman argues that some of these different descriptions, though supposedly of the same reality, are in fact inconsistent with each other. This inconsistency, Goodman argues, shows that belief in realism yields ridiculous (contradictory) results, thus indicating that realism is false. Two examples will be used to illustrate Goodman's view.

The first example involves considering that the objects in figure 1 are all the objects that exist in a particular world.

Figure 1. All the objects that exist in a particular world

So how many objects exist in this particular world? The initial answer is that three seems to be the correct answer. But, as Searle notes, the Polish logician Lesniewski claims there are actually seven such objects. How does he get seven? He counts along the following lines:

---

[5]Searle, *Construction of Social Reality*, 165; see Nelson Goodman, *Ways of Worldmaking* (Indianapolis: Hackett, 1978), 29-40.

$1 = A$

$2 = B$

$3 = C$

$4 = A + B$

$5 = A + C$

$6 = B + C$

$7 = A + B + C$

So are there three objects or seven objects in this imaginary world? Searle rightly notes that "there is no absolute answer to these questions. The only answers we can give are relative to the arbitrary choice of conceptual scheme. The same sentence, e.g., 'There are exactly three objects in the world,' will be true in one scheme and false in the other."[6] Goodman draws the conclusion that we "make reality" or "make worlds" by "drawing certain boundaries rather than others."[7] Goodman thus claims that how many objects there are is relative to a particular world that we have made ourselves. What should we say to Goodman on this matter? Regarding the matter of how many objects there are in the miniworld above, we should say all of the following:

1. There is but one world (it has three circular objects in it, at the least).

2. There is more than one acceptable way to describe this world.

3. One acceptable way is to say it has three objects (there's a certain obvious appeal to this answer).

4. Another acceptable way, Lesniewski's way, is to argue there are seven such objects. This seems less obvious, but a genuine possibility nevertheless.

5. So there is one world, two differing (though not contradictory) conceptual schemes.

It is difficult, very difficult, to see how Goodman's example here might possibly be a problem for the realist. It should be noted that even though there are at least two possible ways to answer the question above, it does not

---

[6]Ibid., 162.
[7]Ibid.

follow there are an infinite number of possibilities. Nor does it logically follow that the two differing approaches are inconsistent with each other. If Anne and Katie see a stoplight from differing perspectives, the shape of what appears to them is different, but that doesn't mean that what one of them sees somehow contradicts (or is inconsistent with) what the other sees. Notice that both Anne's perspective and Katie's perspective are both *of* something else. The fact that they have differing perspectives presupposes that there is something that exists that they can have a different perspective of (in this case, a stoplight).

Searle offers another example to drive home his main point. Suppose we ask an American and a Canadian who are exactly the same size and mass how much they weigh. The American answers "160 pounds" while the Canadian answers "73 kilograms." How can they give different answers without contradicting each other if they are the same weight? The answer is not that difficult. Given that 160 pounds = 73 kilograms, there is no problem here at all. Now 160 pounds actually equals exactly 72.5 kilograms, but we are rounding up. So the same mass is accurately represented by *both* the answer in pounds and the answer in kilograms.

We agree with Searle that Goodman's arguments do not really threaten the truth of realism. For that matter, it is difficult to see how they pose even a modest threat. Consider Searle's reasoning on this matter:

> What counts as a correct application of the term "cat" or "kilogram" or "canyon" (or "klurg") is up to us and is to that extent arbitrary. *But once we have fixed the meaning of such terms in our vocabulary by arbitrary definitions, it is no longer a matter of any kind of relativism or arbitrariness whether representation-independent features of the world satisfy those definitions, because the features of the world that satisfy or fail to satisfy the definitions exist independently of those or any other definitions.* We arbitrarily define the word "cat" in such and such a way and only relative to such and such definitions can we say, "That's a cat." But once we have made the definition and once we have applied the concepts relative to the system of definitions, whether or not something satisfies our definition is no longer arbitrary or relative. That we use the word "cat" the way we do is up to us; that there is an object that exists independently of that use, and satisfies that use, is a plain matter of (absolute, intrinsic, mind-independent) fact. Contrary to Goodman, we do not make worlds; we make descriptions that the actual world may fit or fail to fit. But all this implies that

there is a reality that exists independently of our system of concepts. Without such a reality, there is nothing to apply the concept to.[8]

There is a lot of information in this extended quote, so we summarize Searle's main points as follows:

1. The words we choose to refer to objects are entirely arbitrary. We could have called a "cat" a "schmoo," a "wknd," or whatever.

2. But once we agree that we will use the word *cat* to refer to that particular kind of animal, it is not up to us (or arbitrary) whether any cats exist or not. That is, to speak a bit loosely, up to the world.

3. Goodman wrongly believes that if our choice of words to describe something (e.g., a cat) is arbitrary (we could have called the "cat" a "schmoo"), then the cat's very existence depends on us using the word *cat*. Simply put, our word choices do not create that to which they refer. (The "cat" exists whether we use any word for it or not.)

4. We do not make worlds, as Goodman claims; we merely make descriptions *of* the world that the world may or may not match up with.

It is true, as Searle correctly notes, that we observe external reality from a particular perspective or point of view. But this does not mean that reality itself is perspectival. That would be to confuse *epistemology* (which deals with how we come to know things) with *ontology* (which deals with whether things exist or not).

Goodman is hardly the only one skeptical about the truth of realism. Terry Winograd argues that the sentence "There is water in the refrigerator" can be used "to make a false statement relative to one set of background interests, a true statement relative to another."[9] From this Winograd draws the conclusion "that reality does not exist independent of our representations."[10] Winograd here makes the leap (without any sort of supporting evidence) from how we represent reality to reality itself. This sort of argument, as Searle puts it bluntly, is a non sequitur. There is no logical connection between the arbitrariness of our representations and the world those representations refer to.

---

[8]Ibid., 166 (emphasis original).
[9]Terry Winograd, "Three Responses to Situation Theory," Center for the Study of Language and Information, Report No. CSLI-87-106, 1987, cited in Searle, *Construction of Social Reality*, 159.
[10]Searle, *Construction of Social Reality*, 159.

Hilary Putnam joins with Goodman and Winograd in doubting realism.[11] Putnam writes that "the whole content of Realism lies in the claim that it makes sense to think of a God's Eye View (or better a view from nowhere)."[12] But it is readily apparent that any sort of God's eye view is unavailable to human beings. Given that fact, Putnam can construct the following sort of antirealist argument:

1. If realism is true, then there must be a God's eye view.

2. But there is no such God's eye view.

------

3. ∴ Realism is false.

This is a logically valid argument, meaning that if the two premises are true, then the conclusion must be true. So if we are inclined to reject the conclusion, as we are, we must point out a problem with either premise one or premise two (or both). We grant that premise two is true, at least humanly speaking. But we do not accept premise one as true. Why not? Because Putnam here has confused epistemology with ontology (as Goodman and others did). Remember that realism is simply a claim that the world exists independently of us. There is nothing about claiming realism to be true that requires us to think its truth requires a God's eye view, as Putnam believes. Searle makes the point by noting that realism is not an epistemological claim, but rather a claim about what is (an ontological claim).

We now know that neither of Goodman's two arguments nor Putnam's God's eye view argument succeed in giving us any good reason to doubt the truth of realism. Given that realism does seem to accord with what we might call common sense, and that three prominent attacks on it are all failures, we conclude we are justified in reaffirming the truth of realism.[13]

------

[11]We should note here that Putnam has advanced a number of different positions over the years with respect to realism. Above we are focusing on one of those positions.

[12]Hilary Putnam, *Realism with a Human Face*, ed. James Conant (Cambridge, MA: Harvard University Press, 1990), 23.

[13]There are a multitude of antirealist arguments *out there*. We earlier discussed Latour's position, which is massively antirealist, and saw it was unconvincing. In historiography, a seminal book on the nature of history is Peter Novick's *That Noble Dream: "The Objectivity Question" and the American Historical Profession* (Cambridge: Cambridge University Press, 1988). Novick believes, mistakenly, that in order for the writing of history to be truthful, it must also be fully objective (or have a God's eye view available). But since no such complete objectivity is possible, the goal

Evangelical Christianity is radically undermined if truth/reality is socially constructed. Traditional Christians believe that God is an eternal being, whose existence in no way, shape, or form depends on what humans happen to think about him! Exodus 3:14 tells us that God is "I AM WHO I AM." Many Christian philosophers and theologians have understood this to be both a claim that God exists and a claim as to what kind of being God is. Here it is argued that God is a necessary being. What does that mean? It means that God exists any way reality might have been. By contrast, humans are contingent beings. Our coming into existence depends on a huge number of other conditions happening just so. As a contingent being, our existence depends on factors outside our control. Still, even though we are contingent, our existence supports realism in that we exist independently of any human beliefs about our existence. God, existing necessarily, also is not a socially constructed being (the way a unicorn or Zeus might be), as would be the case if belief in God were entirely the result of wish fulfillment (as Freud and others are inclined to believe). He exists independently of any beliefs about him. So neither our existence nor God's existence is a matter of social construction. Our beliefs about God are socially constructed, but God himself is not.

Others, such as the often-admired Richard Rorty, have offered detailed arguments in support of social constructivism and against realism. It is worth briefly mentioning that Rorty sees his philosophical views as broadly in the pragmatic tradition of John Dewey, Charles Peirce, and others. But a brief glance at his writing shows he neither has cogent arguments for social constructivism nor does he succeed in convincing his fellow pragmatists that he really is a pragmatist.[14]

---

of truth in history writing must be abandoned. Novick's book is a brilliant and learned work, but it is deeply flawed. His argument can be summarized as follows:

If historical truth is attainable, then complete objectivity is possible.
If complete objectivity is possible, then a God's eye view must be available to humans.
But no such God's eye view is humanly possible.

∴ Historical truth is not attainable.

Novick is mistaken that objectivity (which is not an all-or-nothing matter) requires a God's eye view.

[14]On the pragmatist front, see esp. Susan Haack and James Gouinlock, who seriously doubt Rorty is any sort of genuine pragmatist. Haack refers to Rorty as "a vulgar pragmatist." See Susan Haack, *Evidence and Inquiry: A Pragmatist Reconstruction of Epistemology* (Amherst, NY: Prometheus, 2009). Also, see James Gouinlock, "What Is the Legacy of Instrumentalism? Rorty's Interpretation of Dewey," *Journal of the History of Philosophy* 28, no. 2 (1990): 251-69.

We have carefully examined the social constructivist arguments against realism and found them wanting. The arguments of Goodman, Putnam, Winograd, Rorty, and company are far from impressive. They are radically defective and worthy of rejection. So where does that leave us? We might summarize our findings in this chapter as follows:

1. Common sense seems to support the view known as realism.

2. In this sense, realism is the default position.

3. Goodman's arguments against realism are unconvincing. Searle demonstrated that Goodman's arguments rest on an undetected confusion.

4. Putnam's God's eye view argument fares no better.

5. Winograd's claim also fails to persuade.

For all the above reasons, we are clearly justified in maintaining our belief in realism. There really is a reality existing independently of our awareness of it, and the fact that our beliefs are socially constructed hardly means that what the beliefs refer to are also so constructed. The failure of some of the leading constructivist arguments only serves to reinforce what already seemed to be true, namely, that realism is true.

To do justice to postmodernism, there is one more view we need to address. Remember that at the heart of postmodernism is the claim that many influential metanarratives have also been oppressive, and that there are dozens of historical examples to support this claim. Looking at this from a postmodern perspective, consider what might be of concern to them. Their point might be summarized as follows: "The claim that some metanarrative is true usually leads to significant oppression."

Given how obviously wrong such oppression is, how might we prevent such evil from occurring? One distinct possibility, one readily endorsed by many postmoderns, is not only to reject the particular metanarrative but also to take the much more radical step of denying (objective) truth altogether. For if only true metanarratives have been adopted, then the rejection of truth in general will undermine the chain of events that produces oppression. Such a move crucially requires convincing arguments against the existence of objective truth (no small undertaking), but it also helps illuminate the underlying motivation for much postmodern rhetoric. We evangelicals need to not only defend the idea of truth but also, and equally importantly, demonstrate in the real world that a metanarrative such as Christianity does not lead to oppression. Perhaps, then, Christianity will get more serious consideration from those in the postmodern camp.

Summary

1. Introduction to social constructivism

2. Language and belief formation as human social constructions

3. Realism as the idea that reality exists independently of our beliefs about it

4. Three possible reasons for rejecting realism

   A. The historical oppression argument: Fails to convince, as demonstrated in an earlier chapter.

   B. The emancipatory argument: Claims that commitment to external realism is a form of tyranny or oppression. But moral realism, the idea that binding moral principles exist independently of all humans, is anything but oppressive.

   C. The conceptual relativity argument: It is true that our beliefs are relative to our particular language and culture. So conceptual relativity is clearly true.

      i. But the truth of conceptual relativity does not entail the falsity of realism.

      ii. Once we agree on what particular words mean, whether certain words (such as *cat*) genuinely refer to objects in the external world depends entirely on the world and not at all on us.

      iii. So we can and do grant the truth of conceptual relativity, but that is not enough to show realism is false.

5. Goodman's two arguments

   A. Number of objects in miniworld argument (Searle shows this is unconvincing).

   B. Weight-versus-kilogram argument (this is clearly fallacious).

6. Putnam's God's eye view argument

   A. But the truth of external realism in no way requires that a God's eye view of reality be possible.

B. So Putnam's argument also fails.

7. Traditional Christianity is committed to the belief that God exists and does so necessarily. This requires a commitment to realism, as God's existence is in no way a social construction.

8. Given that common sense points toward the truth of realism and that none of the socially constructivist arguments we examined were convincing, we conclude that we are justified in maintaining our commitment to the truth of realism.

9. It was suggested that the postmodern rejection of truth was perhaps aimed more at avoiding oppression than at the nature of truth itself.

Suggested Readings

Boghossian, Paul. "What Is Social Construction?" *Times Literary Supplement,* February 2001.

Goldman, Alvin. *Knowledge in a Social World.* New York: Oxford University Press, 1999.

Goodman, Nelson. *Of Mind and Other Matters.* Cambridge, MA: Harvard University Press, 1984.

Haack, Susan. *Evidence and Inquiry: Toward Reconstruction in Epistemology.* Oxford: Blackwell, 1995.

Hacking, Ian. *The Social Construction of What?* Cambridge, MA: Harvard University Press, 2000.

Latour, Bruno, and Steve Woolgar. *Laboratory Life: The Construction of Scientific Facts.* 2nd ed. Princeton, NJ: Princeton University Press, 1986.

Putnam, Hilary. *Realism with a Human Face.* Edited by James Conant. Cambridge, MA: Harvard University Press, 1990.

Rorty, Richard. *Philosophy and the Mirror of Nature.* Princeton, NJ: Princeton University Press, 1979.

Searle, John R. *The Construction of Social Reality.* New York: Free Press, 1995.

Sokal, Alan, and Jean Bricmont. *Fashionable Nonsense: Postmodern Intellectuals' Abuse of Science.* New York: Picador, 1999.

7

POSTMODERNISM AND THE SELF

There are a lot of things in life that we might question and have serious doubt about. One thing most of us rarely doubt, however, is our "self." That is, we don't normally doubt that we are who we are or that we have continued to exist from one time to the next. And in light of those beliefs, we tend to think of ourselves as specific "selves" that have particular natures and histories. But are these basic intuitions about "ourselves" correct? What, exactly, is a self? Is it an immaterial soul that is independent of our physical bodies? Is it a physical object capable of rational functions and intelligent processes? Or is it merely a collection of characteristics that change and vary over time with experience and influence from the outside world? What is the "self"?

In this chapter, we try to make sense of these questions by doing several things. First, we offer a brief history of the self concept, noting the leading figures in the Western discussion. Second, we discuss the central themes of a postmodern view of the self. Last, we provide a short critique of the postmodern view.

A Brief History of the Self

One of the major aspects of postmodern thought is the way it views the self. In fact, according to Robert Solomon, the issue of the self is one of the most central issues in modern and postmodern philosophy.[1] As we consider the story of the self through these periods, Solomon argues that the "leading

---

[1]Robert C. Solomon, *Continental Philosophy Since 1750: The Rise and Fall of the Self* (New York: Oxford University Press, 1988), 3.

theme of this story . . . is the rise and fall of an extraordinary concept of the self."[2] In the end, we will see how postmodernism rejects traditional premodern and modern views of the self as having a specific nature or as rational beings. Instead, it views the self as something socially constructed from the outside world. But the story does not begin with recent postmodern thinkers. As Calvin Schrag has noted:

> Although the vocabularies employed in the traditional descriptions and definitions of the human self—such as substance and attribute, form and matter, subject, mind, ego, and self identity—have been singled out for sustained attack in the postmodern era, these vocabularies had already come under criticism by certain proponents of modernity.[3]

As such, to better understand postmodern views of the self, in this chapter we will consider briefly the history of the self in Western thought. We will consider how it has been viewed by premodern, modern, and postmodern thinkers alike, paying special attention to the motivations of postmodern thought.

The soul as self: the premodern view. From Plato to the seventeenth century, philosophers, theologians, and most people in general thought of the self as being tied to the individual soul of a particular person. What made Plato, for example, the person (or self) that he was was his immaterial soul. In his thought, the soul could survive the physical death of the person and live apart from the body. John Cooper describes briefly the ancient and early Christian view: "When the body dies the person retains her existence and most likely some kind of consciousness as well. A separation or rendering of that which was so intimately joined in life occurs at death. The person or self or soul or spirit survives the death of the body."[4]

There were some key differences among the perspectives of ancient and early and medieval Christian thinkers like Plato, Aristotle, Augustine, and Aquinas. Plato, for example, held to substance dualism, a perspective that says persons are their souls essentially, and have bodies accidentally. Philosophers like Aristotle and Aquinas, however, were hylomorphists, which held that persons were both souls and bodies essentially. Augustine is often

---

[2]Ibid., 4.
[3]Calvin O. Schrag, *The Self After Postmodernity* (New Haven, CT: Yale University Press, 1997), 3.
[4]John Cooper, *Body, Soul, and Life Everlasting: Biblical Anthropology and the Monism-Dualism Debate* (Grand Rapids: Eerdmans, 1989), 8.

labeled as a substance dualist,[5] but some of his writings suggest that he might better be described as a hylomorphist. Despite these subtle differences, all these philosophers and theologians thought that humans had both souls and bodies, and that our individual identities (our "selves") were tied in some way to the soul.

But there is another important aspect of the premodern view of the self. In this view, human beings possess a nature that bears the image of God. We, of all the creatures of the earth, were said to be like God in some important rational, spiritual, and relational ways. This nature was given by God and, though tainted by sin in the fall, is not determined in any ontological sense by the world. Heath White notes, "The true self, for the pre-modern, is what is given by human nature; it involves a human's destiny, what a person was made for. The various accretions to your personality piled on by family, society, or education are inessential additions, not really part of the self."[6] So then, in the premodern view, the self referred to the soul of the human being whose nature was established by God and was reflective of the divine image. This nature was innate and intrinsic, able to be influenced by external factors, but not determined by them.

The rational self: early modern philosophy. In the modern period, we see a wide variety of perspectives, starting with a rearticulation of the premodern view of the self and ending with the basic ideas that come to be dominant in the postmodern view. Some of the early modern philosophers, for example, continued to think of the self in terms of souls. Yet, hoping to derive beliefs that depended less on theological considerations and more on philosophical foundations, these philosophers tended to use rational argumentation to speak to the nature of the self.

Descartes. Philosophers like René Descartes (1596–1650), for example, argued in favor of substance dualism and the view that persons are one and the same with their souls. He says:

> I do not even know whether I have a body. . . . I might add that I cannot deny absolutely that I have a body. Yet even if we keep all these suppositions intact, this will not prevent me from being certain that I exist. On the contrary, these

---

[5]See Stewart Goetz and Charles Taliaferro, *A Brief History of the Soul* (Malden, MA: Wiley-Blackwell, 2011), 33.

[6]Heath White, *Postmodernism 101: A First Course for the Curious Christian* (Grand Rapids: Brazos, 2006), 69.

suppositions simply strengthen the certainty of my conviction that I exist and am not a body. Otherwise, if I had doubts about my body, I would also have doubts about myself, and I cannot have doubts about that. I am absolutely convinced that I exist, so convinced that it is totally impossible for me to doubt it.[7]

In other words, Descartes thought that there was a substantial difference between his body, which could be doubted, and his soul, which could not be doubted, such that the body and soul must be different kinds of things. And since he could doubt the existence of his mind (which he used interchangeably with the soul), he must be identical with his mind/soul. For him, he existed as a thinking thing. He says, "But what then am I? A thing that thinks. What is that? A thing that doubts, understands, affirms, denies, is willing, is unwilling, and also imagines and has sensory experiences."[8] For Descartes, then, the self is an immaterial soul that is rational and distinct from the body. Like the dualists of old, he also thought that the self persists though various kinds of change without being determined by the world or experiences.

Locke. But this is not the only perspective of the self we find in the modern period. With John Locke (1632–1704), for instance, we see a rather significant shift in the way that persons, souls, and selves were thought about. Locke does not seem to doubt that we are by nature rational beings with conscious experiences. Rather, what he doubts is the idea that the act of thinking described by Descartes requires us to be the kind of substances Descartes thinks we must be. That is, Locke denies that the self is an immaterial soul or mind that is radically distinct from the body and capable of persisting through various kinds of bodily changes. In his view, all that is necessary to account for the self (or what he sometimes calls personal identity) is the continuity of consciousness and memory. As long as these psychological properties are maintained, the self persists. He says:

As far as in the intelligent Being can repeat the *Idea* of any past Action with the same consciousness it had of it at first, and with the same consciousness it has any present Action; so far it is the same *personal self*. For it is by the

---

[7]*Œuvres de Descartes*, ed. Charles Adam and Paul Tannery (Paris: Cerf, 1908), 10:518; English translation in *The Philosophical Writings of Descartes*, trans. John Cottingham, Robert Stoothoff, and Douglas Murdoch (Cambridge: Cambridge University Press, 1984), 2:412, quoted in Peter Markie, "The Cogito and Its Importance," in *The Cambridge Companion to Descartes*, ed. John Cottingham (Cambridge: Cambridge University Press, 1992), 142.

[8]*Œuvres de Descartes*, 7:28; trans. Cottingham, Stoothoff, and Murdoch, *Philosophical Writings of Descartes*, 2:19, quoted in Cottingham, "The Cogito and Its Importance," 140.

consciousness it has its present Thoughts and Actions, that it is *self* to get *self*
now, and so will be the same *self* as far as the same consciousness can extend
two Actions passed or to come. . . . The same consciousness uniting those
distant Actions into the same *Person*, whatever Substances contributed to
their Production.[9]

Here Locke claims that it is the continuation of consciousness and memory
that the self depends on for it's existence. This self is not tied to a particular
substance, whether material or immaterial. That is, what makes a particular
self the self is not the immaterial soul described by the ancient philosophers,
Christian theologians, or by Descartes. Indeed, unlike Descartes, Locke is
less interested in defining the nature of the self and more interested in
understanding its continuation over time.[10] He views the self as a particular
consciousness present in a human being that manages to stay the same
within an organism that is constantly changing. As long as a person main-
tains a continuous consciousness and keeps most of their memories, they
continue to be the person or self that they have always been. But, if they were
to lose their memories or their overall psychological continuity, then they
would cease to be. Thus, on Locke's view, the self is tied directly to psychological continuity. Locke's view tries to account for the persistence and continuation of the self via psychological continuity. In this sense, his view is
not as radical as many of the perspectives that will follow him. Yet his view
does mark a major shift from the earlier perspectives by eliminating the
metaphysical entity of the soul as the seat of the self and by replacing the
soul with nothing more than memories and psychological continuity.

Hume. While some modern philosophers like Joseph Butler and Thomas
Reid were quick to criticize Locke's rejection of the soul and his emphasis on
psychological continuity as the seat of the self, other prominent philosophers
embraced Locke's basic ideas and took them even further. Such was the case
with David Hume (1711–1776). Hume seems to agree that a particular self just
is the thing that is conscious at a given time. But Hume goes further than
this by making it clear that (1) the self is nothing but the collection of perceptions at a given moment, and (2) there is no reason to think that the self
which possesses a given collection of perceptions in the present is the same

---

[9]John Locke, *An Essay Concerning Human Understanding* (Oxford: Clarendon, 1975), 10.
[10]Patricia Sheridan, *Locke: A Guide for the Perplexed* (London; New York: Continuum, 2010),
   66–67.

self as some previous self that may have had the same perceptions. Making it clear that he rejects the earlier views of ancient philosophers, the Christian tradition, and Descartes—the view of persons as souls—Hume says:

> For my part, when I enter most intimately into what I call *myself*, I always stumble on some particular perception or other, of heat or cold, light or shade, love or hatred, pain or pleasure. I never can catch *myself* at any time without a perception, and never can observe anything but the perception. . . . If anyone, upon serious and unprejudic'd reflection, thinks he has a different notion of *himself*, I must confess I can reason no longer with him.[11]

In other words, Hume thought that our perceptions only present what is being perceived at the moment, but they do not present the "I" itself. Because of this, he sees no logical reason to accept the existence of the self. What then, according to Hume, is the self? Hume goes on to explain that the self is nothing more than a bundle of different perceptions at a given moment that we have in experience. He adds:

> He may, perhaps, perceive something simple and continu'd, which he calls *himself*; tho' I am certain there is no such principle in me. . . . I may venture to affirm of the rest of mankind, that they are nothing but a bundle or collection of different perceptions, which succeed each other and inconceivable rapidity, and are in a perceptual flux and movement.[12]

But if the self is nothing more than a collection of perceptions at a given moment, and we have no logical reason to think that the self at the present is the same self as some previous self that had the same perceptions, why are we so inclined to think of our current selves as the same selves as before? If Hume's theory of the self is to have any plausibility, he must offer some kind of reasonable explanation for this inclination. As John Biro notes,[13] Hume thought memory played a key role in giving rise to this continued sense of self. Memory, says Biro, allows current perceptions to be connected back to previous perceptions, giving the sense that the current perceptions are tied back to the same perceptions in the past. But this is nothing more than appearance. In the end, Hume rejects the notion of the self as given by earlier

---

[11]David Hume, *A Treatise of Human Nature*, 2nd ed. (Oxford: Clarendon, 1978), 252-53.
[12]Ibid.
[13]See John Biro, "Hume's New Science of the Mind," in *The Cambridge Companion to Hume*, ed. David Fate Norton and Jacqueline Anne Taylor (Cambridge: Cambridge University Press, 2009).

thinkers and finds no reason to think that the "self" persists from one moment to the next. With Hume, the self is fragmented and reduced to a mere bundle of perceptions.

The transcendent self: romanticism and Kantian idealism. Rousseau. Other modern philosophers were not as pessimistic about the self as Hume had been. Jean-Jacques Rousseau (1712–1778), for example, rejected both the rationalist view of Descartes (who conceived of the self as a thinking thing) and the empiricist view of Locke and Hume (who conceived of the self as a set of memories or perceptions) in favor of a romantic view of the self. In this view, Rousseau emphasized the intrinsic goodness of humanity and applied this universally to all human beings. In other words, the self was characterized by its "inner goodness" as opposed to its rational capacities or its own self-consciousness. As something that was essentially good, Rousseau saw the self as a moral, social, and political force that is projected onto the world. Solomon explains:

> For Rousseau the self was not just introspectible but essentially expressive, projecting into the world and the future. Rousseau's self, in other words, displayed not just the formal features required by the rationalists and empiricists, but the sense of universal personality later required by the romantics. The self was neither the first principle of metaphysics nor a consequence of empiricism; it was first of all our own inner activity—and the most important thing in the world.[14]

There are a few key features of Rousseau's modern view of the self that are important to take note of as we move forward. First, like other modern philosophers after him, Rousseau is incredibly optimistic about human nature and potential for progress. Second, and stemming from the first, Rousseau introduces the idea that the self can project itself onto the world—transcending itself—and into society. This will become an important idea moving forward with thinkers like Kant. And third, like virtually all philosophers before him and most modern philosophers after him, Rousseau still believed that there was such a thing as "human nature" that was universally present in every human being.

Kant. The ideas (1) that the self projects itself onto the world and (2) that there is a "universal human nature" found in each human being (both of

---

[14]Solomon, *Continental Philosophy Since 1750*, 18.

which were affirmed by Rousseau) are reaffirmed and given greater emphasis by Immanuel Kant (1724–1804). It is widely noted by historians of philosophy that Kant introduces his own "Copernican Revolution" into philosophy. This revolution signifies a major shift in the way we think about our perceptions and knowledge of the world, but places the role of the mind and its rational faculties at the center of perception itself.

For Kant, the mind is not a passive entity that merely reflects and represents the world as it is given to us via the five senses—touch, taste, sight, smell, and sound. Rather, the mind actively structures, organizes, and categorizes the data gathered by the senses to give us a representation (Kant called this representation the "phenomena" or the "experience of the thing") of the world (what Kant called the "noumena" or "the thing in itself").[15] In Kant's thought, we know the world as it appears to us (phenomena), but we do not know the world as it actually is (noumena). Rather, the mind uses the categories of the mind to organize the various kinds of sense data that we receive in experience. According to Kant, there were four basic sets of categories, with these categories enabling us to sort out and make sense of all the empirical data introduced through the senses. Thus, according to Kant, the mind imposes itself onto the world by using these categories to structure our sensory inputs and represent the world to us.

For Kant, then, the self is something much more significant than a mere entity capable of passive experience. In his view, the self is transcendent in that it plays an active role and projects itself onto the world of experience. Again, Solomon is helpful:

> The self that becomes the star performer in modern European philosophy is the transcendental self, or transcendental ego, whose nature and ambitions were unprecedentedly arrogant, presumptuously cosmic, and consequently mysterious. The transcendental self was *the* self—timeless, universal, and in each one of us around the globe and throughout history. Distinguished from our individual idiosyncrasies, this was the self we shared. In modest and ordinary terms it was called "human nature." In much less modest, extraordinary terminology, the transcendental self was nothing less than God, the Absolute Self, the World Soul.[16]

---

[15]Immanuel Kant, *Critique of Pure Reason*, trans. Werner S. Pluhar (Indianapolis: Hackett, 1996), 10.

[16]Solomon, *Continental Philosophy Since 1750*, 4.

Kant's "transcendent self" becomes a defining feature of modern perspectives on the self from this point forward, and will become one of the major concepts that postmodern views of the self will reject.

The dissolving self: later idealism, nihilism, and Freud. *Hegel.* There is perhaps no greater German idealist philosopher[17] than Georg Wilhelm Friedrich Hegel (1770–1831). Hegel's contribution to "the self" is wrapped up in is overall philosophical system that centers on his understanding of Geist (roughly "Spirit") and the dialectic. He held to the form of idealist monism, which said reality is just one thing that is spiritual in nature. This spiritual reality is what Hegel called Geist. But, as Hegel makes clear, Geist is not static and immutable. Rather, it is constantly changing and progressing through a process called the dialectic. In his understanding, the dialectic—which was more than just a dialogue between two parties—was a process whereby the one (thesis) faces conflict (antithesis), seeks resolution (synthesis), and becomes something new (a new thesis). Once resolution has come in the form of something new, it then faces new conflict, seeks resolution, and becomes yet something new again. This dialectic process—the ongoing process of thesis, antithesis, and synthesis—was the outflow of Geist.[18]

Read at a remove from the historical discussion prior to him, Hegel strikes most contemporary Western students of philosophy as bizarre and convoluted. But, read within its historical context, and with an eye toward the way civilization, culture, government, and knowledge seem to unfold throughout the events of history, Hegel's philosophy is far more understandable.

But what does this mean for the self? Simply put, since Hegel's philosophy emphasizes the oneness of reality as found in Geist (idealist monism), there is very little place for the "individual self" in his perspective. What is most important is not the way we understand our own individual perspectives, conscious experiences, or abilities to project onto the world around us. Rather, what is most important is the way Geist becomes or unfolds through the process of the dialectic. In fact, as Solomon notes, with Hegel there is no such thing as "human nature," be it rational or transcendent.[19] Any notion

---

[17]A highly speculative philosophical movement, originating in Germany, that stressed the knowing subject and had doubts about the status of all objects external to us.
[18]Bertrand Russell, *The History of Western Philosophy* (New York; Touchstone, 1792), 733.
[19]Solomon, *Continental Philosophy Since 1750*, 67.

of an "individual self" in Hegel's view, originates from the culture, not from something intrinsic to the human being.

Schopenhauer and Nietzsche. The philosophy of Arthur Schopenhauer (1788–1860) serves as a transition in continental philosophy after Hegel. Schopenhauer passionately opposed Hegel's notion of Geist, arguing instead that reality consisted of a dynamic relationship between "idea" and "will." For him, the "will" is something that might be expressed in us individually, but is itself impersonal and should not be confused with the idea of the "individual self" of a given person. There is just the will—a cosmic impersonal will—that gets expressed in and through human beings.[20]

Schopenhauer's emphasis on the will had a substantial impact on the philosophy of Friedrich Nietzsche (1844–1900), who in turn plays an important role in postmodern thought. For Nietzsche, the starting point of all of philosophy is the death of God. He is clear to point out that he does not think that God once existed or at one point passed away. Rather, the very idea of God is no longer possible after the Enlightenment and now the world must move beyond its theological past to embrace the implications of atheism in every respect. If God does not exist, then this calls for the reappraisal of every academic discipline and all cultural norms. What we must do, says Nietzsche, is throw off the idea of God and think anew about everything. As David Michael Levin notes, "Thus, for him [Nietzsche], nihilism consists in the fact that, with the 'death' of God, we are bereft of value and meaning. Since God was the source of all our values and the ground of all possible meaning, the 'death' of God leaves us without any values and any ultimate meaning in life. It summons us to appropriate the power, the omnipotence, of our dying God."[21]

This approach will have much to say about theology, metaphysics, epistemology, ethics, and numerous other things. But perhaps nothing would be more deeply affected than Western anthropology and our understanding of the self. If there is no God, or anything like God, then there is nothing left to define us and each person is left to determine who and what they will be for themselves. As Schrag notes, "In dismantling the concept of God as a

---

[20]Daniel Kolak and Garrett Thomson, *The Longman Standard History of Philosophy* (New York: Pearson, 2006), 746.

[21]David Michael Levin, *The Opening of Vision: Nihilism and the Postmodern Situation* (New York: Routledge, 1988), 22-23.

metaphysical aberration Nietzsche prepared the way for a similar fate be-
falling the concept of man."[22] With Nietzsche, then, intrinsic selves con-
sisting of some predefined nature or essence are denied, and all persons
must create themselves through their own willful choices.

Freud. Sigmund Freud (1856–1939) is another highly important thinker
to note for the history of the self. Like other modern thinkers, he rejected
the idea of the self as soul or spiritual essence, but maintained the idea that
the self is something rooted deep within our intellectual life. With some
similarity to Descartes, Locke, and Hume, Freud centered his approach to
the self on the conscious and unconscious life of the person—the psyche.
But, unlike Descartes or Locke, Freud did not think we had complete
awareness of our beliefs, feelings, and motives. As Freud would explain, the
"psyche" is composed of our conscious and subconscious, and he thought
that the subconscious of a person played the most dominant role in their
choices and actions. And as Freud would explain in a variety of different
works, the psyche could be glimpsed through dreams, and slips of the tongue,
and at least partially understood through the process of psychoanalysis.

It is Freud's view of the subconscious part of our psyche—and the way
this is formed through interaction with culture and society—that is most
important for us to consider here. He believed that the subconscious part of
the psyche composed the vast majority of our mental lives and was deeply
influential on who we are as persons. But, as Freud would argue in the later
phases of his career, the psyche was composed of three distinct parts—the
id, the ego, and the superego.

The id, the first part of the psyche, which is present at birth and dominates
the mental life of a person from roughly ages zero to three, is primarily
motivated by desire for pleasure and for its own needs to be met. In other
words, this is the part of us that gives rise to desire for things like sex, food,
and material possessions. Since this is the only operative part of the psyche
present during the early years of a child's life, the child relates to his or her
parents and everything else in the world in a selfish way. The child cries
when it is hungry, dirty, frustrated, or has particular wants that are unmet,
and does not care who it bothers or how inconvenient the timing might be.
The child is selfish like this, according to Freud, simply because the id is the

---

[22]Schrag, *The Self After Postmodernity*, 2.

only part of the psyche that functions during this time. The id only cares for its wants, and does not care about anything or anybody else.

Freud says that the ego forms next in the person, from ages three to five. The ego is the part of the psyche that recognizes there are other people in the world and that they have needs and wants as well. This part of the psyche, says Freud, is motivated by the reality principle that seeks to navigate our social settings while still satisfying the needs of the id. After this, around the age of five, Freud taught that the superego begins to develop. The superego is often referred to as the conscience of the person because this is the part of the psyche that considers moral and ethical restraints of various kinds. It judges things as good or bad, right or wrong, or ought or ought not. The superego seeks then to repress the desires of the id and restrain our behavior to fit the moral expectations of society and culture. As the superego and the id war with each other (one craving pleasure and the other seeking to repress the pleasures), it is the ego's job to find a balance between the two by meeting the needs of the id, while also going about this in a morally acceptable way to satisfy the superego.

So what does this mean for the self? In short, Freud thought that, though the self was composed of the conscious and the subconscious, the subconscious was the biggest and most important part of the psyche. As Solomon notes, "Freud's theories of the mind virtually all work on the basis of some such fundamental opposition, between antagonistic instincts (for example the sex instinct and the ego-instinct), or between different 'agencies' of the psyche (the 'Ego-Id-Superego' model of his later years)."[23] And it is important to note that the antagonism between the id and superego creates an incredibly difficult job for the ego. In a healthy person, the ego is able to maintain balance. But when either the id or the superego becomes dominant, imbalance comes, the person becomes unstable, and trouble inevitably follows. The struggles of the ego arise from two conflicting desires of pleasure (from the id) and moral instincts (from the superego). These moral instincts are reinforced by our parents, society, and culture. Because of this, much of who (and what) we are will be determined by the struggle between the factions of the psyche. The self, for Freud, is not the soul of antiquity or Christianity, but rather the product

---

[23]Solomon, *Continental Philosophy Since 1750*, 143.

of the struggle of the psyche. And because the self rests deeply within the unconscious of the psyche, the self is not knowable, as Descartes thought it was. The self takes shape as the ego works through the demands and ideals of the id and the superego.

The extinct self: structuralism and postmodernism. Lévi-Strauss. The French anthropologist Claude Lévi-Strauss (1908–2009) is also worth our attention as we continue to explore how the concept of the self changes as we move toward postmodernism. Lévi-Strauss's unique contribution is found in his application of structuralism to the discipline of anthropology. Structuralism was first employed by various linguists to explain the way words take on meaning. As Alan Padgett and Steve Wilkens explain, "The key to structural understanding of human language or any meaning-system is the idea of a deep structure or *code*: an underlying structure which organizes the many and various human symbolic products, whether language, narrative or cultural mores."[24] Or, as Solomon puts it, "Structuralism is the scientific search for objective laws of all human activity, beginning with the classification of its basic elements (actions and words) and the ways in which they are systematically combined."[25]

Structuralism, then, is the quest to understand the structures—genetics, ideas, processes, education, and laws—underneath culture, morality, and the human person. Structuralism held that these structures were universal and objective, applying to all people everywhere. Lévi-Strauss applies structuralism to the human person specifically and seeks to understand the influences on humankind itself that gives rise to various manifestations of humanity within particular people. Like Freud and other modern philosophers, Lévi-Strauss rejects the ancient, Christian, and Cartesian views of the self as a soul or immaterial mind. He goes beyond Freud, however, by completely rejecting the self in its entirety. There is no self as a thing in its own right. Rather, there are various material and cultural factors (structures) that give rise to the various manifestations we call human beings. For him, the self does not so much come to culture (and all its various factors) to interact with it. Rather, the structures of culture and the material world create the

---

[24]Alan G. Padgett and Steve Wilkens, *Christianity and Western Thought: A History of Philosophers, Ideas and Movements*, vol. 3, *Journey to Postmodernity in the Twentieth Century* (Downers Grove, IL: IVP Academic, 2009), 270.

[25]Solomon, *Continental Philosophy Since 1750*, 197.

self. Humanity was a social construction from the universal structures at play on all people everywhere. Again, Solomon is helpful:

> Lévi-Strauss rejects not just the self but the entire first-person framework that had been accepted without question in modern philosophy.... He agrees that there is no escaping our own culture and conceptual context, and maintains that the important truths about ourselves are not to be found in consciousness. They are to be found in the world, and our expressions and creations, in what we produce, including our literature and our stories, our language and our cultures. It is by comparing these—across cultures—that we will get a glimpse of the universal structures of the human mind.[26]

Thus, as an anthropologist, what Lévi-Strauss sought to do was to understand the structures that give shape to humans, and the appearance of the self.

Foucault. Michel Foucault (1926–1984) represents the culmination of the previous discussion and is a clear example of postmodern perspectives of the self. Foucault agrees with Lévi-Strauss's emphasis on the human person as a creation of social and cultural factors, but eventually went further than Lévi-Strauss by rejecting the idea that such forces are universal and objective in all places. In other words, he rejected the idea that there were universal rules, ideas, or moral codes affecting all people everywhere, as Solomon helps us see:

> Foucault is a holist in his insistence that an element can be identified only by its place in a system, and has no identity outside this. But he also insists that, just as one cannot define an element outside the system, so one cannot formulate a table of possible permutations of elements, and one will not find objective laws concerning such permutations that are cross-cultural and timeless. One can only describe actual situations and the changing transformations of meaning.[27]

Instead, for Foucault there was simply power, and power gives rise to individuals. Power sources and structures manipulate, shape, and form the "individual" and make us what we are. What humanity lacks, according to Foucault, is a fixed essence or universal essence shared by all people. Nick Mansfield notes, "The subject does not come into the world with all its nature and scope encapsulated within itself in embryonic form. Subjectivity

---

[26]Ibid., 196.
[27]Ibid., 198.

is made by the relationships that form a human context."[28] Thus there is no such thing as "the real person" in Foucault's thinking. Individual persons are social creations that are primarily formed by the power structures of society and culture. And unlike Lévi-Strauss, these powers structures are not uniform or universal to all cultures. As such, with Foucault we have the death of humanity itself and a complete loss of the concept of "the self."

POSTMODERN THEMES REGARDING THE SELF

So where does this leave us? Now that we've briefly traced the history of the concept of the self, what are some of the major themes in postmodern thought about the self? This is actually a difficult question to answer, as postmodernism itself is extremely nebulous. As Schrag notes, "There is first the obvious truth that we are dealing not with a single, unitary, sharply defined portrait, but rather with a portrait that is itself curiously diversified. What thus appears to be at issue is a multiplicity of profiles and perspectives through which the human self moves and is able to come into view."[29] Even still, numerous themes can be identified. We note three that seem central to postmodern thought: rejection of modernism's optimism regarding reason, loss of essences or "human nature," and an emphasis on social construction and social power.

Dethroning reason and the rational self. However else postmodern thinkers may differ with each other about various and sundry topics, they are deeply unified in their rejection of modernism's high view of reason, especially as it relates to their understanding of the self. As we have seen so far, in the modern period, starting with Descartes and continuing all the way through Kant, reason becomes a central, if not the central, focal point of the self. Descartes, for example, argued that the person or self was an immaterial essence that he referred to as a mind. The mind, in his view, is characterized by an ability to think, reflect, reason, and analyze. And though Locke denied the existence of Descartes's immaterial mind, his own view continued to place a primary emphasis on the mental nature of human beings. For him, the self is characterized by the psychological continuity that persists in a person from moment to moment through memory.

---

[28]Nick Mansfield, *Subjectivity: Theories of the Self from Freud to Haraway* (New York: New York University Press, 2000), 52.
[29]Schrag, *The Self After Postmodernity*, 1.

Hume's own account is very similar to Locke's. He also refers to the beliefs, conscious experiences, and collection of psychological dispositions at a given moment as a way of understanding the self. Unlike Locke, however, Hume did not believe that the person persists through memory from one moment to the next. And like these rational and empirical philosophers, Kant also places major emphasis on reason as he develops his concept of the self. For him, the mind and its rational faculties play an active role in structuring, organizing, and categorizing the data gathered by the senses. But once again, the mental rational faculties are central to his concept of the self.

Despite their differences, for these thinkers the rational mind and the faculty of reason anchored the concept of the self and supposedly stripped away all bias, superstition, and cultural influence, allowing the person to see the world as it really is. Reason was thought to give us objectivity, and rational faculties, of one form or another, were thought to be the bedrock of human nature. As White explains, for these modern thinkers, "reason is the gatekeeper to the mind. At least potentially, reason allows a person to control his thoughts, beliefs, feelings, and intentions by evaluating each one, keeping and pursuing those that are rational and rejecting those that are irrational."[30] And given the way reason allows persons to understand, it is not surprising that the mind is such a fundamental feature of modern views of the self.

Postmodern thinkers, however, completely reject such views, contending that modernism's great confidence in reason is misplaced and in error. In their view, the modern emphasis on reason is grossly naive. They believe that modern views fail to account for the way bias, culture, power structures, experience, and a host of other things do in fact shape the way we think. For them, rational faculties do not provide a basis for objectivity and therefore do not give us a basis for understanding the self.

Loss of essence, loss of the self. Postmodern thinkers are also deeply unified in rejecting the very idea of human nature. They deny that there is any fixed set of characteristics that can be found in all humans. White helps us see the contrast with modernism, saying, "Postmoderns insist that there is *no* essence to being human; that there is no human nature, only human history; that reason is influenced by culture more than the other way

---

[30]White, *Postmodernism 101*, 70.

around."[31] And as Thomas J. Altizer has noted, this loss of human essence comes as a direct correlation with the death of God in the modern period:

> The night brought on by the death of God is a night in which every individual identity perishes. When the heavens are darkened, and God disappears, man does not stand autonomous and alone. He ceases to stand. . . . The death of the transcendence of God embodies the death of all autonomous selfhood, an end of all humanity which is created in the image of the absolutely sovereign and transcendent God.[32]

As we have labored to show in this chapter, this conclusion did not arise as an abrupt departure from the long consensus of Western thought. Rather, the concept of the self slowly dissolved, as various thinkers developed their accounts of the self in response to each other over time. As we have seen, from Plato and even up through Freud, philosophers have struggled to identify the one thing that it means to be a human being or to be a self.

With Plato and the early Christian philosophers, for example, the self was thought of as a sort of spiritual essence located in the soul. Descartes shared a similar view, but shifted the locus of the self from the soul to the mind, giving the self a more rational foundation. Locke and Hume pointed to psychological properties. With Hegel, however, the self is located within Geist, the one Spirit that is unfolding in all things through the process of the dialectic. This significant shift in the concept of the self undermines the idea of "individual selves" in favor of a more unified and universal self—Geist— in all things. Yet the concept of the self dissolves further with thinkers like Schopenhauer and Nietzsche. In their thought, the self is found in the will, or specifically, the will to power. The self is not some spiritual or rational thing as others had thought, but is instead conceived of as a volitional force played out in the choices we make in the world.

Freud and Lévi-Strauss bring additional shifts of magnitude for the concept of the self. Freud, for example, fully rejects the idea of spiritual, rational, or volitional essences. For him the self is merely a thing that is shaped by the struggling and conflicting development of the id, the ego, and the superego. This tripartite psyche may never be known fully or sufficiently,

---

[31]Ibid., 73.

[32]Thomas J. Altizer, *The Descent into Hell; a Study of the Radical Reversal of the Christian Consciousness* (Philadelphia: Lippincott, 1970), 153-4.

but Freud did believe dreams and psychoanalysis give us glimpses into the basic structure. The psyche, he thought, developed through the internal conflict of the tripartite desires, and by interaction with the external world. But Freud still believed there was a self there to be known, even if we can only know it partially.

Lévi-Strauss had one final critical development for the self concept. He completely rejects the idea that there is anything there to be known, and argues that the self is nothing more than a social construction brought about by universal structures and influences found in all places. There may not be some thing called a self to be studied and analyzed, but there were, he thought, real forces and influences in place to create or construct "selves." In his thought the self—as a metaphysical, spiritual, rational, volitional, or psychological essence—was completely lost, and only universal structures are left to study.

Like Lévi-Strauss, Foucault protests and rejects the idea of human nature. In fact, Foucault and other postmodern thinkers go beyond Lévi-Strauss by also rejecting the uniform social forces found in all cultures that shape individuals. There are no shared essences or shared influences in Foucault's view of the self. All there is is power—manifesting itself in various ways from one place to the next—which creates and shapes individuals.

While this history shows an ever-dissolving concept of the self, all views prior to postmodernism share a conviction that there is still some underlying thing, universally shared by all people, called the self. Their differences express the long history of trying to find what the self is and to possess a basic understanding of its nature, even if only vaguely. As White puts it, "Whereas for moderns and premoderns the central fact about human beings is what they have in common, for postmoderns that central fact is the variations and differences among human beings. Emphasizing the common— the alleged human nature, or the faculty of reason—is another way of suppressing differences."[33] Foucault himself says it this way:

> One thing in any case is certain: man is neither the oldest nor the most constant problem that has been posed for human knowledge. Taking a relatively short chronological sample within a restricted geographical area—European culture since the sixteenth century—one can be certain that man is a recent invention within it.[34]

---

[33]White, *Postmodernism 101*, 73.
[34]Michel Foucault, *The Order of Things* (New York: Vintage, 1994), 386.

And as he goes on to say, if the power sources that gave rise to humankind ever disappeared, "Man would be erased, like a face drawn in the sand at the edge of the sea."[35] Thus the self concept has evolved and morphed over time from thinker to thinker, until it is finally denied altogether by Foucault and other postmodern philosophers. The self is lost and the search for such things is met with contempt and outrage.

Social power and social construction. The denial of human nature leads us to a final point of emphasis in postmodern thinking. If there is no such thing as human nature or human essence, then how should we understand the human being? As our previous discussions about Lévi-Strauss and Foucault suggest, the self in postmodern thought is nothing more than a social construction.[36] Individuals are not shaped by an internal essence innate to all people, but rather by the world they live in, and by the interactions they had with other people, situations, and influences. The human being is an open-ended specimen, able to take any form or adapt to any social influences from one culture to the next. He is defined by these influences, not by a specific nature.

But there is more to say about this social construction of the self. As Foucault argues, the social forces at play in shaping the selves differ and vary from one context to the next. Since there is no uniform essence or nature nor are there any uniform structures or processes, or any true self at all, there is nothing that can be objectively studied or analyzed to help us understand the self. There is nothing, that is, other than power. As Padgett and Wilkens explain, "Foucault makes the radical claim that divisions between truth and untruth, good and evil, pleasure and unhappiness are always already implicit systems of power and individuation."[37] In other words, any attempt to "explain" what it means to be a human is really nothing more than a power grab by those who want to control and hold power over other people. White offers some helpful examples of just how this plays out in postmodern thought.

> Since the 1970s, postmoderns have discerned many more power relationships
> in society than simply the haves and have-nots: men have power over women
> (hence feminism); whites have power over minorities (hence racial politics);

---

[35]Ibid., 387.

[36]So we lack both a common human nature and a concrete self, which is a subset of the characteristics of human nature.

[37]Padgett and Wilkens, *Journey to Postmodernity*, 296.

straights have power over homosexuals (hence gay and lesbian political activism). Identity politics is a challenge to the claims about human nature or reason that reinforce these differences in social power: "Men are naturally in authority over women," "Whites are superior (intellectually or otherwise) to blacks," "Homosexuality is unnatural."[38]

As White helps us see, Foucault and other postmodern philosophers are highly suspicious of "human nature" because it is a concept often employed as a tool to shape people and gain control over them. The self concept, in their view, is constructed by power and foisted on us; it is not something within us by nature.

A Christian Response

Without question, postmodern views of the self differ wildly from more traditional Christian notions of the self (we shall turn to those differences in a moment). And given the stark contrast between Christian and postmodern views of the self, most Christians will have nothing but criticism and scorn for what we have just described in the last few pages. While we offer some criticisms ourselves, we also want to note some important insights that postmodern thinkers have brought to our attention.

Some helpful insights. There are, despite first appearances, some positive aspects of postmodern views of the self. First, postmodernism rightly pushes back on some of the problematic ideas of modernity. In modern thought, for example, philosophers shifted to a rationalistic view of the self and overconfidence in human reason. It was thought that we could strip ourselves of all cultural influence, personal bias, and superstition to see things as they really are—that we could be completely and perfectly objective in our view of reality. But of course, this is naive and unrealistic. As postmodern thinkers argue, we are deeply influenced by our culture and by other factors such that we see things in different ways. This is not to say that we side with postmodern thinkers and their antirealist views. Surely there is a real world before us that can be known, even if only partially. But postmodern thinkers have offered legitimate critiques of the supposed objectivity guaranteed by modernity. Whatever other concerns one might have with postmodernity, modernity is not the answer.

---

[38]White, *Postmodernism 101*, 74-75.

Second, as postmodern thinkers have noted, not only do cultural influences affect the way we see the world, but they also have an impact on the shape of the human being in general. That is, culture also has an impact on what we become as individual persons. But this is a problematic claim that needs clarification, as we are not siding with postmodernism and its denial of human nature. But it is true that human beings take on many different shapes, have wildly different ideologies, and manifest vastly different personas. Surely culture and society have a major part in this, exerting influence in many different ways.

We might note any kind of deep divisions in society as evidence of this. We could consider, for example, divisions over political issues like same-sex marriage, abortion, war, immigration, or health care to see this influence. Or we might also look at the different purposes to which people give their lives and the reasons they see themselves living. That these differences arise from cultural and social influences there seems to be no doubt. On this postmodern observations help us make sense of these differences, even if we differ with them about there being such a thing as human nature.

Third, postmodern thinkers have helped us see the way power can be abused. Whether we like to admit it or not, those who hold cultural or social influence are often the most powerful brokers in the economy of human life. Throughout history, this power has been used in horrible ways to manipulate, distort, injure, and kill people. Examples are not hard to come by. Consider, for example, the way social power was used in the United States to oppress African Americans. This oppression is highlighted by slavery in the seventeenth through nineteenth centuries, but the oppression hardly ended there. White supremacists continue to use a distorted concept of human nature to hurt and oppress African Americans. The same has been true in the oppression of Jews, Christians, women, and many more through recent history. In each case, one group with significant influence—perhaps the majority of influence—uses a distorted concept of the self as a weapon of power to disenfranchise other people. Postmoderns rightly protest such abuses and help us see our errors.

Some differences and concerns. In our estimation, postmodernism gets some things right regarding the self. There are, however, some important problems associated with their denial of the self.

First, while their understanding of social influence helps us make sense out of how major differences between people on issues such as purpose, meaning, and moral conviction might arise, the final conclusion of post-modernism—the denial of human nature—is overstated and counter-intuitive. Sure, social and cultural factors shape the way we approach, understand, and feel about things, but this hardly means that there is no such thing as human nature itself. Something is there—namely persons—to be shaped and influenced, and despite whatever else may differ among them, these persons have much in common. They laugh, they love, they feel, they think, they reason, they plan, they act, they regret, they mourn, and much more. Persons, no matter what differences may be manifested among them, do all these things. And these similarities tell us that there is something common to all people. To say that there is no such thing as human nature or the self is to commit oneself to absurdity. Postmodernism helps us make sense out of what makes us different. But it fails to address what we are by denying that we are anything at all.

Second, for those committed to a Christian worldview, the postmodern conclusion—the denial of the self—is extremely problematic. Simply put, the Christian tradition not only affirms the existence of human nature but also has very clear things to say about that nature. Just one quick passage will help us see this. One of the most central statements in all of Christian Scripture comes from Genesis 1:26-27. Here the Bible says,

> Then God said, "Let Us make man in Our image, according to Our likeness; let them have dominion over the fish of the sea, over the birds of the air, and over the cattle, over all the earth and over every creeping thing that creeps on the earth." So God created man in His *own* image; in the image of God He created him; male and female He created them. (NKJV)

Here the author of Genesis tells us that (1) human beings possess a specific nature, (2) that this nature is after God's own image—the *imago Dei*—and (3) that this nature is shared by both male and female.

That we possess this particular nature becomes even more important in the Christian tradition as we consider the church's teaching about Christ's own human nature. In the incarnation, John tells us that "the Word became flesh" (Jn 1:14). This, as understood by the councils of the church, means that Jesus had a real human nature of the same kind as human beings today. The Council of Chalcedon is helpful. It says, "We . . . teach men to confess one and the same Son, our Lord Jesus Christ, the same perfect in Godhead and also perfect in manhood; truly God and truly man, of a reasonable [rational] soul and body; consubstantial [coessential] with the Father according to the Godhead, and consubstantial with us according to the Manhood; in all things like unto us, without sin."[39]

A simple glance at both Christian Scripture and Christian theological history demonstrates that the idea of human nature—that there is such a thing as a self—is central to this tradition. Postmodern thinkers are free to reject this idea, but for those who wish to affirm postmodern ideas while at the same time hold to some form of Christianity, this is a significant problem. One simply cannot have it both ways. And since the postmodern denial of human nature appears to be counterintuitive and overstated, perhaps it is best to simply forsake that view. As we have tried to note in this chapter, rejecting the postmodern rejection of the self does not mean that we cannot learn from this perspective. Indeed, their perspective helps us in some ways, even if it overstates its case along the way.

Conclusion

In this chapter we offered a brief history of the concept of the self, noting key figures throughout Western history. The history begins with Plato's concept of the soul, but ends with Foucault's rejection of the very concept. In postmodern thought, the concept of human nature is completely lost and replaced with social forces and powers. While postmodernism may help us understand what makes us all very different and the way culture and society shape us, it overstates its case and affirms something counterintuitive. The demise of the self seems not to have happened after all. Despite its anger and protest, the postmodern conclusion seems false.

Summary

1. In both classical philosophy and the Christian era, philosophers like Plato and theologians like Augustine viewed the self as being one and the same with the immaterial soul.

2. In the early modern period, philosophers like Descartes continued to view the self as an immaterial substance, thinking of it in more intellectual terms as a mind.

---

[39]"The Creed of Chalcedon, A.D. 451," in *The Creeds of Christendom: With a History and Critical Notes*, ed. Philip Schaff, rev. David Schaff (Grand Rapids: Baker, 1996), 62.

3. Locke and Hume brought a major shift in the way modern thinkers viewed the self, arguing that the self was a collection of psychological properties found in memories. But whereas Locke believed that this self could persist in existence, Hume denied it altogether.

4. Rousseau and Kant brought further shifts in thinking about the self. For them, the self was something that projected itself on the world.

5. Hegel again emphasizes a spiritual view of the self that was wrapped up in his understanding of Geist, leaving little space for the notion of an individual self.

6. Freud located the self in the psyche and the subconscious struggle among the id, the ego, and the superego.

7. Lévi-Strauss emptied the notion of the self completely, arguing that there is no universal "essence" or "whatness" of the self. Rather, the self is something that forms through engagement with culture and the universal structures of power and influence.

8. Foucault takes Lévi-Strauss one step further by not just rejecting the notion of a universal human nature but also rejecting the notion of universal structures that can be studied and understood.

9. Despite significant differences among postmodern thinkers about the self, they rally around the following ideas: the rejection of reason and the rational self, the rejection of "human nature," and the affirmation of socially constructed selves.

10. Postmodernism is helpful in that it highlights the various factors that shape and influence individuals and groups, and in that it shows us how power can corrupt.

11. The postmodern rejection of "human nature" seems committed to an absurdity. Social construction alone is an inadequate understanding of the self. Something—the self—must exist to be shaped. If it exists, it must have a nature.

12. The postmodern rejection of "human nature" is irreconcilable with the Christian doctrines of anthropology and Christology. In the incarnation, the Son took on human form, and the creeds declare that he still has a genuine human nature. One cannot affirm both postmodernism and Christianity together.

SUGGESTED READINGS

Anderson, Walter Truett. *The Future of the Self: Inventing the Postmodern Person.* New York: Penguin Putnam, 1997.

Hall, Donald E. *Subjectivity.* New York: Routledge, 2004.

Mansfield, Nick. *Subjectivity: Theories of the Self From Freud to Haraway.* New York: New York University Press, 2000.

Schrag, Calvin O. *The Self After Postmodernity.* New Haven, CT: Yale University Press, 1997.

Solomon, Robert. *Continental Philosophy Since 1750: The Rise and Fall of the Self.* New York: Oxford, 1988.

8

REALISM AND ANTIREALISM,
OBJECTIVITY AND SUBJECTIVITY

How well do we comprehend the world? Do we see it as it really is, or are there factors at play that skew our perspectives and cause us to see it in a particular way? And if there are, does this mean that we never see the "real"? Is our knowledge of reality reflective and representative of how things really are, or is it merely a collection of ideas fabricated by our own subjective minds? Answering questions like these about the concrete world of everyday objects is hard enough. But as we probe a bit deeper to consider issues of truth, morality, the meaning of life, spirituality, or any worldview claim in general, these questions become all the more important and significant. Are our moral convictions, for example, reflective of what is objectively right and wrong for all people? Or are they social constructs that have been created by our own unique and subjective situation in life? Questions about truth and knowledge are at the heart of epistemology and many of the debates surrounding postmodernism. More specifically, the questions above are fundamental in the debate between realism and antirealism, and its corollary debate between objectivity and subjectivity.

In what follows we will navigate through these debates by offering a brief account of the various historical perspectives that have spoken to these questions. After this, we will look at some of the strengths and weakness of the postmodern critiques of objectivity and realism. But first, some terminology will be helpful.

TERMINOLOGY

So what, exactly, do we mean by terms like *realism, antirealism, objectivity*, and *subjectivity*, and what is their relationship to each other? This is an especially important question since terms like *objectivity* and *subjectivity* can a have a variety of meanings, depending on the kind of philosophical issue at hand. In metaphysics, for example, *objective* tends to refer to an external reality outside the mind, whereas *subjective* refers to persons themselves. In moral discussions, *objective* is typically used to denote a moral standard that is not socially constructed or dependent on social factors, and *subjective* refers to a moral norm that may differ from person to person or group to group. And again, in the philosophy of mind, *objective* refers to qualities of a particular kind that can be observed by all, whereas *subjective* refers to those subjective experiences that can only be experienced by the one having them. In this case, the subjective qualities found in our conscious experiences are often used by philosophers of mind to argue in favor of the existence of the soul. As you can see then, terms like *objective* and *subjective* need to be defined within the context we are using them. What do these terms mean in epistemology, most generally, and in the discussion of modernity and postmodernity, more specifically?

As noted above, within epistemic discussions, these terms represent two different debates in the history of philosophy that run parallel to each other. Generally speaking, those who hold that we can be objective in the way we see the world also hold to a form of realism. And likewise, those who think our grasp of the world is subjective tend toward antirealism. So what do these terms mean? Roughly speaking, we might define these terms within epistemic discussions as follows:

> **Objectivity:** Objectivity is the view that we have the ability to be objective in the way we see the world and in our truth claims. It denies that social, cultural, or our subjective mental idiosyncrasies prevent us from grasping what is really there. As Robert Audi puts it, objectivism is the view "that there is an objective method for ascertaining whether beliefs about the world are true, that is (roughly speaking), a method which can be used by any competent investigator and tends to yield the same results when properly applied by different competent investigators to the same problem."[1]

---

[1]Robert Audi, *Epistemology: A Contemporary Introduction to the Theory of Knowledge* (New York; Routledge, 1998), 255.

Realism: Realism is the view that our grasp of the world is of the truly existing world and that we can have genuine knowledge of it. It denies that the world is mind-dependent. As such, our knowledge and understanding reflects, in at least some genuine fashion, the world as it is. Alister McGrath offers a helpful description of the view: "The term 'realism' denotes a family of philosophical positions which take the general position that there exists a real world, external to the human mind, which the human mind can encounter, understand and represent, at least in part. There is an objective world, quite apart from the human thinker, which exists independently of our thoughts, fears, longings and musings."[2]

Subjectivity: Subjectivity is the view that denies the possibility of epistemological objectivity and says that our perspective of the world is always *determined* by and situated within our own unique intellectual idiosyncrasies. John Searle explains, "A statement is epistemically subjective if its truth depends essentially on the attitudes and feelings of observers."[3]

Antirealism: Antirealism is the view that claims all knowledge is mind-dependent. It does not deny the existence of an external world and real objects in the world. It simply says that our knowledge is not of those things.[4] Rather, it says that knowledge is of the phenomena of the things. Or as Lawrence Cahoone has put it, antirealism claims "that knowledge is made valid not by its relation to its objects, but by its relation to our pragmatic interests, our communal perspectives, our needs, our rhetoric, and so on."[5]

We will elaborate on these terms and concepts as we proceed throughout the chapter, introducing a few other concepts and alternatives along the way as well. But before we begin considering the history of these perspectives, let us note one important thing about their relationship. For modern and postmodern thinkers, it has typically been assumed that objectivity and realism rise and fall together. That is, if we are successful in seeing the world objectively, then we have good reason to think that we are seeing reality itself, and that realism is true.

---

[2] Alister E. McGrath, *A Scientific Theology*, vol. 2, *Reality* (Grand Rapids: Eerdmans, 2002), 126.

[3] John R. Searle, *Mind, Language and Society: Philosophy in the Real World* (New York: Basic Books, 1998), 44.

[4] In one important sense, then, antirealists are skeptics concerning knowledge.

[5] Lawrence E. Cahoone, "Introduction to Part 1," in *From Modernism to Postmodernism: An Anthology*, ed. Lawrence E. Cahoone (Malden, MA: Blackwell, 1996), 17.

But, by contrast, if we have reason to be suspicious of our ability to know objectively due to social, cultural, historical, or other idiosyncratic factors that prevent a direct and immediate apprehension of reality, then realism must be false and antirealism must be true.

In large part, this has been the story of the modern and postmodern perspectives. Moderns, on the one hand, tended to think that objectivity was possible and thus realism was true. Postmoderns, on the other hand, were deeply suspicious of objectivity and concluded, therefore, that antirealism is true. Moderns and postmoderns tend to agree about these relationships. However, this assumption has been challenged more recently by those who argue that knowledge is mediated by various factors, but continue to insist that some form of realism is true. In other words, they reject the idea that complete objectivity and realism rise and fall together, arguing that our knowledge is indeed mediated to some degree, but that realism is also true.

We will say more about the relationship of realism and objectivity as we move on. For now, let us turn our attention to the way these ideas developed and evolved through the premodern, early modern, and late modern/postmodern periods.

A Brief History of Objectivity and Subjectivity, Realism, and Antirealism

During the premodern period, realism was largely assumed by intellectuals within the Western world. Scientists, theologians, philosophers, and lawyers held that we are largely successful in understanding the world and that knowledge was not only a possibility but also an actuality. Yet, as we will see, it is not as clear that thinkers in this period sought for a perfectly objective vantage point for their knowledge, as many were willing to allow ideas unique to their perspectives to shape their theories and truth claims. As such, the realism of the premodern period was not naive about our ability to have a perfect grasp of the world. That is, most thinkers prior to modernity understood the possibility of epistemic error.

In the early modern period, philosophers continued to assume realism, but made strident efforts to attain methodological objectivity. They largely rejected the premodern approach that allowed one to start from within a particular perspective—religious, metaphysical, or cultural—and work from there. For modern thinkers, unless we are able to strip away all subjective factors, we will be blinded by our biases and our efforts to understand reality are doomed to failure.

In the late modern and postmodern periods, ideological shifts took place that caused many to grow suspicious of our ability to see the world objectively. The recognition that social, cultural, historical, and various personal factors play an inevitable role in the shaping of our views and theories became more common. Postmodern philosophers rejected the notion of objectivity, and with it they also rejected realism. For them, all knowledge, perspectives, and theory are dependent on cultural and personal idiosyncrasies that prevent us from being objective or attaining the "view from nowhere." As such, antirealism—the thesis that all knowledge is mind dependent—became the mantra of the movement.

Premodern views of realism and objectivity. Prior to the seventeenth century, from Thales to Francis Bacon and René Descartes, philosophers, scientists, and theologians assumed a form of realism. They thought that the external world existed apart from our minds and our ability to perceive it, and that this world would exist even if we were not there to experience it. For example, realism is seen in the way that Thales and Anaximenes (Greek thinkers in the fifth century BC) theorized about the "ultimate stuff" being water or air. Their attempt to identify the primal material of reality assumed a "realistic" view of the world in which things exist apart from our perceptions and where we are able to attain genuine knowledge of it. Pythagoras, by contrast, assumed realism in his understanding of number and harmony as fundamental to reality. These were mind-independent entities that gave shape to the world and could be known. Heraclitus and Parmenides (also fifth-century-BC Greeks), again assume realism in their debate regarding change and continuity. And Plato and Aristotle assume realism in the way that they understand and argue for forms and universals. As Mortimer Adler has rightly noted, "In the history of Western thought . . . a profound understanding of truth has prevailed from the time of Plato and Aristotle to the present. This understanding rests upon a single supposition; namely, that there exists, quite independent of the human mind, a reality which the human mind thinks about and tries to know."[6]

---

[6]Mortimer J. Adler, *Truth in Religion* (New York: Macmillan, 1990), 116.

Alan Padgett also argues that realism was "the viewpoint of almost all religious believers" in the premodern period.[7] For these believers, he says, the God "that they worship and live for must be real in order for it to be worshiped and for prayer to make sense."[8]

So the premodern thinkers were realist, but what about their view of objectivity? Did they also assume an objectivist approach to knowledge? Richard Rorty thinks so. He says, "The tradition in western culture which centers around the notion of the search for truth, a tradition which runs from the Greek philosophers through the enlightenment, is the clearest example of the attempt to find a sense of one's existence by turning away from solidarity to objectivity."[9] He further explains with some examples:

> Herodotus' willingness to take the barbarians seriously enough to describe their customs in detail may have been a necessary prelude to Plato's claim that the way to transcend skepticism is to envisage a common goal of humanity— a goal set by human nature rather than by Greek culture. The combination of Socratic alienation and platonic hopes gives rise to the idea of the intellectual as someone who is in touch with the nature of things, not by way of the opinions of his community, but in a more immediate way.[10]

While premodern thinkers were clearly realist, it is less clear that Rorty is correct in saying that they were also committed to objectivism. As Stephen Gaukroger notes, the strong commitment to objectivism is an emphasis that took shape much more in the modern period. "This development dates from no earlier than the start of the 19th century, when the West's conception of its superiority shifted from its religion—Christianity—to its science."[11] Moreover, one can easily find examples in the Christian era of those who do not seem to fit the objectivists' expectations. Colin Brown argues, for example, that Christian thinkers have regularly allowed their approach to knowledge and theory to be shaped by factors explicitly centered on their theology. He says that for many Christians throughout history, "the proper starting place . . . for the philosophy of the Christian religion is not outside

---

[7]Alan G. Padgett, *Science and the Study of God* (Grand Rapids: Eerdmans, 2003), 36.
[8]Ibid.
[9]Richard Rorty, "Solidarity or Objectivity," in *Objectivity, Relativism, and Truth: Philosophical Papers* (Cambridge: Cambridge University Press, 1991), 21.
[10]Ibid.
[11]Stephen Gaukroger, *Objectivity: A Very Short Introduction* (New York: Oxford University Press, 2012), 2. Descartes and Bacon are clearly exceptions here.

it but within it. Its primary data is the Christian experience of God in Christ."[12] He also says, "The approach to truth of the reformers is essentially a continuation of that of Anselm and the authors of scripture. It is summed up in the words: 'I believe so that I may understand.'"[13]

In other words, Christian thinkers did not seem to share the conviction that they had to rid themselves of all religious assumptions and convictions as they explore the world and developed arguments. In fact, these theologians assumed that one must start with certain assumptions before anything else could make sense. This is not to say that premodern thinkers thought of themselves and their approach as being radically subjective. They did care about intellectual error and understood that biases could impinge on their ability to understand the world. Nevertheless, it is not clear that Rorty can so easily describe the Western mind from Herodotus forward as being committed to objectivism. In short, then, the premodern thinkers were committed to realism, but it is less clear that they embraced the naive objectivism of the later modern thinkers to whom we now turn.

Early modern views of realism and objectivity. Whereas premodern thinkers assumed realism but seemed less concerned with total objectivity in their approach to reality and knowledge, things changed with the modern period as thinkers made decisive shifts toward objectivism. That is, modern thinkers intentionally adopted a perspective that required them to "stand back from our perceptions, our beliefs and opinions, to reflect on them, and subject them to a particular kind of scrutiny and judgment. Above all, it requires a degree of difference in judging that may conflict with our needs and desires."[14] And, as many have noted, "science was seen to embody objectivity in its purest form."[15] Michael Polanyi argues, for instance, that the "prevailing conception of science, based on the disjunction of subjectivity and objectivity, seeks—and must seek at all costs—to eliminate from science such passion, personal, human appraisals of theories, or at least to minimize their function to that of a negligible by-play."[16] But how, exactly, did this

---

[12]Colin Brown, *Philosophy and the Christian Faith* (Downers Grove, IL: InterVarsity Press, 1968), 47.

[13]Ibid.

[14]Gaukroger, *Objectivity*, 1.

[15]Ibid., 2.

[16]Michael Polanyi, *Personal Knowledge: Towards a Post-critical Philosophy* (Chicago: University of Chicago Press, 1974), 15-16.

idea develop in the modern period? We shall attempt an account momen-
tarily, but before we proceed, a quick word of qualification is in order. It is
somewhat difficult to identify the exact moment when the objectivist
movement began and then started to decline. We will mention several
thinkers that emphasized this ideal, and several that argued against it. Interestingly, the time frame of its dominance and downfall is not linear—rather,
they overlap at key moments and even in individual thinkers.

There are plenty of philosophers we might mention, but our very brief
excursion into the rise of objectivity will mention just a few quick examples:
Descartes, Bacon, Immanuel Kant, and Karl Popper. We begin with Descartes. In the seventeenth century, Descartes sought for a way to find sure
and certain knowledge that was not plagued by the same kinds of intellectual errors of the philosophers and thinkers in the centuries before him.
In the *Discourse on Method*, he describes, with some distaste, the lack of
certainty and overall confusion that existed in the Western world prior to
his time. He says:

> I have been nursed by books since I was a child, and because I was convinced
> that, by using them, one could acquire a clear and certain knowledge of every-
> thing that is useful for life, I had great desire to study them. But as soon as I
> had concluded the course of studies at the end of which one is usually admitted
> to the ranks of the learned, I changed my mind completely. For I found myself
> so overcome by so many doubts and errors that I seem to have gained nothing
> from studying, apart from becoming more conscious of my ignorance.[17]

Frustrated and underwhelmed by the lack of intellectual progress of
previous thinkers, Descartes sought for a new way of thinking to help him
achieve absolute certainty in all his knowledge. For this, he looked to
mathematics as an example of how we might reason. Descartes did not
think himself to be giving a universal method. Instead he simply described
his approach as one that requires us to set aside any ideas or beliefs that
could have any possibility of doubt until one is left with only those ideas
that are clear, distinct, and indubitable. Once these ideas are identified, one
can then proceed to build a system of thought on these clear and distinct
ideas. Only through such methodological doubt, Descartes believed, could
one be assured that they have removed any possibility of error. Or put

---

[17]René Descartes, *Discourse on Method*, trans. Desmond M. Clarke (New York: Penguin, 2003), 7.

another way, this method of systematic doubt allowed him to be objective about his knowledge.

Similar themes can be found in Francis Bacon, even though his general epistemic approach is fundamentally different. Descartes, for example is known as a rationalist while Bacon is generally described as an empiricist. Yet, like Descartes, Bacon was frustrated with the epistemic failures of the philosophers before him and drew special attention to the way various kinds of biases impinge on our ability to see the world correctly and objectively. Bacon pointed to and identified the *idols of the mind* in an effort to rid himself, and all scientific inquiry after him, of the epistemic biases that cause us to mis-see the world in our scientific investigations. According to Bacon, these idols include:

1. Idol of the Tribe: the negative influence of human nature that distorts perceptions and understanding.

2. Idol of the Cave: the tendency for us to let various social, historical, cultural, and ideological factors shape our view of the world.

3. Idol of the Marketplace: epistemic difficulties that arise from human language.

4. Idol of the Theatre: prior ideological allegiances to particular schools of thought.[18]

For Bacon, these "idols" of the mind plagued the deductive method and all scientific endeavors before him. To fix the problem, Bacon suggests a new method of induction. In this method, observers saturate their quests for understanding and attempts to formulate scientific theories in the particulars of the natural world. For example, if one wants to have a good theory of what swans are like, then one must not start with some prior theory about swans that may or may not be steeped in ideology, but rather, they must strip away all previous assumptions and go investigate swans. As Bacon would argue, only after extensive and exhaustive investigation of the actual objects of nature can one begin to move toward theory. He says that "true induction is certainly an appropriate way to banish idols and get rid of them."[19] In his view, induction strips away the idols and allows the scientist to be more objective in her approach.

---

[18]Francis Bacon, *The New Organon* (Cambridge: Cambridge University Press, 2000), 41-49.
[19]Ibid., 41.

We must also say something about Immanuel Kant's influence on the matter of objectivity. As McGrath notes, "Kant had argued, in what now seems a somewhat optimistic manner, for transcendental criteria of judgment, valid for all minds and across all cultures and traditions at all time."[20] He continues by saying that the Enlightenment—typified in the Kantian perspective—took "the view that human reason elevated the intelligent and the enlightened individual above the shadows and clouds of tradition, and allowed the 'big picture' to be seen with unprecedented clarity. In the light of this comprehensive overview of the totality of things, reliable judgments could be made concerning religions, traditions and other such outmoded ways of thinking and behaving."[21]

This emphasis is also evident in a variety of ways within Kant's works. First, in his famous *What Is Enlightenment?*, Kant argues that Enlightenment is the courageous move away from superstition and tradition and the decision to use one's own reason. He sees superstition exemplified in pastors and legal authorities, while reason is exemplified in the scholar. He says, "Likewise the clergyman is obliged to teach his pupils and his congregation according to the creed of the church which he serves, for he has been accepted on that condition. But as a scholar, he has full freedom, in fact even the obligation, to communicate to the public all his diligently examined and well-intentioned thoughts concerning erroneous points in that doctrine and concerning proposals regarding the better institution of religious and ecclesiastical matters."[22] In other words, Kant understood the Enlightenment to be the era where people threw off previous ways of thinking and allowed reason and experience to guide them in their search for truth.

A kind of objectivity is also found in his approach to ethics, or more specifically, the way he sought to ground ethics. In an age when the West had thrown off metaphysics and religion, philosophers now had the task of finding a way to ground morality. In the Christian tradition, this had typically been done by way of reference to a God who was the source of goodness, fairness, and other such moral ideals. But since such beliefs about God had

---

[20]McGrath, *Reality*, 57. These would be standards that transcended any particular culture—they would appeal to all reasonable people from all cultures, no small feat.

[21]Ibid., 58.

[22]Immanuel Kant, "What Is Enlightenment?," in *Basic Writings of Kant*, ed. Allen W. Wood (New York: Modern Library, 2001), 137. Part of Kant's point is that the clergy are hired by the state to teach a particular set of doctrines—they are not free to do otherwise.

been jettisoned, philosophers were no longer able to situate and ground morality with reference to God. Ethics had been unhitched from its theological wagon. Kant, like other philosophers of his time, looked for a way to universalize and objectivize our moral inclination—or at least our method for making moral judgments—without making them dependent on the previous theological basis of the past. Kant's proposal is the "categorical imperative."

To help convey the idea of the categorical imperative, Kant set it in contrast to a hypothetical imperative. These were commands that we might follow under certain circumstances if we desired a particular outcome. For example, a hypothetical imperative might say, "If you want to be popular [hypothetical], don't insult people [imperative]." These are not universal. A categorical imperative, by contrast, is a command (imperative) that applies to all people, at all times, everywhere (categorical). Kant argues that there is only one such imperative, but that it has multiple applications for our actions. He summarizes the categorical imperative as follows: "Act only according to the maxim whereby you can at the same time will that it should become a universal law."[23] The categorical imperative, for Kant, was a way of identifying, universalizing, and objectivizing moral judgments that could be used by all people everywhere. It assumed that people everywhere have the same preferences for the human condition and attempted to construct an objective basis for morality on those preferences. But as we will see, these assumptions would ultimately be challenged by postmodern thinkers. Moreover, whereas Kant's work contributes at least in part to the movement toward objectivism, his work would also be influential in its downfall.

We have mentioned the specific examples of Descartes, Bacon, and Kant in relation to the rise of objectivity. But we might also say something about the general association of modern science with objectivism. As Gaukroger notes, as far back as Galileo in the sixteenth century, scientists were beginning to characterize their approach as being objective. He says, "Galileo, for example, charged his opponents with having preconceived ideas, construed as a form of vested interests, and Aristotelians are presented as people with an ax to grind, unable to argue a case on its merits and so having to rely on a philosophical system, which is treated as a form of intellectual dishonesty and

---

[23]Immanuel Kant, *Grounding for the Metaphysics of Morals*, trans. James W. Ellington (Indianapolis: Hackett, 1993), 30.

lack of objectivity."[24] While other English and French scientists took a similar view of science in the seventeenth and eighteenth centuries, Gaukroger notes that the objectivist movement finds greatest emphasis in the twentieth century with the logical positivists and the works of Karl Popper.

In keeping with objectivist ideals, A. J. Ayer and the logical positivists followed David Hume's empiricism and his distinction between analytic and synthetic truths.[25] Analytic truths are those truths that we know by definition—"a bachelor is unmarried." Synthetic truths are truths we can know by way of empirical investigation—"the ball is red." The logical positivists employed the verification principle as a way of excluding all metaphysical and religious claims as contenders for truth. In their view, only those statements that can be verified either analytically or synthetically can be regarded as true. Statements such as "God exists" were relegated to a third category of nonsensical. That logical positivism would be rejected later on the grounds that the verification principle is itself neither analytic nor synthetic is not central to our survey of the history of objectivity. What is important at this point is to note that for the logical positivists, the verification principle was an attempt to strip away the biases of religion and metaphysics and find truth via science and logic. It too was an important phase in the quest for objectivity.

Like the other thinkers we have mentioned, Popper looked for a way to ensure the objectivity of scientific inquiry. But he differed significantly with his predecessors. Whereas the logical positivists sought objectivity in their verification principle, Popper rejected this principle and replaced it with a principle of his own—the falsification principle. In *Realism and the Aim of Science*, Popper notes:

> Objectivity is not the result of disinterested and unprejudiced observation. Objectivity, and also unbiased observation, are the result of criticism, including the criticism of observational reports. For we cannot avoid or suppress our theories, or prevent them from influencing our observations; yet we can try to recognize them as hypotheses, and to formulate them explicitly, so that they may be criticized.[26]

---

[24]Gaukroger, *Objectivity*, 17.

[25]For the record, it was Kant, not Hume, that assigned the labels of "analytic" and "synthetic." Yet, it was Hume who noted the concepts and so we have mentioned them in relation to Hume. What Kant and everyone thereafter referred to as "analytic," Hume referred to as "statements of relations of ideas." And, what Kant and everyone thereafter called "synthetic," Hume referred to as "statements of fact."

[26]Karl Popper, *Realism and the Aim of Science* (Totowa, NJ: Rowan and Littlefield, 1983), 48.

Criticism and the possibility of falsifying a theory were key to Popper's thought. He says, "I shall certainly admit a system as empirical or scientific only if it is capable of being tested by experience."[27] That is, he thinks that a theory can only be counted as scientific if it is tested in such a way that it can be shown to be false. If a given theory is able to stand up against such tests, then it is granted the status of being scientific. Or as he says, "I shall not require of a scientific system that it shall be capable of being singled out, once and for all, in a positive sense; but I shall require that its logical form shall be such that it can be singled out, by means of empirical tests, in a negative sense: *it must be possible for an empirical scientific system to be refuted by experience.*"[28]

So where does this leave us? From at least Descartes forward (and some like Rorty would argue from well before Descartes) we see various philosophers looking for ways to ensure an objective approach to knowledge that allows them to rid themselves of superstition and bias. Descartes employed rationalism and modeled his approach on the methods used in mathematics. Bacon employed induction, Kant employed reason and the categorical imperative, the logical positivists used verification, and Popper employed falsification. There is far more to be said about each of these thinkers and the ideas we have mentioned. And there are more philosophers that could be added to our brief survey. But this quick selection highlights the quest for objectivity that arose in the modern period. By one method or another, the modern period is marked by its appetite for objectivity. We now turn to the decline of objectivity.

From modernity to postmodernity. Objectivity received great emphasis in the modern period, but it would be called into question by late modern and postmodern thinkers. There are numerous factors that led to the rejection of objectivity, but we should mention at least three important developments: philosophical shifts beginning with Immanuel Kant, historical observations by thinkers like Thomas Kuhn, and a growing sociological awareness of cultural and perspectival differences.

Interestingly, just as our account of the rise of objectivity must say something about Kant, a discussion about its decline must also start with Kant. With his emphasis on universal human reason and the categorical imperative,

---

[27]Karl Popper, *The Logic of Scientific Discovery* (New York: Harper & Row, 1968), 40.
[28]Ibid., 40-41. Emphasis original.

Kant's work makes an important contribution to modernism's ideal of objectivity. But at the same time, much of Kant's work cuts the legs out from under the quest for objectivity, and has a significant influence on the postmodern move away from realism toward antirealism. Specifically, Kant's distinction between noumena and phenomena coupled with his suggestion that the mind is active as opposed to passive proved catastrophic to objectivism.

Thomas Nagel notes that "Kant's position is that we can conceive of things only as they appear to us and never as they are in themselves: how things are in themselves remains forever and entirely out of the reach of our thought."[29] Kant argued that phenomena (appearances of things) and the noumena (things in themselves) are two fundamentally different things. And moreover, he noted that what we have access to in our mental life is the "appearance of things" and not the "things in themselves," since we are never able to step outside of our perceptions to grasp reality directly. In his own words, "Our rational cognition applies only to appearances, and leaves the thing in itself unrecognized by us."[30]

But there is more with Kant that must be noted. Kant also had much to suggest about the role of the mind in perception. Whereas previous thinkers had been inclined to take a passive view of the mind in perception, Kant suggested that the mind is active. If the mind is passive in perception the way previous thinkers had thought, then we can be fairly confident in the representations the mind offers us about the world we see in perception. After all, if the mind is passive, then it alters nothing in perception. It merely takes what is there and reflects it in our perceptions of the world. In other words, a passive mind leads to a rather straightforward and accurate portrayal of the outside world. But if, on the other hand, the mind is active, then it is structuring, ordering, and possibly even distorting the data collected by the senses as it "represents" the outside world. What this means is that there is a very real possibility for a sharp disconnect between reality and the representations of reality found in our perceptions. So, with the distinction between noumena and phenomena and his suggestion of an active mind, Kant helped usher in the postmodern rejection of objectivity and realism.

---

[29]Thomas Nagel, *The View from Nowhere* (New York: Oxford University Press, 1986), 98.
[30]Immanuel Kant, *Critique of Pure Reason*, trans. Werner S. Pluhar (Indianapolis: Hackett, 1996), 10.

Kuhn highlights another development that challenges the modern confidence in objectivity. While scientists from the Enlightenment forward championed the idea that their theories were formulated objectively via the scientific method, Kuhn, a historian of science, demonstrated the deep and unavoidable influence that current presuppositions of the scientific community have on the formulation and development of theory. He challenged the notion that scientific progress happens gradually and smoothly over time as each scientist discovers and then further develops a given theory, and he showed instead that scientific progress has tended to come in dramatic and sizable jumps from one way of thinking to another, which he called paradigm shifts. When a paradigm is adopted, scientists within the community use that paradigm as a way of seeing and thinking about things. The paradigm is used for a period of time, during which new bits of data are collected that support the paradigm, and still other bits of data are collected that challenge the paradigm. What Kuhn noted is that there is often great resistance to reformulating the paradigm in light of new data that challenges it. Only as the data mounts against a given paradigm and it comes to a tipping point will the scientific community shift to a new paradigm.

Kuhn's observations are troublesome for those who assume that the scientific enterprise is purely objective. What Kuhn shows is that ideology and social factors are always at play in the doing of science. He notes that when scientists are instructed

> to examine electrical or chemical phenomena, the man who is ignorant of these fields but who knows what it is to be scientific may legitimately reach any one of a number of incompatible conclusions. Among those legitimate possibilities, the particular conclusions he does arrive at are probably determined by his prior experience in other fields, by the accidents of his investigation, and by his own individual makeup.[31]

He then adds,

> Observation and experience can and must drastically restrict the range of admissible scientific belief, else there would be no science. But they cannot alone determine a particular body such as belief. An apparently arbitrary element,

---

[31]Thomas Kuhn, *The Structure of Scientific Revolutions* (Chicago: University of Chicago Press, 1962), 3-4.

compounded of personal and historical accident, is always a formative ingre-
dient of the beliefs espoused by a given scientific community at a given time.[32]

In other words, despite what many modern thinkers had thought about
scientists and the scientific method, there are a variety of factors that influence a scientist's thinking and prevent pure objectivity. Kuhn's observations had a profound impact on the decline of objectivity. McGrath is again
helpful, noting that "there is widespread agreement that his analysis of the
development of the sciences makes it virtually impossible to affirm that
there has existed, and still exists, a concept of rationality which is independent of time and space, so that scientific progress can be considered to
be purely and unproblematically cumulative."[33]

Kuhn was not, however, the only one to recognize and articulate this
insight. Michel Foucault points to the same shifts and draws similar conclusions. While discussing the way medical advances have taken place, he notes
that since the eighteenth century, shifts have occurred not just in the propositions that were once thought to be true but even "the ways of speaking and
seeing, the whole ensemble of practices which served as support for medical
knowledge. These are not simply new discoveries, there's a whole new
'regime' in discourse and forms of knowledge. All this happens in the space
of a few years."[34] He then adds, "My problem was not at all to say, 'Voila,
long live discontinuity, we are in the discontinuous and a good thing too,'
but to pose the question, how is it that at certain moments in certain orders
of knowledge, there are these sudden take-offs, these hastenings of evolution,
these transformations which fail to correspond to the calm, continuist image
that is normally accredited?"[35] Foucault's point is not to say that scientists
are not engaged with the natural world. Rather, his point is that their engagement with the natural world is—despite protestations to the contrary—
laden with presuppositions and theoretical commitments, rendering the
natural sciences less objective than modern thinkers had thought. With this,
Foucault asks an important question. "It is a question of what governs statements, and the way in which they govern each other so asked to constitute

---

[32]Ibid., 4.
[33]McGrath, *Reality*, 61.
[34]Michel Foucault, *Power/Knowledge: Selected Interviews and Other Writings, 1972-1977* (New York:
    Pantheon, 1980), 112.
[35]Ibid.

a set of propositions which are scientifically acceptable, and hence capable of being verified or falsified by scientific procedures. In short, there is a problem of the regime, the politics of the scientific statement."[36] Kuhn and Foucault represent a growing awareness that the natural sciences are not as objective as was long believed by modern thinkers.

There is one other important development that we must note regarding the decline of objectivity, namely, the growing sociological awareness of cultural and perspectival differences. Simply put, by the beginning of the twentieth century, sociologists in particular, and intellectuals in general, began to see that one of the more significant assumptions of the modern period was false. As seen with Kant and the categorical imperative, modern thinkers tended to believe in a universal rationality that was shared by all people everywhere. In this view, modern philosophers believed that all people everywhere thought and reasoned the same way and followed the same rational process. A careful study of culture, however, would suggest otherwise. McGrath explains, saying that the "empirical study of cultural rationalities disclosed a very different pattern—namely, that people possessed and possess contested and at times incommensurable notions both of what is 'rational,' 'true and right,' and how those qualities might be justified."[37] That is, once we began to study various cultures and investigate the way different people groups actually think and reason, the modern assumption of a universal rationality could no longer be sustained. Polanyi agrees, noting that the concept of objectivity

> would be shattered if the intuition of rationality in nature had to be acknowledged as a justifiable and indeed essential part of scientific theory. That is why scientific theory is represented as a mere economical description of facts; or as embodying a conventional policy for drawing empirical inferences; or as a working hypothesis, suited to persons' practical convenience—interpretations that all deliberately overlook the rational core of science.[38]

Despite the confidence of modernism that humanity could be objective and pure in its approach to the world, that confidence was eroded by the Kantian understanding of perception, the arguments of Kuhn and Foucault

---

[36]Ibid.
[37]McGrath, *Reality*, 57.
[38]Polanyi, *Personal Knowledge*, 16.

that question the objectivity of the natural sciences, and the growing sociological awareness of the perspectival differences from one culture to another.
There are surely other factors that could be mentioned that have contributed
to the decline of objectivity. But these are three factors that must be noted.

One additional point should be made before moving forward. As noted
at the beginning of the chapter, in the history of this discussion, objectivity
and realism have tended to rise and fall together. That is, if one believed they
could be objective in their grasp of the world outside of themselves, they
also assumed that the world outside of themselves was there to be known.
Because of that, as postmodern thinkers grew more uncertain of our ability
to be objective, they also tended to move away from realism toward antirealism. In short, if our grasp of the world is tainted by subjective factors, then
how can we be certain of what we think we see in the world of our perception? Knowledge, on the postmodern view, was increasingly understood
to be something that is mind dependent.

What should we think about all of this? In most discussions, evaluations
tend to be one-sided. Supporters of postmodern thought have tended to
celebrate the ideal of the movement without recognizing the problems that
come with it. And opponents of postmodernism have tended to offer scathing
criticism without recognizing the important insights of the movement. In
what follows, we shall try to set forth what we think is a more balanced and
fruitful evaluation that recognizes both the benefits and the problems of
postmodern views on objectivity, subjectivity, realism, and antirealism.

A POSITIVE CRITIQUE OF POSTMODERN VIEWS
OF OBJECTIVITY AND REALISM

We will turn to some concerns associated with postmodernism in just a
moment. But first, the positives. One positive aspect of postmodernism is
that it forces us to be intellectually honest about the way culture, education,
experience, upbringing, and a host of other factors play on our formulation
of theory. We are not as objective as we might think we are.

Of course, this is not to say that modern science and the scientific method
have not made significant strides in helping us move toward objectivity.
They have indeed. But it is to say that no matter how hard we might try to
strip ourselves of our presuppositions and biases, we are still culturally and
historically situated as knowers and are always affected by theoretical factors

at the outset of our investigations. In other words, we come to our observations with theory already in hand and already at work. As Alan Padgett has put it, "All our knowing arises from our location, from our point of view and cultural context. Even the natural sciences are located in culture, language, and history. None of us has a God's-eye view, a 'view from nowhere.' Any approach that hopes to grasp the object of our studies will need a host of contrasting, alternative points of view on that object."[39] McGrath illustrates how culture and history affect our perspectives.

> Yet the Enlightenment vision died with the recognition that the Enlightenment itself was just another human tradition, possessed of the particularity and corrigibility of the rival traditions it sought to critique and judge. Far from rising above traditions, the Enlightenment simply represented yet another tradition, distinguished perhaps by its arrogance and presumption rather than its epistemic status. It was only a matter of time before it would be humbled and chastened.[40]

He then adds:

> One of the most basic beliefs of the Enlightenment was the autonomy of human reason, and its universal capacity to arrive at justified beliefs. This axiom of the Enlightenment was shaken to its foundations through the growing awareness that reasoning was not a universal, neutral medium, shared by all of humanity at all times and in all places, but was situationally specific. What the Enlightenment took to be universal was actually ethnocentric—even Eurocentric—reflecting the historically determined views of Western culture, including its canons of rationality. What was once thought to be globally valid was gradually realized to be historically situated and socially constructed.[41]

The rationality once thought to be the product of universal patterns of reason was now discovered to be deeply influenced by particular aspects of people groups at a given moment in history. As Esther Meek notes, "Every knower's interests and culture and outlook significantly shape what he or she is knowing."[42] That is, the concerns of the day in a given community tend to

---

[39]Padgett, *Science and the Study of God*, 24.
[40]McGrath, *Reality*, 58.
[41]Ibid., 58-59.
[42]Esther Lightcap Meek, *Longing to Know: The Philosophy of Knowledge for Ordinary People* (Grand Rapids: Brazos, 2003), 31.

dictate the very things we explore and investigate. Postmodernism helps us to recognize this. As a movement, it has given serious and helpful attention to our situatedness and allows us to avoid gross naiveté. As a result, we are far more likely to acknowledge and engage other perspectives as valuable contributors to conversation and the development of theory.

There are, however, some concerns with postmodern views of objectivity and realism. To these we now turn.

Some Concerns with Postmodernism

The criticism of postmodernism's view of objectivity and realism is multifaceted and multilayered. Critics have come from various disciplines and offered substantial pushback against some of the sweeping conclusions reached by the movement. Despite whatever value is to be found in the way postmodernism helps us to see the situatedness of our perspectives, it nevertheless suffers from several significant problems. Here are three specific concerns.

First, whereas postmoderns have made some helpful observations about our lack of total objectivity, they have often acted as if this were enough to undercut realism as well. And as a result, the arguments from postmodernism against realism are often vague or just plain weak. As critic John Searle says, the "arguments against our commonsense idea that there exists an independent reality are often vague and obscure. . . . What exactly are the propositions being asserted? What exactly are those denied? And what exactly are the arguments for both assertion and denial? You will look in vain for answers to these questions in most discussions of these matters."[43] Most arguments against realism are actually just observations about the mediated nature of knowledge—denial of objectivity—that then attempt to connect objectivity and realism. They assume that objectivity and realism rise and fall together without proving that they do.

But as Searle points out,

> From the fact that our knowledge/conception/picture of reality is constructed by human brains in human interactions, it does not follow that the reality of which we have the knowledge/conception/picture is constructed by the human brain in human interactions. It is just a non sequitur, a genetic fallacy

---

[43]John Searle, *The Construction of Social Reality* (New York: Free Press, 1995), 158.

to infer from the collective neurophysiological causal explanation of our knowledge of the external world to the nonexistence of the external world.[44]

In other words, it doesn't follow from the concerns postmodernism raises with objectivity that we must jettison realism. We may well lack the ability to be totally objective in our grasp of the world and still be able to grasp the world that is there to behold.

Second, postmodern antirealism—which states that knowledge is *of* the way things appear to us, not the way things really are—is hard to maintain in light of the successes of modern science. Imagine for just a moment that antirealism is actually true. If it were, then it becomes difficult to explain how science has allowed us to do remarkable things like put a man on the moon, perform open heart surgery, fly aircraft across oceans, split atoms, and much more. How is any of this possible if our knowledge is only of the way things appear to us and not of the way things really are? If our knowledge is of appearances only, and the appearances are different from the way things actually are, then all scientific calculations and predictions would be in serious error, making it impossible to do what we have been able to do in science. Imagine, for example, a team of astronomers planning the launch of a satellite or rocket with astronauts heading for the moon. If, as antirealism would suggest, they only know how things appear, then disaster would strike in every attempted launch. Architects and engineers take the real world into account when they design and build a building. The building does not stay up by sheer luck and coincidence, but rather because the architect and engineer understood the specific realities that need to be considered in constructing a building. The same would be true in all other kinds of scientific experiments. Now surely scientists make mistakes and experiments sometimes fail. But they also succeed in many cases. This success is a curious thing if in fact we never have knowledge of the real world as it really is.

McGrath makes this point with considerable force. He says, "The credibility of realism arises directly from the experimental method, which discloses patterns of observational behavior which seem to be best accounted for on the basis of a realist point of view."[45] He later notes that because of this, realism "remains the most satisfying and resilient account of the

---

[44]Ibid., 159.
[45]McGrath, *Reality*, 123.

outcome of the human engagement with the natural world, despite the rhetoric of scorn directed against it by postmodern thinkers and others. The natural sciences are widely judged to have successfully seen off postmodern criticisms of their fundamental assumptions."[46] Elsewhere he adds, "It seems to many that the success of the natural sciences shows that they have somehow managed to uncover the way things really are, or to lock into something which is fundamental to the structure of the universe."[47] As Mc-Grath helps us see, natural science—or more specifically, the successes of natural science—does not seem possible if antirealism is true. And yet, we live in a world filled with the benefits that come from natural science. Natural science rests on a realist account of the world and our knowledge, making postmodern antirealism seem to be entirely implausible.

Third, the antirealism of postmodernism is contrary to our basic intu-itions of the way our perceptions relate to the world. It might be true that various people groups approach the world in different ways and with dif-ferent assumptions. But one assumption that is shared by people all over the world is that we see what is there, not just what appears to us. And based on these intuitions and assumptions, we engage the world to learn all kinds of things that are true. As Meek has put it,

> For knowing nothing at all, you and I seem to know quite a lot. Or at least we seem to live like it—that is, when it isn't more personally advantageous to be skeptics. Vast portions of our lives and jobs and society are devoted to infor-mation, learning, and discovery. What's more, we continually make advances from unknowing to knowing, whether in the classroom or the science lab or in the ordinary affairs of life.[48]

No one, including the postmodern antirealist, lives as though we have no way of grasping the actual world. We operate, explore, act, and behave in ways that betray the antirealist's intuitions and confirm the realist's intu-itions. No matter what questions might be raised about our ability to have total objectivity, we nevertheless operate as if realism is true. Most people generally think—and rightly so—that a mind-independent world exists that we can know and understand. And as a result, postmodern antirealism is irresponsible and reckless.

[46]Ibid., 197.
[47]Alister E. McGrath, *The Science of God* (Grand Rapids: Eerdmans, 2004), 126.
[48]Meek, *Longing to Know*, 31.

CONCLUSION

This chapter has covered a lot of terrain. We introduced the concepts of objectivity, subjectivity, realism, and antirealism; noted how objectivity and realism have typically been understood to rise and fall together; offered a brief history of their development; and concluded by offering an assessment of the postmodern concerns with objectivity and its endorsement of anti-realism. Postmoderns have raised legitimate questions about our historical and cultural situatedness. If we are intellectually honest, we have to admit that we are not as objective as modern thinkers had hoped we could be.

At the same time, three important points must be kept in mind as we make this admission. First, to say that we are not, or cannot, be totally objective is not the same as saying we have no objectivity at all. Indeed, we can and should strive to be as objective as possible in our intellectual pursuits. Scientists, theologians, historians, and other intellectuals can work to minimize bias and unhelpful cultural influences that cause us to misspeak. Second, it doesn't follow from our lack of total objectivity that realism is false. As Searle has argued well, postmodern arguments on this point are vague and weak. It looks like postmodern "attacks" on realism give us no good reason for setting this long-established assumption aside. Third, as we have outlined in the last section, the postmodern alternative to antirealism is plagued by some menacing problems. And so we conclude that despite protestations by postmoderns to the contrary, realism fits with our basic intuitions about the way our perceptions relate to the outside world and continues to be the only viable epistemological perspective for our intellectual lives.

SUMMARY

1. Throughout most of history, intellectuals have agreed that objectivity and realism rise and fall together.

2. Premoderns were clearly realists, but it was not always true that phi-losophers felt the need to rid themselves of certain epistemic starting points. This is especially true with Anselm and the Reformers.

3. Realism continued to be assumed by modern thinkers, but now the desire for objectivity emerges with great force in thinkers like Des-cartes, Bacon, Kant, and Popper, to name just a few. Each had different

ways he sought to secure objectivity, but the quest for objectivity is found in all of them nonetheless.

4. By the end of the modern period, and in the thinking of Kant, a major shift regarding objectivity took place. Kant insisted, and postmodern thinkers follow, that all we ever know is the way things appear to us, not the way things actually are. Perception, and thus knowledge, is mind dependent.

5. Historical observations by thinkers like Kuhn and Foucault call the supposed objectivity of science into question. Historical, cultural, and experiential idiosyncrasies of the scientist play an unavoidable part in the formulation of theory, leading postmodern thinkers to reject the notion of objectivity in favor of a far more subjective understanding of knowledge.

6. In the twentieth century, a growing sociological awareness of the way various people groups in different places and times actually think and reason casts further doubt on the notions of universal reason and objectivity.

7. In the wake of their concerns regarding objectivity, and following the historical tendency to say that objectivity and realism rise and fall together, postmoderns believe that the lack of objectivity disproves realism.

8. Postmodernism raises important questions about objectivity and forces us to acknowledge the way various factors shape our theories. Yet the lack of total objectivity does not mean that all knowledge and theory is subjective.

9. The tendency to say that objectivity and realism rise and fall together is questionable, and we have argued that is not necessarily the case. It is possible to still gain a proper knowledge of the outside world despite our situatedness. Even without total objectivity, we don't have sufficient reason to reject realism.

10. The alternative to realism—postmodern antirealism—has several plaguing problems. It is undercut by the successes of modern science and is contrary to our basic intuitions about the relationship between our perceptions and the world itself. These problems were serious enough for us to reject antirealism.

11. Realism continues to be the only viable epistemic perspective suitable for our intellectual lives.

SUGGESTED READINGS

Burge, Tyler. *Origins of Objectivity*. New York: Oxford University Press, 2010.

Daston, Lorraine, and Peter Galison. *Objectivity*. New York: Zone, 2010.

Gaukroger, Stephen. *Objectivity: A Very Short Introduction*. New York: Oxford University Press, 2012.

McGrath, Alister E. *A Scientific Theology*. 3 vols. Grand Rapids: Eerdmans, 2001–2003.

Rorty, Richard. *Objectivity, Relativism, and Truth: Philosophical Papers*. Cambridge: Cambridge University Press, 1991.

Searle, John R. *The Construction of Social Reality*. New York: Free Press, 1995.

9

ON METANARRATIVES
AND OPPRESSION

Central to understanding postmodernism is grasping its take on what are called metanarratives. There are a number of crucial issues that merit our attention here. To adequately address all these issues we will devote both this chapter and the next to examining them. In this chapter we focus on the historical treatment of four groups in the United States. In the next chapter we examine the broader questions of whether postmoderns are correct in claiming that all metanarratives are oppressive, and thus deserve our rejection.

Christianity is, among other things, a *metanarrative*. It is a worldview, a comprehensive way of looking at the world that seeks to discover what is real (metaphysics), how we know (epistemology), how we should live (ethics), what humanity is (anthropology), and how we should think (logic).[1] As evangelical Christians we are committed to the truthfulness of the Christian worldview—there *really is* a Creator God, who revealed himself in Jesus Christ, inspired the biblical authors, and continues to accomplish his redemptive plans today. Many thinkers with postmodern inclinations have major doubts about metanarratives in general. They believe that metanarratives are inextricably bound up with oppression by those in power over those who lack power. The noted French thinker Michel Foucault, for example, writes that "we cannot exercise power except

---

[1]These five categories are not the only things worldviews address, but they are among the most important.

through the reproduction of truth."[2] For Foucault, the relation between knowledge and power "is central to the discussion around truth."[3] Christianity, Marxism, Enlightenment modernism, modern science (at least in the West) can all reasonably be understood as comprehensive stories (or metanarratives) claiming to accurately represent reality in all its complexity. If some of the postmoderns are correct, then *all* metanarratives are guilty of exploitation and oppression, a consideration that would weigh heavily against any truth claim made by these metanarratives. In this chapter we will explore a specifically American metanarrative to determine how oppressive it has (or hasn't) been over the past few hundred years. More specifically, we will ask *how* America has treated four particular groups: African Americans, women, Jews, and the disabled.[4] The treatment will be unduly brief, but detailed enough to get a feel for what the answers to this central question are. After a brief look at the treatment of these four groups, the focus will shift to the key question: Are metanarratives necessarily (automatically) exploitive?

AFRICAN AMERICANS IN AMERICAN HISTORY

Frederick Douglass, one of the leading African Americans in the nineteenth century, wrote a few years before his death of "the growing repression, the triumph of disenfranchisement, lynching terror, and white indifference."[5] He wrote that "I cannot shut my eyes to the ugly facts before me."[6] It is worth noting that Douglass said this some thirty years after the Emancipation Proclamation, and some twenty years after the passage of the Fourteenth Amendment, two significant events that were intended to better the life of African Americans in the United States. There are many watershed events in African American history, but here we will limit our attention to four: the so-called Three-Fifths Compromise, the reality of Jim Crow laws in the post-Reconstruction South, the *Brown v. Board of Education* decision

---

[2]Michel Foucault, *Power/Knowledge: Selected Interviews and Other Writings, 1972-1977* (New York: Pantheon, 1980), 93.

[3]Lloyd Pettiford and Melissa Curley, *Changing Security Agendas and the Third World* (London: Pinter, 1999), 65.

[4]Some of the other groups that could be included here include Catholics, the Chinese, Latinos, gays and lesbians, Italians, the Irish, the poor, Native Americans, and organized labor. There is a rich literature addressing the treatment of all these groups in American history.

[5]Leon Litwack, *Trouble in Mind: Black Southerners in the Age of Jim Crow* (New York: Knopf, 1998), xv.

[6]Ibid.

of 1954, and the lynching of fourteen-year-old Emmett Till in Mississippi in August of 1955.

The Three-Fifths Compromise. In 1777 the Continental Congress met and drew up the forerunner of the US Constitution, namely, the Articles of Confederation. The Congress meeting initially decided to assess taxes not on the basis of population, but on the basis of land values. But the states consistently undervalued their land so as to reduce the tax burden. In the context of this debate, a committee was appointed that decided to levy taxes on the basis of population. One might think that one could simply count the number of people in a particular colony, but that would be based on the idea that all persons were to be treated equally. Southerners generally viewed African Americans not as fellow humans (with the right to vote, etc.), but as property, something they owned. There was initially much disagreement, but eventually they decided on a ratio suggested by James Madison, specifically a five-to-three ratio (or the Three-Fifths Compromise). Every five African Americans would count as three persons for the purpose of congressional representation. It is not difficult to see how such a compromise degrades all African Americans and stamps them as inferior from the cradle to the grave. The words *slave* and *slavery* "did not appear in the Constitution—a concession to the sensibilities of delegates who feared they would 'contaminate the glorious fabric of American liberty.'"[7] As Eric Foner notes, the document "prohibited Congress from abolishing the African slave trade for twenty years. . . . And it provided that three-fifths of the slave population would be counted in determining each state's representation in the House of Representatives and its electoral votes for president."[8]

Jim Crow laws. After the Civil War, the Emancipation Proclamation, and the Thirteenth through Fifteenth Amendments, many saw the American South as moving toward a more civil and tolerant view toward African Americans. But by the time Reconstruction ended (in 1877), a time when the South had been occupied by Union troops and African Americans both voted and ran for office, many Southerners rose up in bitter and often violent opposition to the idea of full equality for black persons. Whites

---

[7]Eric Foner, *Give Me Liberty! An American History* (New York: Norton, 2005), 1:250.
[8]Ibid.

perceived in the behavior of "uppity" (and invariably younger) African-Americans a growing threat or indifference to the prevailing customs, habits, and etiquette. Over the next two decades, white Southerners would construct in response an imposing and extensive system of legal mechanisms designed to institutionalize the already familiar and customary subordination of black men and women.[9]

Whites and African Americans went to segregated schools, sat in different parts of restaurants, had separate drinking fountains, separate restrooms, and segregated seating in theaters. They were separate in virtually all things, yet equal in very few. And African Americans who violated these rigid social customs were subjected to beatings and even lynchings, the ultimate form of violence. Between 1882 and 1950 there were more than 4,700 documented lynchings in the South, the majority of them directed against African Americans. Martin Luther King Sr. witnessed a black man being beaten to death for being "sassy," a term "commonly used by whites to identify trouble-making, 'uppity,' and 'impudent' African-Americans."[10] Many Southern black towns lacked black high schools, and much more money was spent on white students than black. In South Carolina in 1908–1909, the state spent roughly $1.6 million to educate 154,000 white students, but only $308,000 to educate 181,000 black students.[11] Furthermore, African Americans were systematically excluded from voting in Southern states by way of poll taxes, literacy tests, and other nefarious devices designed to keep African Americans out of power and "in their place." The American Dream of working hard, making it, and being a contributing citizen in a diverse and multicultural society was effectively denied to African Americans in the South in the latter part of the nineteenth century and well into the twentieth.

Brown v. Board of Education. The Supreme Court Case *Plessy v. Ferguson* (1896) established "separate but equal" as the law of the land and dominated Southern culture until 1954. Then in an unprecedented decision, the court (unanimously) struck down *Plessy* and ruled that "separate but equal" was unconstitutional. The ruling was greeted with elation in the black community, especially in the South. Southern whites, on the other hand,

---

[9]Litwack, *Trouble in Mind*, 230.

[10]Ibid., 13.

[11]Nell Irvin Painter, *Creating Black Americans: African-American History and Its Meanings, 1619 to the Present* (New York: Oxford University Press, 2007), 166.

reacted with horror and indignation that their very way of life had been undermined by the Supreme Court. As promising as all this seemed, the court did not establish a timetable for the implementation of the *Brown* decision, and the South, especially the Deep South, was in no hurry to comply with this federal ruling. When the Democratic Party began pushing for civil rights on the national level in 1948, a number of white Southerners broke off from the Democratic Party and founded the Dixiecrats, Southern Democrats who were passionately opposed to anything that might be seen as promoting racial equality (or "race mixing"). The Dixiecrat presidential nominee, Strom Thurmond of South Carolina, carried four Southern states, and garnered more than 87 percent of the vote in Mississippi, a state with a high black population and a long history of oppressing its African Americans.[12] In response to *Brown*, the White Citizen's Council was formed in Mississippi in 1954. Mississippi also had a Sovereignty Commission, which used taxpayer money "to prevent desegregation through intimidation and harassment."[13] In 1955 the Reverend George Lee was shot to death in Mississippi for his civil rights activism, yet the local newspaper headlined the story "Negro Leader Dies in Odd Accident."[14] The intent of the *Brown* decision did begin to bear fruit in Little Rock in 1957 and in other states in the late 1950s, but the South did a masterful job of dragging its feet when it came to complying with the court.

Emmett Till's Murder. Mississippi consistently offered the most opposition to complying with *Brown*. What made this painfully clear was the brutal murder of Emmett Till in Money, Mississippi, in August of 1955.[15] Till, a fourteen-year-old boy from Chicago, was visiting his cousins in Mississippi in the summer of 1955. Till was unfamiliar with the region's customs governing the interaction between African Americans and whites. As recounted by some, Till went into the local grocery and on his way out reportedly said, "Bye, baby" to the white woman behind the counter, Carolyn Bryant. Bryant reported this violation of Southern mores to her

---

[12]Though Thurmond consistently campaigned against civil rights, it is now known (and acknowledged by his family) that Thurmond had an affair with Essie Mae Washington, a black domestic in the Thurmond household, and had a daughter with her.

[13]Painter, *Creating Black Americans*, 267.

[14]Ibid.

[15]Recent scholarship has brought into question whether Carolyn Bryant, the woman in the grocery store, told the truth about what happened with Emmett Till. See Timothy Tyson, *The Blood of Emmett Till* (New York: Simon & Schuster, 2017).

husband, Roy. Roy and his half brother J. W. Milam went out to where Till was staying and asked for "the boy" who had done all that talking. The initial idea appears to be that Bryant and Milam would beat Till up, teach him a lesson, and go on their way. But things didn't happen that way. Till, apparently not realizing the mortal danger he was in, pulled a picture from his school of a friend of his, a white girl. "Milam was outraged and decided to kill him, 'Chicago boy,' he remembered—out of the courtroom—saying, 'I'm tired of 'em sending your kind down here to stir up trouble. Goddamn you—I'm gonna make an example of you—just so everybody can know how me and my folks stand."[16] Milam shot Till, they attached a cotton-gin fan to his body, and dumped the body in the Tallahatchie River, a river with a long history of human bodies deposited in it. Till's mother, Mamie Till, insisted on an open casket. Pictures of Till's mangled and mutilated body were soon seen nationwide, as the rest of America began to realize the magnitude of the problem in the Deep South. Finally, an all-white, all-male jury found Bryant and Milam not guilty, to the cheers from the white section of the segregated courtroom in the segregated state in the country that stands for liberty and equality.[17]

WOMEN'S RIGHTS

In the history of the United States women have been marginalized, viewed as inferior in multiple ways, denied the right to vote, and generally not accorded the full range of constitutional protections belonging to white males. As with the treatment of African Americans, we will briefly present four noteworthy events to serve as a very brief introduction to a much larger topic. The four events will include the *Bradwell v. Illinois* case, the *Muller* rulings, inequality in wages, and the need for Title IX.

Bradwell v. Illinois (1873). In the early 1870s Myra Bradwell applied for admission to the Illinois bar, having both a law degree and being a person of good character. But the Illinois Supreme Court denied her admission, arguing that the "strife" of the bar would undermine her femininity. She filed suit, arguing that the Fourteenth Amendment guaranteed her equal protection under the law. The US Supreme Court ruled (in an eight-to-one

---

[16]Stephen J. Whitfield, *A Death in the Delta: The Story of Emmett Till* (Baltimore: Johns Hopkins University Press, 1988), 21.

[17]Many other events are worthy of inclusion. They include the Dred Scott case, the Colfax massacre, the Scottsboro trial, the murders of Medgar Evers and Dr. King, and a host of others.

decision) that the Fourteenth Amendment did not cover the equal right to practice a profession. Justice Bradley wrote that "the natural and proper timidity and delicacy which belongs to the female sex evidently unfits it for many of the occupations of civil life. . . . The paramount destiny and mission of women are to fulfill the noble and benign offices of wife and mother. This is the law of the Creator." Bradwell, so it seems, could be a mother or an attorney, but not both. Well into the twentieth century, many law schools and medical schools had quotas that severely limited the number of women pursuing that profession.

The Muller Case. In the early 1900s the Supreme Court delivered a number of rulings often known as the Lochner cases.[18] Lurking in the background was a push for equal rights for women. Some women wanted full-fledged equality with men when it came to job possibilities, wages, job advancement, voting, and the full rights of an American citizen under the authority of the Constitution. Other feminists wanted the courts to make laws that specifically protected women. Women did need protection, but other feminists argued, not as a specifically designated group, for this worked with the assumption that women were (in many ways) the weaker sex, and thus in need of special protectionist legislation. In *Muller v. Oregon*, the attorney Louis Brandeis, later a Supreme Court justice, argued that "the two sexes differ in structure of body, in the function to be performed by each, in the amount of physical strength [and] in the capacity for long-continued labor." The difference, Brandeis asserted, justified special legislation regulating women's hours of work. In its decision, the court adopted the reformers' position and articulated a theory of women's nature hardly designed to please feminists."[19] To be labeled as weaker in a number of ways undermined the position of the other feminists who sought full equality in all of life. This view of women as weaker continued to be a factor throughout much of the twentieth century.

Wage inequality. One of the most basic forms of discrimination in human history is to pay one group of workers less money than another group doing the exact same job.[20] So if group A gets $12 an hour for doing job J, while

---

[18]The cases focused on (among other things) the extent to which states could regulate the hours of workers as opposed to understanding the liberty of contracts to be an overriding concern.

[19]William H. Chafe, *The Paradox of Change: American Women in the 20th Century* (New York: Oxford University Press, 1991), 57.

[20]And taking into account other relevant factors such as experience and skill level.

group B gets $9.50 an hour for the very same work, then we have a straight-forward case of (arbitrary) wage discrimination. Well, throughout much of the twentieth century women were paid less for doing the same job as men. It is very difficult to find cases where men were paid less than women for equal work. But the cases where women were paid less are legion, documented and otherwise. At the end of World War II "women workers continued to receive appreciably lower wages than men. . . . Women in manufacturing earned 66 percent of what men were paid. A female laundry worker in Illinois took home $0.55 an hour; a man $1.10."[21] Some prominent men introduced legislation to address these issues. Senator Wayne Morse sponsored a federal equal-pay bill, but it failed to pass.[22] Though the income gap has narrowed since World War II, there continue to be well-known examples of wage discrimination. For example, Smith Barney paid out $33 million in 2008, and Merrill Lynch paid $39 million in 2013 to settle class action lawsuits brought forward by many female employees. It is true that the number of female CEOs of Fortune 500 companies has climbed to twenty, a new high, though that number is a mere 4 percent of the total. Even allowing for the fact that more women choose to stay home after having children than men do, the ongoing gap is a massive one. One recent case that reveals how far there is to go to reach equality is the *Ledbetter* case. Lily Ledbetter was a worker for Goodyear Tire in Alabama for a number of years. She later found out she was getting paid less than men who did the same work with comparable experience. Her case went all the way to the US Supreme Court, where they rejected her claim in a five-four decision, on the grounds that the suit had not been filed within the statute of limitations for such suits. Given the majority's decision, Goodyear served to benefit by keeping information about wages secret, so that if anyone found out about the wage inequalities it would be too late to sue! This is not unlike the boy who kills both parents and throws himself on the mercy of the court as he is an orphan!

Title IX. In the late 1960s at American high schools, boys could pursue football, basketball, baseball, wrestling, track, cross country, soccer, tennis, and a number of other sports. At many high schools, the athletically inclined girl could choose between cheerleading or no involvement in sports. The

---

[21]Ibid., 164.
[22]Ibid.

contrast was a stark one. In 1972, some 295,000 girls were involved in high school athletics in the United States, compared to 3.67 million boys, a ratio of approximately one to twelve. Presently the number of girls participating is about 3.2 million, while the number of boys is at 4.5 million. This (vastly improved) ratio is about seven to ten. Still, there is a ways to go. Female athletes "at the typical Division 1-FBS (formerly division 1-A) school receive roughly 28% of the total money spent on athletics, 31% of the recruiting dollars, and 42% of the athletic scholarship dollars. In addition, at the typical FBS school, for every dollar spent on women's sports, about two and half dollars are spent on men's sports."[23]

In a country with no female presidents in its history, only a handful of female Supreme Court justices, few female CEOs, and ongoing concerns with wage inequality and Title IX,[24] full equality remains a goal on the horizon, one perhaps now visible, but not too near.

ANTI-SEMITISM

Anti-Semitism, sadly, has a long and brutal history in the United States. As one scholar notes, "Many Americans still believe that Jews control the national economy, are pushy and dishonest, are clannish, and are power hungry."[25] In the United States "it was not uncommon for Jews to find their path to higher education blocked by laws that either limited the number of Jewish university students or prohibited their entry altogether. Formal Jewish quotas were published in university policy statements during the 1920's, and became particularly restrictive during the 1930's."[26] Bastions of progressive liberal and humanistic values, the Ivy League schools were not exceptions to general practice. Harvard, Yale, and Princeton all used ethnically restrictive quotas to severely limit the number of Jews admitted to their schools.[27] In the mid 1930s the Detroit Tigers had a gifted first baseman named Hank Greenberg, a talented and hard-working player liked by all. But though he had some of the best hitting numbers in baseball history, one year

---

[23]"Title IX: 40 Years and Counting," National Women's Law Center, June 2012, 2.

[24]It needs to be noted that these are but a few facts that need to be seen as representative of a much broader problem. It should also be noted that Title IX upholds equitable opportunities for any educational program, not just athletics.

[25]Juan L. Gonzalez, ed., *Racial and Ethnic Groups in America*, 5th ed. (Dubuque, IA: Kendall Hunt, 2003), 364.

[26]Ibid.

[27]See Jerome Karabel, *The Chosen: The Hidden History of Admission and Exclusion at Harvard, Yale, and Princeton* (New York: Mariner, 2006).

he was left off the American League all-star team despite having his best season. Why would that happen? It's simple. Hank Greenberg was Jewish, and many held that against him.

SS St. Louis. In May of 1939, a German ship called the *St. Louis* sailed from Hamburg, Germany, for Havana, Cuba. There were 938 passengers on board, almost all of them Jews fleeing persecution in Germany and Eastern Europe. The majority of the passengers were German citizens. Many of the passengers planned to stay in Cuba only until they could get visas to enter the United States. None of them would ever make it. Cuba denied permission for the ship to dock, only allowing 28 (who already had US visas or were Spanish citizens) to leave the ship. The remaining 900-plus people stayed on board as the *St. Louis* slowly sailed toward Miami and up the East Coast.

> The State Department and the White House had decided not to take extraor-
> dinary measures to permit the refugees to enter the United States. A State
> Department telegram sent to a passenger stated that the passengers must
> "await their turns on the waiting list and qualify for and obtain immigration
> visas before they may be admissible into the United States." US diplomats in
> Havana intervened once more with the Cuban government to admit the pas-
> sengers on a "humanitarian" basis, but without success.[28]

Denied permission in both Cuba and the United States, the *St. Louis* returned to Europe. Great Britain admitted 288 of the remaining passengers, all but one of whom survived the war. But of the 620 who returned to Germany, some 532 were trapped in Germany when the war began in the fall of 1939. Of that number, 254 died during the war (most in the death camps), while only 278 survived. The fact that the United States denied entry to fellow human beings who were being persecuted dovetails with public opinion polls in the late 1930s. A 1938 poll showed that "60 per cent of the respondents held a low opinion of Jews, labeling them 'greedy,' 'dishonest,' and 'pushy.'"[29] One wonders how a ship full of the Irish, or Italians, or the French might have fared in comparison.

Ivy League anti-Semitism. Geoffrey Chaucer once wrote, "If the gold rust, what then will iron do?" The idea is that if even the best things (gold) dete-

---

[28]"Voyage of the St. Louis," *Holocaust Encyclopedia*, United States Holocaust Memorial Museum, accessed December 26, 2013, www.ushmm.org/wlc/en/article.php?ModuleId=10005267.
[29]*Fortune*, July 1938, 80.

riorate, then it goes without saying that lesser things will as well. Over the last one hundred years or so (and beyond), the Ivy League universities have cultivated the image of being progressive, tolerant, broad-minded, and the like. These are all genuine virtues, and to be greatly admired. But if we look at the admission policies of the Big Three (Harvard, Yale, and Princeton) during much of the twentieth century, they leave us shaking our heads. In the early twentieth century, the admissions policies of the Big Three were essentially merit oriented. But after World War I there was increasing fear of immigrants, political radicalism, and those who simply were "different." In response to such fears Congress permanently limited European immigration to 150,000 per year, with special restrictions for those from southern and eastern Europe.[30] In signing the 1924 law, President Calvin Coolidge expressed popular sentiment when he said, "America must be kept American."[31] Along similar lines, the Big Three worried about increasing Jewish presence among undergraduates and sought to develop policies that quietly but effectively limited Jewish access to their institutions. Robert Nelson Corwin, who served as chairman of Yale's board of admissions from 1920 to 1933, was troubled by the increase of Jews and wrote that the Jews were lacking in "manliness, uprightness, cleanliness, native refinement, etc."[32] Corwin especially wanted to limit the admission of New Haven Jews to Yale, seeing them to be an "alien and unwashed element" that "graduates into the world as naked of all the attributes of refinement and honor as when born into it."[33] Corwin gave the admissions office the discretion to include matters of "personality and character," two highly subjective standards that would enable Yale to keep Jewish presence to a minimum. By 1924, the number of Jews in the freshman class dropped from 115 the year before to 88—"a figure that just so happened to constitute precisely 10 percent of all entering students."[34] Under Corwin's leadership (and the approval of the board of trustees), it would be almost forty years before the percentage of Jews in the freshman class would reach the level attained in 1923.[35] Princeton, also

---

[30]The underlying rationale was that they were "less like us" than those from western and northern Europe.

[31]Foner, *Give Me Liberty*, 2:683.

[32]Karabel, *The Chosen*, 111.

[33]Ibid., 112.

[34]Ibid., 115.

[35]Ibid.

concerned about the "Jewish problem," added the interview element to their admissions. This device made it possible to minimize and/or screen prospective students who were Jews and to limit "undesirables" in general.

The Holocaust. Though the United States was not directly culpable for the slaughter of the Jews during the late 1930s and in World War II, the German hatred of the Jews can be seen as dovetailing with common American attitudes toward Jews and other minorities. Jews, along with African Americans and women, were still second-class citizens in many respects. The Germans saw Jews as less than fully human, and throughout the 1930s, after Hitler was democratically elected president in 1933, the Jews were systematically stripped of their rights and their dignity. By 1945 when the war ended, some 5.85 million Jews had been murdered by the Germans and the monstrous war machine they had created. Roughly one out of every three Jews living in Europe was killed, many of them in factories of death such as Auschwitz, Buchenwald, and Dachau. Although Germany's horrific response to the Jewish "problem" was not replicated in the United States—indeed, Americans fought and died to overthrow the Nazi regime and in the process liberated Jews and others from concentration camps—that does not mean that Jews did not or do not face discrimination in America.

One can profitably understand the very popular Harry Potter stories as an extended commentary on race, hatred, and human behavior in the twentieth century. Voldemort and his minions are focused on those not of pure blood, and seek to exclude and ultimately to subjugate or kill all those who fail to meet his monstrous standards. And just as Hitler and his cronies had massive popular support, so Voldemort is revered (and worshiped) by the many who see his policies of hate and exclusion as acceptable and desirable.

THE DISABLED

Just as African Americans, women, and Jews have not fared well in American history, the physically and mentally disabled have often been subjected to abuse, discrimination, and exclusion from mainstream American society. In the early 1900s politicians, educators, and others became concerned about the rapid influx of immigrants, and there was increased vigilance not to allow those with physical and/or moral defects to enter our country. As Kim Nielsen says, it was widely believed that "criminality, feeble-mindedness, sexual perversions, and immorality, as well as leadership, responsibility, and proper expressions of gender, were hereditary traits."[36] She goes on, "Conveniently, this argument blamed the huge economic disparities between the small numbers of the rich and the large numbers of the poor on the deficiencies of poor people."[37] Harry Olson, an influential judge in Chicago, warned in 1911 that "the success of the United States depended on limiting its undesirable elements—degenerate immigrants being only one of the many undesirable categories."[38] In Indiana, Dr. Henry Clay Sharp of the Indiana Reformatory worried about the spread of (hereditary) degeneracy in the United States. According to Sharp, the "degenerate" class included "most of the insane, the epileptic, the imbecile, the idiotic, the sexual perverts; many of the confirmed inebriates, prostitutes, tramps, and criminals, as well as the habitual pauper found in our county poor asylums; also many of the children in our orphan homes."[39] This mentality was widespread, as was the belief in the importance of eugenics—the idea that the superior races/groups (especially the white Anglo-Saxon Protestants) needed to be cultivated while "degenerates" and "undesirables" (two commonly used terms) needed to be minimized and/or weeded out. How was the country to pursue such momentous goals? Well, two of the leading "solutions" were seen as severely restricting immigration and sterilizing those mentally and/or morally unfit to have children. It goes without saying that the sterilizations would mostly be involuntary and, in many documented cases, done without anesthesia! Those from southern and eastern Europe were most likely to be scrutinized at Ellis Island as they came to the United States. First-class passengers were the least scrutinized, as they clearly had the means to succeed and would not become a public liability. The great scientist Charles Steinmetz made it past the Ellis Island officials only because of the persistent pleas of an insistent and well-to-do friend. Steinmetz himself, given the mentality of the times, had multiple strikes against him. He was four feet three inches tall, had a hunched back, and was Jewish. He was clearly a person of "poor physique," a commonly used category to keep undesirables out of our "physically fit" country.[40]

---

[36]Kim Nielsen, *A Disability History of the United States* (Boston: Beacon, 2013), 101.
[37]Ibid.
[38]Ibid.
[39]Ibid., 102.
[40]This mentality persisted for some time, and helps explain why Franklin Roosevelt, a polio victim and four-time president, never publicly alluded to his disability or to the fact he could scarcely

Moische Fischmann was a talented thirty-year-old African American smith. He already had gainfully employed siblings in the United States who vouched for him. He even had a letter from an employer guaranteeing him work. Yet the board at Ellis Island unanimously voted to deport Fischmann, for Fischmann was deaf. Despite an eloquent appeal, the board maintained that "there can be little doubt that the applicant's certified condition will seriously interfere with his earning capacity." So, Fischmann was deported. The fact that Fischmann was also Jewish may well have contributed to him being rejected as a person of "poor physique."[41] In a similar fashion, immigrant women were also expected to have bodies suitable to perform physical labor. This is especially puzzling given that the majority of adult women in the United States did not work (outside the home) at that time.[42]

Alice Smith lived in New Jersey in the early 1900s. In 1911 a four-person board decided that the twenty-seven-year-old Smith should be sterilized and that "procreation by her is inadvisable." The board represented the New Jersey Board of Examiners of Feeble-Minded (Including Idiots, Imbeciles, and Morons), Epileptics, Criminals, and Other Defectives.[43] The state was seeking to enforce a law recently signed by then governor of New Jersey Woodrow Wilson, soon to be a two-term president and traditionally seen by historians to be an above-average president.[44] Smith had been legally committed at various times to the New Jersey State Village for Epileptics in Skillman, New Jersey. Her most recent committal occurred despite the fact she had not had a seizure in over five years. In 2014 the great majority of epileptics can have their seizures controlled by medication and live a full and productive life. Unfortunately for Alice Smith epilepsy was heavily stigmatized in the early 1900s and was often seen as linked with other physical and/or moral "defects." Harry Laughlin, a leading eugenics advocate, claimed that Smith was "congenitally defective, and [had] also inherited the epileptic tendency from her parents." To allow her to return to her home would be a "crime against society" and "most wasteful to the nation and State to allow

---

walk. One wonders if Roosevelt had contracted polio as a child in Europe, then sought admission at Ellis Island, whether he would have been allowed into the United States in the first place.

[41]Ibid., 108.

[42]Ibid.

[43]It's hard to believe, but that was the actual name of this erstwhile commission.

[44]It should be noted that President Wilson's legacy has been in decline for some time now, in part because of his blatantly racist ideas toward blacks and for being a force in the resegregation of Washington, DC, when he was president (1913–1921).

this defective to wander about, as it would entail perpetuation of her kind, and other evils due to this lack of proper care and segregation."[45] So for the good both of Alice Smith and society, Alice Smith needed to be sterilized. Sterilization actually became fashionable, as more than thirty states passed forced-sterilization laws. For the good of the patient, for the good of the country—just an all-around excellent idea.

The treatment of those with disabilities combined elements of racism, sexism, ethnocentrism, bad science, and ignorance with a general and genuine contempt for those who were "different" or "defective" or "degenerate." Christians more than anyone should realize that all human beings suffer from a serious and deeply rooted disability, namely, *sinfulness*.[46] Apart from God's grace shown through the life and death of Jesus Christ, this disability dominates the lives of all people.[47] The fact that some people have more disabilities than others is irrelevant in the eyes of God, and should do nothing to lessen our love and concern for our fellow human beings.[48]

METANARRATIVES AND OPPRESSION

This very brief overview of the treatment of four groups of human beings makes the fairly obvious point that many groups of our fellow humans have been treated poorly, very poorly, in American history.[49] Traditional histories of the United States, insofar as they omitted discussion of all these groups, failed to do justice to the varied and rich history of average Americans and to those who often lacked the power and influence of many of their fellow Americans.

The issue now before us is whether postmoderns are correct that believing in a particular metanarrative inevitably results in the oppression and marginalization of people groups out of the mainstream. If they are correct, then there are excellent reasons for having doubts about the truthfulness of each and every metanarrative, including evangelical Christianity.

---

[45]Ibid., 115.

[46]I am not making this point to be cute, I am making it because it is *true*, and the recognition of our sinfulness is a crucial first step in coming to realize our deep need for a Savior both to atone for our sins and to make us right with God.

[47]Is 53; Rom 3 and 5; and Eph 2:1 all testify to our utter lostness apart from God's saving grace.

[48]As I write, I presently have three major disabilities: sinfulness, nearsightedness, and a significant hearing impairment.

[49]And I know of no reason to think the United States is particularly unusual here. Human sinfulness mixed with ignorance and other factors often results in the marginalization and oppression of those who are "different."

Michel Foucault has argued that "truth . . . is produced only by virtue of multiple forms of constraint."[50] In other words, where there is "truth," there is always power (or authority) lurking in the background. The noted historian Joan Wallach Scott agrees with Foucault here. She claims that "gender is a primary way of signifying relationships of power."[51] Keith Jenkins, a Marxist historian, argues that "history is theory and theory is ideological and ideology is just material interests."[52] Put in clearer English, Jenkins is claiming that history represents a point of view (an ideology or worldview), and that all points of view are adopted because they benefit the person adopting it. So truth is not the bottom line in adopting views of the world, but rather power and selfish desires. Now Foucault, Scott, and Jenkins are not exactly evangelical Christians making criticisms from a Christian point of view. But this hardly means we should automatically reject what they say as false. Note they also believe 2 + 2 = 4 and that Voltaire lived in the 1700s. And we accept these claims because there is overwhelming evidence for both—they are true, their claims accurately line up with (or correspond to) reality. Many prominent Christians have readily acknowledged that metanarratives have often been intimately linked with oppression and inhumane practices. The historian Mark Noll writes that "history-writing has always served political purposes."[53] The facts don't speak for themselves; they need to be placed into a larger context/story, and that story is often one that makes those writing history look pretty good. The evangelical theologian Millard Erickson, in considering the idea that metanarratives have been oppressive, notes that "[there is] a strong measure of truth in this contention."[54] Finally, the noted Christian philosopher Alvin Plantinga agrees when he writes that

> other themes of postmodernism can only elicit enthusiastic applause from a Christian perspective: one thinks of sympathy and compassion for the poor and oppressed, the strong sense of outrage at some of the injustices our world displays, celebration of diversity, and the "unmasking" of prejudice,

---

[50]Foucault, Power/Knowledge, 131.

[51]Joan Wallach Scott, Gender and the Politics of History, rev. ed. (New York: Columbia University Press, 1999), 42.

[52]Keith Jenkins, Re-thinking History (London: Routledge, 2007), 9.

[53]Mark Noll, "Traditional Christianity and the Possibility of Historical Knowledge," Christian Scholar's Review 19, no. 4 (1990): 389.

[54]Millard Erickson, Truth or Consequences: The Promise and Perils of Postmodernism (Downers Grove, IL: InterVarsity Press, 2001), 276.

oppression, and power-seeking masquerading as self-evident moral principle and the dictates of sweet reason.[55]

So Foucault, Scott, Jenkins, Noll, Erickson, and Plantinga are all in agreement on this crucial point—that traditional metanarratives have often been oppressive.[56] The argument (which we shall label the oppression argument) might be summarized as follows:

1. All metanarratives are oppressive.

2. All oppressive metanarratives should be rejected.

3. Christianity is a metanarrative.

_____

4. ∴ Christianity should be rejected.

The argument can be symbolized as follows:

1. All As are Bs.

2. All Bs are Cs.

3. m is an A.

_____

4. ∴ m is a C.

So is this a good argument? Is it an argument that Christians and non-Christians alike should endorse? We first need to determine if the argument is a logically *valid* one, where a *valid* argument is one where the conclusion follows logically (or necessarily) from the premises. In other words, is it possible for all the premises (1-3) to be true and the conclusion false? The answer is a definite no. Consider a straightforward geographical argument that uses this same structure of argument:

---

[55] Alvin Plantinga, "Postmodernism and Pluralism," in *Warranted Christian Belief* (New York: Oxford University Press, 2000), 423.

[56] The fact that all six make the same claim *doesn't* prove it to be true. While it may be true that "great minds think alike," it is also true that "fools seldom differ." The key here is that there is excellent evidence in support of the claim we are making here. As noted earlier, deconstruction can also be read as a device or tool for undermining the truth claims by those who use language traditionally. Deconstruction seeks to place those on the fringes and margins of society on a more equal footing with those who possess the power in that society.

1. All people living in Minot live in Ward County.

2. All people living in Ward County live in North Dakota.

3. Carla lives in Minot.

---

4. ∴ Carla lives in North Dakota.

All this makes evident that the argument above is a valid one—the conclusion has to be true if all the premises are true. The second thing to do is now to determine if the argument is not only valid, but also *sound*. A *sound* argument is one where the argument is valid and all the premises are true. So are all the premises in the oppression argument true? Beginning with the third premise (because it is the most obvious), it is definitely true that Christianity is a worldview. Many Christian scholars have written extensively on this topic,[57] and there is a strong consensus that Christianity is a comprehensive view of the nature of reality, knowledge, morality, human nature, and a host of related issues. So what about the second premise? Should we automatically (without further analysis) reject any and every metanarrative that is oppressive? There may be some controversy on this matter, but we think there are good reasons[58] to reject all oppressive metanarratives. So we readily concur that the second premise is also true. So with both the second and third premises recognized as true, the overall success (or soundness) hinges on the truth of the first premise. Should we agree with Foucault and company that all metanarratives are oppressive? We think not. We have granted that many metanarratives have been oppressive at various times in the past (and present). But it is a long, long way from the claim

Some metanarratives are oppressive

to the much stronger universal claim

All metanarratives are oppressive

---

[57]See, for example, Ronald H. Nash, *Worldviews in Conflict: Choosing Christianity in a World of Ideas* (Grand Rapids: Zondervan, 1992); David K. Naugle Jr., *Worldview: The History of a Concept* (Grand Rapids: Eerdmans, 2002); James W. Sire, *The Universe Next Door: A Basic Worldview Catalog*, 5th ed. (Downers Grove, IL: IVP Academic, 2009); and D. A. Carson, *The Gagging of God: Christianity Confronts Pluralism* (Grand Rapids: Zondervan, 2002). See also N. T. Wright's online class, "Worldviews, the Bible, and the Believer," N. T. Wright Online, accessed June 5, 2017, http://ntwrightonline.org/portfolio-items/worldviews/?portfolioCats=35.

[58]Scripture offers a number of moral principles that oppressive views violate.

The following claims are all true:

1. Some humans believe zombies exist.

2. Some humans live in Max, North Dakota.
   and

3. Some humans are over seven feet six inches tall.

But now consider the much stronger claims that correlate with these claims:

4. All humans believe zombies exist.

5. All humans live in Max, North Dakota.

6. All humans are over seven feet six inches tall.

While claims one through three are all obviously true, claims four through six are, by contrast, all obviously false. To make claim five false, we only need one example to the contrary—one person who does not live in Max. Given (among other things) there are 1.2 billion people presently living in China, claim five is false. So can we think of any metanarratives that are not oppressive? Yes, indeed. We can think of one excellent candidate for a nonoppressive metanarrative: biblical Christianity. We believe that Christianity is not only not oppressive but also, more importantly, that it is a positively liberating worldview. Humans are sinful creatures. As Augustine, Martin Luther, Jonathan Edwards, and many others have argued, apart from God's saving grace in and through Jesus of Nazareth, humans live in bondage to their sinful natures. As humans who live after the fall of Adam we are not able to not sin. And apart from God's grace, we do not choose God; we are not even able to do so, as Romans 8:7 makes evident (see also Eph 2:1). Consider the following verses that support the idea that Christianity is both nonoppressive and liberating:

1. Galatians 5:1: "It is for freedom that Christ has set us free."

2. Romans 7:25: "Thanks be to God, who delivers me through Jesus Christ our Lord!"

3. Ephesians 2:1: "As for you, you were dead in your transgressions and sins."

4. Romans 6:17-18: "But thanks be to God that, though you used to be slaves to sin, you have come to obey from your heart the pattern of

teaching that has now claimed your allegiance. You have been set free from sin and have become slaves to righteousness."

5. John 8:32: "Then you will know the truth, and the truth will set you free."

6. Luke 4:18-19: "The Spirit of the Lord is on me, / because he has anointed me / to proclaim good news to the poor. / He has sent me to proclaim freedom for the prisoners / and recovery of sight for the blind, / to set the oppressed free, / to proclaim the year of the Lord's favor."

Apart from the grace of God, we are spiritually dead (Eph 2:1), unable to choose God in our own power (Rom 8:7), and under God's wrath (Eph 2:3). We are also slaves to sin—we cannot help but sin, as Augustine eloquently argued seventeen hundred years ago. Apart from God our yoke (burden in life) is immeasurably heavy; through faith in Jesus Christ, by contrast, the yoke is easy and the burden light (Mt 11:30). The hope of the gospel, Jesus Christ and his substitutionary death on the cross, sets us free both from the power (bondage) of sin and the penalty of sin, for the wages of sin is death (Rom 6:23). The twentieth century, perhaps more than any other century, has witnessed human cruelty to other humans on a scale never seen before. Now more than ever those apart from Christ, living under both the power and penalty of sin, need some hope, both for now and for the future.

SUMMARY

1. We examined the claim that all metanarratives are oppressive.

2. Christianity, Marxism, secular humanism, and Buddhism (for example) are all metanarratives.

3. The United States has a long history of oppression against African Americans, women, Jews, and the disabled.

4. But there is no good reason to make the jump from "some metanarratives are oppressive" to "all metanarratives are oppressive."

5. Biblical Christianity is not only not oppressive but also liberating.

6. The twentieth century is testimony to the need for humans to embrace the gospel.

Suggested Readings

Appleby, Joyce, Lynn Hunt, and Margaret Jacob. *Telling the Truth About History*. New York: Norton, 1995. A lucid account of the development of American history in the context of Western culture. Both informative and challenging.

Chafe, William. *The Paradox of Change: American Women in the 20th Century*. New York: Oxford University Press, 1992. An excellent and highly readable overview of women in the United States in the twentieth century.

Foner, Eric. *Reconstruction: America's Unfinished Revolution*. New York: HarperCollins, 2002. A detailed history of Reconstruction by a prominent scholar. The picture painted here is not a pretty one.

Foucault, Michel. *Madness and Civilization: A History of Insanity in the Age of Reason*. New York: Vintage, 1988. One of Foucault's major works. Very much worth reading, though dense and difficult at times.

Jenkins, Keith. *Re-thinking History*. New York: Routledge, 2003. A sustained assault on the evils of capitalism by a historian working in the Marxist tradition. Some of his more worthwhile points are obscured by the language and rhetoric he uses.

Karabel, Eric. *The Chosen: The Hidden History of Admission and Exclusion at Harvard, Yale, and Princeton*. New York: Mariner, 2006. A well-researched and clear overview of anti-Semitic admission policies at our three most prestigious universities.

Litwack, Leon F. *Trouble in Mind: Black Southerners in the Age of Jim Crow*. New York: Knopf, 1998. A powerfully written overview of the development of Jim Crow laws in the American South. The writing is clear and accessible.

Nielsen, Kim E. *A Disability History of the United States*. Boston: Beacon, 2013.

Sire, James W. *The Universe Next Door: A Basic Worldview Catalog*. 5th ed. Downers Grove, IL: IVP Academic, 2009. An articulate and even-handed critique of the major worldviews by an evangelical writer. Sire is always a pleasure to read.

Whitfield, Stephen J. *A Death in the Delta: The Story of Emmett Till*. Baltimore: Johns Hopkins University Press, 1991. One of the best treatments of the Till murder and the broader Southern culture that made such incidents possible.

10

DOUBTS ABOUT METANARRATIVES

In this chapter we examine the claim by Jean-François Lyotard (1924–1998) that metanarratives are worthy of rejection. We will first look at what a meta-narrative is, then examine three reasons for questioning/rejecting meta-narratives, and conclude with some general observations about one particu-larly promising metanarrative.

A narrative is a story. "Once upon a time there were three bears" is the opening to a story familiar to most Americans: Goldilocks and the Three Bears. The narrative includes the story line, the cast of characters, and a number of other factors. A metanarrative (*le grand récit*) is a big story, a worldview so to speak. A metanarrative often includes claims about what reality is, what knowledge is, how we should live, what is most important, and so forth. Marxism, Buddhism, the Enlightenment commitment to science and progress, and Christianity can all plausibly be seen as examples of metanarratives. Postmoderns such as Lyotard and Michel Foucault have both philosophical and political reasons for being skeptical about the pos-sibility of any metanarrative being true. Lyotard famously summed this up in his claim that postmodernism amounts to "incredulity towards metanarratives."[1] Some more radical postmoderns have gone beyond Lyotard to proclaim that metanarratives have a "secretly terroristic function to ground and legitimate the illusion of a 'universal' human history."[2]

---

[1]Lyotard, *The Postmodern Condition*, A Report on Knowledge, trans. Geoff Bennington and Brian Massumi (Minneapolis: University of Minnesota Press, 1984), 7.

[2]Terry Eagleton, "Awakening from Modernity," *Times Literary Supplement*, February 20, 1987, 194.

For example, one of the major narratives in the West has been the white, Eurocentric version of history.[3] In the late 1800s much of Africa had been colonized by the leading European powers, and many of those African countries did not achieve independence until the 1960s. Many came to realize that the very countries that officially preached democracy, Christianity, and the equality of all human beings had used their technological and military superiority to exploit the colonies' lands and labor "for naked economic and military advantage."[4] These Western metanarratives were used to massively oppress blacks, women, colonies, Jews, and many, many others. Three broad reasons can be identified as to why many postmoderns are skeptical of metanarratives.

1. The Historical Claim: All metanarratives have been politically and morally oppressive. They have marginalized women, blacks, and countless others. Somehow white European males always came out on top in these sweeping narratives. Marxism, the Enlightenment commitment to science and progress, and Christianity are all seen as oppressive metanarratives.

2. The Epistemic Claim: There may be a true story (worldview), but we humans are unable to know it. Due to our natural limitations, enmeshment in our particular cultures, and the limits of human language, we are simply unable to rise above our situation in life and discover any one metanarrative to be true.

3. The Moral/Political Claim: Metanarratives by their very nature label and marginalize the "other" in society, oppressing them and cheating them both of the opportunity for self-discovery and of equal economic and social opportunities. Though the moral claim and the historical claim are often intertwined, they are logically distinct and capable of being true without the other one also being true.

EVALUATING THE THREE CLAIMS

So what should we think about these various claims? The first of the three, the historical claim, is worthy of serious consideration. Heath White nicely summarizes the historical claim as follows,

---

[3]What follows is indebted to my analysis of metanarratives in Stewart E. Kelly, *Truth Considered and Applied: Examining Postmodernism, History, and Christian Faith* (Nashville: B&H Academic, 2011), 128-33.

[4]Heath White, *Postmodernism 101: A First Course for the Curious Christian* (Grand Rapids: Brazos, 2006), 44.

Postmodernism comes after the most violent century in history, and it carries an ethical impulse. In Africa and Asia and South America it has seen the exploitation of black and brown people in the name of the white man's burden; in the United States it has seen the mistreatment and exclusion of minorities in the name of social cohesion; in Germany it has seen genocide in the name of national destiny; in the Soviet Union, China, and Cambodia it has seen mass murder in the name of political ideology; it has seen multiple wars fought in the name of religion. Postmodernism diagnoses each of these great sins as the oppression of one group by another (which is pretty obvious), but furthermore, as oppression encouraged by some universal moral code or social or political guide: "We have a duty to civilize the backward tribes." "The races must not mix." "We must eliminate the bourgeoisie in order for the dictatorship of the proletariat to commence." "The Germans ought to rule Europe; the Jews ought to be eliminated."[5]

Since the onset of World War I in 1914, the world has seen inhumanity to fellow human beings achieve epic proportions. Genocide, persecution, mass slaughter, nuclear bombs, chemical weapons, hatred of others (seen as different and inferior) have all occurred far too often. Anyone seriously entertaining the belief that humans are somehow fundamentally decent creatures is pressed on all sides by the carnage of the twentieth century to explain how good creatures could behave so badly so often. In the West in the past two hundred years or so, white European males, especially those from western and northern Europe, may be the only group of humans not massively oppressed! Those entertaining the idea that the United States has somehow risen above all these massive failings needs to take some serious classes in American history. The history of the treatment of fellow human beings with "black" skin in the American South since the 1600s has been one of massive oppression, a savagery beyond imagination, a sustained pattern of violence that is diametrically opposed to the values of human decency, respect, and regard for our fellow human beings.[6] Unfortunately, the United States has not been an exception to the pattern of oppression in the West, but has more than held its own in terms of systematic inhumanity toward our fellow

---

[5]Ibid., 56.
[6]For lucid and compelling accounts of this sustained brutality, the works of Leon Litwack are an excellent place to start. See Leon Litwack, *Trouble in Mind: Black Southerners in the Age of Jim Crow* (New York: Knopf, 1998), and Litwack, *Been in the Storm So Long* (New York: Vintage, 1980).

human beings. The Civil War, the civil rights movement, the ever-present reality of lynching, and the repeated videos depicting police brutality toward blacks combine to hammer home the sad truth that racism is a long-standing problem with no immediate signs of substantial improvement. And though blacks have long been victims of oppression in the United States, they are— unfortunately—hardly the only group to be treated poorly. Women, Jews, Catholics, the Irish, Hispanics, Asians, Italians, Native Americans, the dis- abled, labor unions, and many others have received less than decent treatment at the hands of mainstream white America. One does not have to be politically liberal or way to the left (politically speaking) to recognize how many groups have been treated poorly. Blacks were enslaved, denied the right to vote, and lynched with regularity. Women were denied the right to vote and the right to own property, subject to inferior wages, and generally treated as second-class citizens.[7] Asians were singled out for excessively restrictive immigration laws,[8] interned during World War II, and often viewed with suspicion and distrust.

All this makes clear that the metanarrative of the United States (which can be said to include the idea of the American Dream: "work hard and get ahead") has often involved the poor treatment of its peoples. Sadly, such treatment is not limited to people within our American borders. The American treatment of the Filipinos, the Mexicans, and many of the peoples of Central America has also been less than virtuous.[9]

So what should we think about the historical claim? Given all the evi- dence, we need to begin by humbly acknowledging that many, many groups of our fellow human beings were not treated well over the cen- turies. Examples of oppression abound, and to reject the historical claim would be to ignore massive amounts of evidence and the history of in- justice and oppression toward our fellow humans. And if we add the study of Marxist countries to our list, the list grows exponentially. For massive oppression and inhumanity, the behavior of Joseph Stalin in the Soviet Union (from the early 1920s through 1953) and Mao in China are stunning examples of oppression.

---

[7]See William Chafe, *The Paradox of Change: American Women in the 20th Century* (New York: Oxford University Press, 1992).

[8]See the Chinese Exclusion Act of 1882.

[9]On the Filipinos, see Leon Wolff, *Little Brown Brother: How the United States Purchased and Pacified the Philippine Islands at the Century's Turn* (Camp Hill: History Book Club, 2006).

So does all this mean we should affirm the historical claim as true? We don't think so. Why not? Because the historical claim is a broad and sweeping historical generalization. Note that the historical claim affirms that "all metanarratives have been politically and morally oppressive." Claims with the word *all* only need one exception to make them false. So when we read that "all men never take out the garbage," we know this is false, because there was one man in Indiana who took the garbage out once! Not every metanarrative in every era of human history has been characterized by significant and ongoing oppression, though this is not to claim that any metanarrative (or human society) ever approached anything close to perfection. So we should grant there is significant truth in the historical claim, but reject it insofar as it makes a broad generalization allowing for no exceptions.

How should we think about the epistemic claim? The epistemic claim is an example of serious skepticism, where skepticism is the idea that we humans are justified in believing little if anything about the world around us. It doesn't claim there is no reality beyond us, but only that we humans are not in a position to know this reality. There is a kernel of truth in the epistemic claim, namely, that humans can know very little with any significant degree of certainty. René Descartes thought we could know quite a bit with a high level of certainty, but few philosophers nowadays would agree with him. So if knowing some belief to be true requires we know it with (what is often called) Cartesian certainty, then the epistemic claim looks rather promising. But why should we set the bar so high for genuine human knowledge? We can know many beliefs with a very high level of probability, and such a level is sufficient to say we know that belief to be true. In other words, knowledge does not require Descartes's level of certainty. One can begin with the idea that we clearly know many things to be true.[10] For example, consider the following:

1. Columbus sailed west in 1492 (a historical claim).

2. 2 + 3 = 5 (a mathematical claim).

3. Red Bank is in New Jersey (a geographical claim).

---

[10]The line of thought we are defending here is indebted to the philosopher Roderick Chisholm and to the New Testament scholar N. T. Wright. Both thinkers believe it is obvious that we know certain things to be true, and that a serious burden of proof is on the skeptic who denies we have any such knowledge.

4. A computer monitor in front of me now (a perceptual claim).

5. Objective moral standards exist (a moral claim).

Can we say we know all these claims to be true? Well, there is excellent evidence for claim one; there are ample historical records to show that Columbus really did sail west in 1492. And claim two is universally accepted by mathematicians as true, and can also be proved. Any decent map of the United States will show that Red Bank is in Monmouth County near the Atlantic Ocean, and if you went to that particular latitude and longitude you would run smack into Red Bank. As to a computer monitor presently being in front of me, there is very good evidence for that being true. I see what looks like such a monitor, I can touch it, its existence is what makes my present typing of these words evident to me, and I have no good reasons (such as powerful prescription medications or drugs illegal everywhere but Colorado) to doubt the above. So I am justified in making my computer-monitor claim.

Finally, what about the claim about the existence of objective moral standards? This is more complicated than the other four claims, and at least mildly controversial in philosophical circles. Having said that, we think there are persuasive reasons for thinking claim five is also true. If God exists, and there are adequate reasons for believing in God, then we can argue that the character of God provides a strong foundation for making some claims about objective moral standards. On a more practical level, almost everybody thinks that some actions are wrong, and that implies there are moral standards. For example,

1. Hitler was a bad man.

2. Helping the less fortunate is morally good.

3. We all claim "That's not fair" when one person is giving preferential treatment over others for no good/adequate reason.

Given the above considerations, and that we Christians believe that the Bible is an authoritative revelation of the one true God (whom we can know), we conclude that the epistemic claim is false and worthy of our rejection. So we reject it.

Finally, what should we think about the moral/political claim? Are meta-narratives by their very nature guilty of marginalizing and/or oppressing people? Here we can begin by noting our comment above that there *are* many examples of historical oppression. But it is a much stronger claim to say that all metanarratives are inherently (morally) oppressive. The moral claim ignores the power of the gospel (God's good news in Christ) to free people from the power and bondage of sin. Many years ago the Protestant Reformer Martin Luther claimed that people apart from God are in bondage to sin. In an ongoing dialogue with the great Dutch scholar Desiderius Erasmus, Luther affirmed what is known as the bondage of the will. This is the claim that though non-Christians have the ability to choose between options (what is often called "free will"), they do *not* have the ability apart from God to do that which is pleasing in God's sight, because their hearts are fundamentally selfish (sinful) and unable to put God first apart from God's saving grace in and through Jesus Christ.

Evangelical Christians should take all three claims seriously, especially the historical and moral claims. But advocates of those two claims overstate their case when they make sweeping generalizations about the claims. Anyone who is historically informed should grant that there is much truth in both the historical and moral claims, but the idea that metanarratives are inherently oppressive "ain't necessarily so," as there are plenty of exceptions that can be documented.

THE CHRISTIAN METANARRATIVE AND OPPRESSION

Christianity is a metanarrative. Some Christian scholars have denied this, but we believe their arguments are unconvincing. If something walks like a duck and sounds like a duck then the chances are decent it is a duck. And if something looks and acts like a comprehensive worldview (or metanarrative), then there is good reason to think it actually is a metanarrative. We think it is far more prudent to admit that Christianity is a metanarrative and then deny it is oppressive rather than to deny that it is a metanarrative in the first place. Traditional Christianity makes substantive claims about all of the following:

1. Whether there is a supreme being

2. Who/what caused the beginning of our universe

3. That human beings are made in God's image

4. That humans fell through Adam

5. That God mercifully provides a way for humans to be reconciled to God through the person and work of Jesus Christ

6. That it provides a foundation for making morally objective claims

7. That there is a trustworthy and knowable revelation (the Bible)

8. That reality is both material (physical) and spiritual (immaterial) in nature

The brief list above makes clear that Christianity makes claims of the following sort:

1. Metaphysical (claims about the nature of ultimate reality)

2. Moral (providing a basis for moral standards)

3. Epistemological (addressing whether we can know or not)

In a nutshell it tells us what exists, who we are, what we can know, how we should live, what the meaning of human existence is, and what our hope for salvation consists in. And this is just for starters. This clearly suggests that Christianity should be considered a metanarrative.

It now remains to see whether it is an oppressive metanarrative or a liberatory one (or somewhere in between). We will argue that there is a strong case for claiming both that it is not oppressive and that it is positively liberating. Furthermore, there is no other metanarrative we know of that rivals Christianity in its ability to offer people genuine hope and liberation from the shackles of sin and our sinful human natures.

Our belief, though not unanimous among evangelical Christians, is not an unusual one. One of the best books on Christianity and the idea of worldview in the past thirty years or so is James Sire's book *The Universe Next Door*, a lucid and fair-minded analysis of the leading eight or nine worldviews (metanarratives) in the world. It seems worth asking whether Sire considers Christianity a worldview. Let's begin by seeing what Sire thinks a worldview is. He writes,

> A worldview is a commitment, a fundamental orientation of the heart, that can be expressed as a story or in a set of presuppositions (assumptions which may be true, partially true or entirely false) which we hold (consciously or subconsciously, consistently or inconsistently) about the basic constitution of reality, and that provides the foundation on which we live and move and have our being.[11]

---

[11]James Sire, *The Universe Next Door*, 5th ed. (Downers Grove, IL: IVP Academic, 2009), 16.

So what exactly does a worldview involve? We are glad you asked! It involves, Sire thinks, something like the following seven questions:[12]

1. *What is prime reality—the really real?* This is the most fundamental question; it sets boundaries on the answers to the other six. This is the branch of philosophy known as metaphysics. Christians, of course, claim that the eternal Creator God, eternally existing as three persons in one being or substance, is the ultimate or prime reality.

2. *What is the nature of external reality, that is, the world around us?* Do we see the world as created or autonomous, chaotic or orderly? This is another aspect of metaphysics.

3. *What is a human being?* This comes under the heading of anthropology.

4. *What happens to a person at death?*

5. *Why is it possible to know anything at all?* This can be labeled as an epistemological question, where epistemology is simply a fancy word for the study of knowledge.

6. *How do we know what is right and wrong?* This is the study of ethics, where we examine principles for evaluating human behavior and seek to determine what is most important in life (often called the study of the good).

7. *What is the meaning of human history?* This is the Big Enchilada (or Kahuna). This is a comprehensive question seeking to figure out how everything fits together into a coherent whole/story.

Christianity clearly addresses all seven of the fundamental questions that Sire suggests are at the heart of a worldview. This then, we suggest, is true because Christianity really is a worldview (or metanarrative). Some prominent Christian thinkers argue that Lyotard had worldviews other than Christianity in mind, and that we should not think that Christianity is a worldview. Both Michael Horton and James K. A. Smith have expressed doubts about whether Christianity is a metanarrative/worldview.[13] Horton,

---

[12]Ibid., 17-18.

[13]See Michael Horton, *The Christian Faith: A Systematic Theology for Pilgrims on the Way* (Grand Rapids: Zondervan, 2011), 16-19, and James K. A. Smith, *Who's Afraid of Postmodernism? Taking Derrida, Lyotard, and Foucault to Church*, The Church and Postmodern Culture (Grand Rapids: Baker Academic, 2006), for more on this matter.

for example, argues along the following lines:

1. Lyotard has in mind metanarratives that are grounded in autonomous human reason.

2. But Christianity is not grounded in this manner.

3. So, Christianity is not a metanarrative.

He admits it is a *mega* narrative or big story, but it is yet not a metanarrative. There are three (among other) reasons he offers in support of his conclusion: First, to be a metanarrative a narrative must be grounded in autonomous human reason. Since Christianity is not, it is not a metanarrative. Let us call this the autonomous grounding claim. Second, metanarratives are grounded in dispensable myths. Christianity is grounded in an indispensable myth (a nonnegotiable story), so it is not a metanarrative. Let us call this the indispensable myth condition. And third, he claims metanarratives give rise to ideologies that resort to violence if necessary. Christianity transcends all such ideology, Horton claims, and also does not sanction violence to achieve its ends. We will label this the ideology plus violence connection.

Should we be persuaded by his general argument? We don't think so. Not only do we think that the autonomous grounding claim should be rejected, but also the indispensable myth condition and the ideology plus violence connection. All three claims fail to persuade. Let's briefly examine the reasons why.

We reject the autonomous grounding claim because there are a number of metanarratives besides Christianity that do not ground themselves in autonomous human reason. The main branches of Buddhism and Hinduism can hardly be said to be based on autonomous reason. Many Buddhists and Hindus have a deep distrust of the sort of reason endorsed by the leading lights of the European Enlightenment (Descartes and Locke come to mind here). Horton's claim here might apply to *most* Western metanarratives other than Christianity, but many Eastern views are not so inclined. One particular branch of Buddhism, the branch known as Madhyamika Buddhism, is notorious for its low view of (autonomous) human reason. Yet it is rightly thought of as a worldview or metanarrative. Horton can only support his claim by limiting himself to Western metanarratives, and we see no good reason to limit ourselves in such a fashion.

What about the indispensable myth connection? Does it fare any better? Not that we can tell. Two examples should be sufficient here. Traditional Buddhism is grounded in the person and teachings of Gautama Siddhartha, better known as the Buddha. This powerful story (or "myth") is no more dispensable for Buddhists than the teachings of Jesus are for Christians. Furthermore, Western science rose to prominence grounded in the empirical method and a significant confidence in human reason. Newton, Galileo, Boyle, and others clearly saw this as a bedrock foundation, anything but dispensable.[14]

Finally, the ideology plus violence connection also does not survive careful scrutiny. The word *ideology* has (at least) two central meanings:

1. A negative or derogatory sense as used by many Marxists. Here it means a worldview that is adopted largely to further one's own selfish aims in life.

2. A neutral sense in which it roughly means *worldview* or the like.

Even if we suppose it is true that many Marxist and non-Marxist versions of secular humanism allowed and/or resorted to systematic violence in support of their authority, it is yet false that this is true of all non-Christian worldviews. Historically speaking, most branches of Buddhism (which clearly is a worldview or metanarrative) are decidedly pacifistic, and would not resort to violence under any imaginable conditions. So yes, Buddhism is a metanarrative (and thus an ideology), but fundamentally opposed to the sort of violence that Horton sees connected with such metanarratives.[15] If we understand an ideology as "a system of ideas and ideals," as the *Oxford English Dictionary* defines it, then it is hard to see why we should object to Christianity being labeled an ideology.

---

[14]For a learned account of the prominence of science and reason in the Enlightenment, see the works of Jonathan Israel, Margaret Jacob, and Roy Porter. One certainly doesn't get the impression from reading these three scholars that science saw its foundation as anything but dispensable. See Jonathan Israel, *Radical Enlightenment*; Joyce Appleby, Lynn Hunt, and Margaret Jacob, *Telling the Truth About History* (New York: Norton, 1994), esp. the sections on the heroic model of science; and Roy Porter, *The Creation of the Modern World: The Untold Story of the British Enlightenment* (New York: Norton, 2000).

[15]See Keith Yandell and Harold Netland, *Buddhism: A Christian Exploration and Appraisal* (Downers Grove, IL: IVP Academic, 2009).

The Liberating Christian Metanarrative

Let us return to Luther and the bondage of the will. What does he mean by this? He means that the human will cannot help but sin if the human heart of that person has not been regenerated ("born again") by the power of the Holy Spirit. Luther agreed with the Dutch scholar Erasmus, saying, "You are no doubt right in assigning to man a will of some sort, but to credit him with a will that is free in the things of God is too much."[16] Luther thought our will was perfectly capable of making everyday sorts of choices, but he was convinced humans lacked the ability even to accept God's offer of salvation in Christ. For Luther, the bondage of humans can be described as follows:

> The will is like a beast standing between two riders. If God rides, it wills and goes where God wills. . . . If Satan rides, it wills and goes where Satan wills; nor can it choose to run to either of the two riders or to seek him out, but the riders themselves contend for the possession and control of it.[17]

Timothy George writes that "herein is the tragedy of human existence apart from [divine] grace: We are so curved in upon ourselves that, thinking ourselves free, we indulge in those things that only reinforce our bondage."[18] The upshot of all this is that we all are in bondage (apart from God's grace), and we lack even the ability to turn to God for help in our own strength. So if someone does not reach down to rescue us, we are utterly lost, left to our own devices. John Stott, one of the leading evangelicals of the past one hundred years, sums up the human predicament in the following: "Outside Christ man is dead because of trespasses and sins, enslaved by the world, the flesh, and the devil, and condemned under the wrath of God."[19] This is an awful predicament: we are spiritually dead (see Eph 2:1), enslaved to sin, and condemned before the one true God. And if that is not bad enough, we are unable to do anything to extricate ourselves from our predicament. This is Bad News of the greatest possible magnitude.

Then, in Ephesians 2:4, is one of the greatest pieces of Good News that one could possibly imagine. Paul writes, "But God, being rich in mercy,

---

[16]E. Gordon Rupp and Philip S. Watson, eds., *Luther and Erasmus: Free Will and Salvation* (Philadelphia: Westminster, 1969), 170.

[17]Ibid., 140.

[18]Timothy George, *Theology of the Reformers*, rev. ed. (Nashville: B&H Academic, 2013), 77.

[19]John Stott, *The Message of Ephesians* (Downers Grove, IL: InterVarsity Press, 1979), 79.

because of His great love with which He loved us, even when we were dead in our transgressions, made us alive together with Christ (by grace you have been saved)" (Eph 2:4-5 NASB). One could loosely paraphrase all this as follows: There is really bad news, but there is even better news present in the good news of the gospel and what God has (already) done for us in Jesus Christ. This is the central Christian message in a nutshell. God liberates us from the power and penalty of sin by allowing his one and only Son to die in our place that we might be born again (breaking the bondage) and now accepted in God's eyes because when he looks at us he no longer sees our sin, but rather the sacrifice by Jesus Christ on our behalf. Let's take a brief look at some of the key elements of the Christian gospel:

1. It is good news delivered in the context of very bad news.

2. The fact that we were in bondage accentuates our dramatic deliverance from the power and penalty of sin by God in Christ.

3. If God docs not take action in our regard, we are utterly without hope.

4. God gets the credit and the glory for sending Christ to save us. We have no merit before God and no claim on him. He gives his grace freely.

5. The third person of the Trinity, the Holy Spirit, convicts us of sin and regenerates our hearts, making us born again.

6. With this new Spirit-empowered nature, (1) we are no longer in bondage; we have been set free; and (2) we are now able to bear supernatural fruit, the fruit of the Spirit, by abiding in God through the power of the Spirit.

It is hard to see, given the above, how Christianity would be guilty of being oppressive. We have already granted that many Christians have acted very badly over the years, but that is not an indictment of Jesus or the Christian message as such, but rather of many of its adherents. We have also seen that Christianity offers genuine hope to an otherwise lost humanity, and offers the only hope for being freed from the bondage of the will that so concerned Luther. Rather than being oppressive, the gospel of Jesus Christ sets us free from the power and penalty of sin. Paul writes in Romans 8:2: "because through Christ Jesus the law of the Spirit who gives life has set you free from the law of sin and death."

Summary

1. There are three reasons why postmoderns are skeptical of metanarratives.

    A. Historical claim: historically, all metanarratives have been oppressive.

    B. Epistemic claim: we humans are unable to know any metanarrative as true.

    C. Moral claim: metanarratives by their very nature are oppressive.

2. Evangelicals should take all three claims seriously, especially the historical and moral claims. But both of these claims are sweeping generalizations that don't allow for exceptions, and there clearly are exceptions to both claims.

3. Christianity and Metanarratives

    A. Is Christianity a metanarrative? James Sire argues that Christianity is a metanarrative/worldview.

    B. Both Michael Horton and James K. A. Smith argue that Christianity is not a metanarrative.

    C. Horton offers three arguments in favor of his claim that Christianity is a *mega* narrative but not a metanarrative:

        i. Christianity is grounded on considerations that rule it out as a metanarrative.

        ii. Christianity is based on a nonnegotiable story, while metanarratives are based on negotiable stories.

        iii. Metanarratives allow for ideologies that resort to violence to maintain their authority. Christianity doesn't do this, so (again) it's not a metanarrative.

    D. None of these three arguments are persuasive.

    E. Sire's take on worldviews/metanarratives combined with the failure of Horton's three arguments gives us ample reason for concluding that Christianity is very much a metanarrative.

4. Christianity is a Liberatory metanarrative.

    A. Apart from God, humans are in bondage to sin (Luther).

    B. They cannot escape this bondage on their own efforts.

    C. But God reaches down to save us and breaks the bondage of sin through the death and resurrection of Jesus (and the faith that individuals place in him).

D. Christianity, by the work of the Holy Spirit, gives each believer in Christ a new heart and the indwelling presence of the Holy Spirit. This new nature and the power of the Spirit gives the believer genuine freedom to do what is pleasing in God's sight (bearing the fruit of the Spirit). So, as Christians, we no longer sin no matter what (due to our bondage), but have been set free to live obediently to God through faith in Christ and the power of the Spirit.

E. All of the above shows that Lyotard has no good or sufficient reason for expressing incredulity toward all metanarratives, as Christianity offers not oppression but genuine liberation and the daily power to live virtuously.

SUGGESTED READINGS

Eagleton, Terry. "Awakening from Modernity." *Times Literary Supplement.* February 20, 1987, 194. A defense of a radical form of postmodernism. Not easy reading.

George, Timothy. *Theology of the Reformers.* Rev. ed. Nashville: B&H Academic, 2013. An outstanding overview of some of the key Protestant Reformers.

Horton, Michael. *The Christian Faith: A Systematic Theology for Pilgrims on the Way.* Grand Rapids: Zondervan, 2011. An excellent book by a leading evangelical theologian.

Kelly, Stewart E. *Truth Considered and Applied: Examining Postmodernism, History, and Christian Faith.* Nashville: B&H Academic, 2011. Contains an extended analysis of metanarratives.

Lyotard, Jean-François. *The Postmodern Condition: A Report on Knowledge.* Translated by Geoff Bennington and Brian Massumi. Minneapolis: University of Minnesota Press, 1984. The classic critique of metanarratives.

Packer, James I. *Keep in Step with the Spirit: Finding Fullness in Our Walk with God.* Grand Rapids: Baker Books, 2005. A clear and careful presentation on the idea of Christians abiding in the Holy Spirit by a leading evangelical theologian. Highly recommended.

Rupp, E. Gordon, and Philip S. Watson, eds. *Luther and Erasmus: Free Will and Salvation.* Philadelphia: Westminster Press, 1969. Two leading scholars writing on the debate between Luther and Erasmus.

Sire, James. *The Universe Next Door: A Basic Worldview Catalog.* 5th ed. Downers Grove, IL: IVP Academic, 2009. A readable and articulate overview of the leading worldviews today.

Smith, James K. A. *Who's Afraid of Postmodernism? Taking Derrida, Foucault, and Lyotard to Church.* The Church and Postmodern Culture. Grand Rapids: Baker Academic, 2006.

Stott, John R. W. *The Message of Ephesians.* Downers Grove, IL: InterVarsity Press, 1979. Still one of the best commentaries on the book of Ephesians.

White, Heath. *Postmodernism 101: A First Course for the Curious Christian.* Grand Rapids: Brazos, 2006. A brief and readable introduction to the main postmodern themes.

11

TRUTH, FAITH, AND
POSTMODERNISM

What is truth?

John 18:38

Such a thing [truth], however, has been notoriously elusive.

Paul Horwich, "Theories of Truth," in
A Companion to Epistemology

I am the way and the truth and the life.

John 14:6

The concept of truth is one of the most complicated and most controversial issues in the history of philosophy. Both philosophers and theologians disagree whether there is such a thing as truth,[1] and also whether such truth is knowable by human beings. In this chapter we will examine some of the leading theories of truth, evaluate some postmodern views of truth, and also discuss why the very idea is especially important to those who call themselves Christians. There is an enormous philosophical literature on the nature of truth, and what we present here is both highly selective and not intended to be an exhaustive analysis of all the issues connected with truth. For our purposes, we will examine four theories of truth: (1) the pragmatic

---

[1]Though it is clearly true that the great majority of contemporary philosophers think something like "truth" exists.

theory, (2) the coherence theory, (3) two postmodern views of truth, and (4) the correspondence view of truth, the one we think is most defensible.

Christianity and Truth

Evangelical Christians believe that the Bible is a truthful book, that it contains no claims that, properly understood, are false.[2] They also believe that we worship a God who is morally perfect, a God that not only does not lie, but also cannot lie.[3] And finally, Christians believe that it is true that God created the universe, that the Son of God became incarnate, that he died for our sins on the cross, and that he bodily rose again on the third day. These four truths are central to biblical Christianity and to the truth of the gospel. If any of the four are false, then traditional Christianity is in big, big trouble. The apostle Paul recognizes this when he writes about the resurrection of Jesus in 1 Corinthians 15. Paul's words are worth quoting at length here:

> But if it is preached that Christ has been raised from the dead, how can some of you say that there is no resurrection of the dead? If there is no resurrection of the dead, then not even Christ has been raised. And if Christ has not been raised, our preaching is useless and so is your faith. More than that, we are then found to be false witnesses about God, for we have testified about God that he raised Christ from the dead. But he did not raise him if in fact the dead are not raised. For if the dead are not raised, then Christ has not been raised either. And if Christ has not been raised, your faith is futile; you are still in your sins. Then those also who have fallen asleep in Christ are lost. If only for this life we have hope in Christ, we are of all people most to be pitied.

Here Paul makes a number of important truth claims:

1. If Jesus has not been raised, then our faith is useless.

2. If he has not been raised, then we are false witnesses about God.

3. If he has not been raised then we all are dead in our sins.

4. If he has not been raised, then we are most to be pitied.

---

[2]See 2 Tim 3:16 for a familiar passage on the inspiration (and inerrancy) of Scripture. Some evangelicals and many more liberal theologians might doubt all this. See Craig L. Blomberg, *The Historical Reliability of the New Testament: Countering the Challenges to Evangelical Christian Belief* (Nashville: B&H Academic, 2016), and N. T. Wright, *Jesus and the Victory of God* (Minneapolis: Fortress, 1997).

[3]See Num 23:19. God neither lies nor is he even capable of lying. This is radically different from human beings, who both can and do lie, some with amazing regularity.

This passage makes clear that Christianity is not just about having warm-fuzzies about God, or just having faith; it is also very much about a truthful and loving God who has acted in history by sending Jesus to die on our behalf and then rise from the dead. Consider the set of truth claims presented in table 1.

Table 1. Major truth claims of Christianity

	CHRISTIANITY	SECULAR WORLDVIEWS*
God exists	True	False
God created the universe	True	False
Jesus was the incarnate Son of God	True	False
Jesus died for our sins	True	False
Jesus rose from the dead on the third day	True	False

*It should be noted that some worldviews, such as Deism, believe that there is a god, but it is not the all powerful, all loving, Creator God of traditional Christianity. Deism believes in a sort of second-rate god who is on extended holiday!

It is the truth of these five (and other) important claims that separates Christianity from other worldviews.[4] If truth does not exist, or it exists but is not knowable by us human beings, then traditional Christianity would be seriously undermined. The claim that Jesus rose from the dead is not *merely* a claim about what we Christians believe, though it does involve belief; rather it is a claim about a particular human being (the incarnate Jesus, fully God and fully human) who lived in a real time, in a real place, and died on a real cross, and then bodily rose from the dead, leaving a totally empty tomb behind. If someone had been in Jerusalem in AD 30 or 33,[5] they would have had the opportunity to personally witness the brutal crucifixion of Jesus, to see his empty tomb on Sunday, and to bear witness to a Jesus bodily risen.

Christians make claims about the way the world is, about what has happened in the past, and about genuine transformation in the lives of billions of Christians over the centuries. So if, as some claim, there is no truth, then Christians are at least mistaken, possibly deluded, and have grounded their hopes in something no more real than a unicorn, the existence of Hogwarts,

---

[4]Some worldviews such as Islam would view the first two claims in table 1 as true, though it is not entirely clear that the God of Christianity and the God of Islam (Allah) are one and the same being.

[5]The two most likely dates for the crucifixion of Jesus.

or Uncle Bubba's miracle cure for gout, arthritis, apparitions, lumbago, and predicting the future of the stock market.

So, much is at stake here. It is not just some academic philosophers and theologians debating some particularly complicated matter,[6] but ultimately a matter of life, death, and the hope we Christians have, which is grounded in the eternal God who has revealed himself in Scripture and creation. Kevin Vanhoozer notes that "Scripture itself employs a rich and varied vocabulary of truth."[7] Scripture presents God as the one true God (see Jer 10:10), and truth "is first and foremost an attribute of God that emphasizes divine reliability and steadfastness. Truth is grounded in who God is, especially in relation to his covenant word. God is trustworthy just because he acts faithfully, and God's word is God's bond."[8]

Many postmoderns emphasize that humans are situated interpreters, that we always approach the Bible and what it says from a particular angle or viewpoint. But we have also seen that nothing about being a situated interpreter makes it impossible for us to know the truth. Though we may "see through a glass, darkly" (1 Cor 13:12 KJV), we *do* see. And though some postmoderns have "an endemic aversion to truth,"[9] even most postmoderns recognize there is such a thing as facts and a correct description of historical events.[10] Mark Dever writes that "our God is not a mute God. Not only is he active in history, but he has spoken. And so we must care about cognitive truth. God has revealed himself as a personal God, and part of that personhood is his communication to us of truth."[11] The Bible is not only God's personal communication to us, more importantly it is the truthful communication of the one true God. To read and understand the Bible is to grasp important truths about the human condition (our genuine sinfulness), our need for a Savior (we are objectively guilty before God), that God sent his

---

[6]Such as how many angels can dance on the head of a pin.

[7]Kevin J. Vanhoozer, "Truth," in *Dictionary of Theological Interpretation of the Bible*, ed. Kevin J. Vanhoozer (Grand Rapids: Baker Academic, 2005), 819.

[8]Ibid.

[9]Alister E. McGrath, "The Challenge of Pluralism for the Contemporary Church," *Journal of the Evangelical Theological Society* 35 (1992): 366, cited in D. A. Carson, *The Gagging of God: Christianity Confronts Pluralism* (Grand Rapids: Zondervan, 1992), 167.

[10]Even the well-known postmodern philosopher Richard Rorty recognizes there are genuine facts, though he doubts our ability both to know those facts and to arrange them into any kind of coherent picture of reality.

[11]Mark E. Dever, "Communicating Sin in a Postmodern World," in *Telling the Truth: Evangelizing Postmoderns*, ed. D. A. Carson (Grand Rapids: Zondervan, 2009), 144.

only Son, Jesus, in the flesh to die on our behalf (the truths of the crucifixion and the atonement), that Jesus really did rise from the dead (as Thomas and others demonstrated) and will one day really return to judge the living and the dead. All this is to suggest that the concept of truth is central to Christianity and that it is equally important we be able to know these truths.

COMMON SENSE AND TRUTH

There is such a thing as *common sense*, where common sense can be understood to be a basic ability to understand life and reality and to grasp certain obvious features of the reality we daily experience. For example, common sense supports all of the following basic claims:

1. All humans die.

2. If you work hard your chances for success improve.

3. There is no free lunch.

4. Treating other people badly often comes back to get you (some degree of karma, colloquially speaking, is true).

5. Money cannot buy happiness (or love).

6. Being loved is a good thing.

7. Some foods taste better than others.

8. Soccer is a popular sport.

9. Dogs can be good companions.

10. Pursuing a baby bear with its mother in the area is not a great idea.

Now many of these claims admit of exceptions and are no more than accurate generalizations about life and reality. Still, if someone denied the truth of all ten of the claims above, we would be justified in doubting whether they have both oars in the boat. Actually, we might be justified in claiming they aren't anywhere near the boat either! So far none of this is particularly questionable. But common sense also has a connection with the idea of truth, which is what we are focused on in this chapter. Besides lending support to the ten claims above, common sense also clearly supports the idea that there is such a thing as truth, and that certain claims are true. So what sorts of claims does common sense support? The following might be a good start:

1. Material objects exist (even people who deny their existence regularly duck when walking through a low doorway).

2. John Kennedy was assassinated (some deny it, but there is no decent evidence to support their belief).

3. The United States is one of the wealthier countries in the world, while Haiti is not.

4. Many trees have green leaves.

5. Cars can be helpful getting from point A to point B (or from getting from point B to point A).

Anyone who doubted all five claims would earn our serious skepticism. Common sense does not *prove* any of these five claims are true beyond a shadow of a doubt, but it does place a heavy *burden of proof* on those who deny one or more of these claims. If one person is talking to another, and person A appeals to common sense in support of one of these claims, that places the responsibility on person B for showing otherwise. So the upshot of the above is this: Those who reject claims supported by common sense have the responsibility to provide excellent evidence why common sense is mistaken on a particular point. Just as Great Britain was on our side during World War II, so common sense is on our[12] side when we affirm that certain claims are true and that there is such a thing as truth. We truth affirmers could all be mistaken in all our common-sense beliefs, but we think this is highly improbable. You and I have a better chance of winning the Powerball lottery or being given a billion dollars by an anonymous rich person than we do of showing all common-sense beliefs are false. Juries convict people because it seems true they committed a crime. People feel angry when they think it is true they have been treated shabbily, and people rejoice with glee when they think it true that their favorite sports team has truly won some important championship. Most of what we do on a daily basis is closely tied to our beliefs about what we think is true. Consider the following examples:

1. We get up early because we believe it is true that our job starts at eight in the morning.

2. We eat food because we think it is true that it will (among other things) satisfy our hunger.

---

[12]Here "our" refers to those who affirm the existence of truth.

3. We brake suddenly when a young child darts out in front of our car, for we believe it is wrong to intentionally drive over another human being, and we think it is true that braking hard will truly decrease our chances of hitting the child.

4. We make eye contact when shaking hands with the boss because we believe it is true that making eye contact is a sign of respect and good manners in our country.

5. We pray daily to God, because we believe it is true that God exists and that Scripture commands us to pray daily.

So truth is not just a topic relevant for philosophers and theologians who have nothing better to do and need to get a life. It is also of immense importance for how we live our lives day in and day out. And for evangelical Christians it is obviously very important that our Christian beliefs be true, for this is (and should be) the basis of much we do and how we approach life and make plans for our future. We now turn to the difficult matter of the nature of truth and to examining leading theories of truth to see which theory might be most reasonable.

THEORIES OF TRUTH: THE PRAGMATIC THEORY

One of the leading theories of truth in recent times has often been called the pragmatic theory of truth.[13] It has had many able defenders over the years, including William James (1842–1910), Charles Peirce (1839–1914), John Dewey (1859–1952), and many others. Defenders of the pragmatic theory view truth differently than do supporters of either the correspondence theory or the coherence theory. Pragmatic theories of truth should be viewed as both a large family of views and individual/particular theories that vary somewhat from other members of the family. Here we will briefly focus on two of the better-known representatives: James and Peirce.

James's view. It is probably accurate to say that James's expression of the pragmatic theory is less sophisticated than Peirce, and probably Dewey too. It is also not easy to take all of James's writings on truth and put them into a single coherent picture. The overall idea that James advances is along the lines of the following:

---

[13]This section is heavily indebted to the following: Alvin I. Goldman, *Knowledge in a Social World* (New York: Oxford University Press, 1999); Richard L. Kirkham, *Theories of Truth: A Critical Introduction* (Cambridge, MA: MIT Press, 1995); and Steven B. Cowan and James S. Spiegel, *The Love of Wisdom: A Christian Introduction to Philosophy* (Nashville: B&H Academic, 2009).

A proposition is true if and only if it is useful to believe it, that is, useful to the prospective believer.

We should begin by noting that James is correct in thinking that true beliefs do tend to be useful or helpful. If a car salesperson tells you that car X will reliably get you from Sheboygan, Wisconsin, to Bayonne, New Jersey, and it is true, that is a useful piece of information. And similarly, false beliefs can have negative consequences. So if it turns out the salesperson is unreliable and untruthful, and the car only makes it from Sheboygan to the Sheboygan suburbs, you may be stranded, out a lot of money, and muttering to yourself, asking why you listened to that salesman anyway! But James's version of pragmatism also runs into a number of serious problems, which follow.

First, it is counterintuitive to think that truth is simply what is useful. For starters, some true beliefs are not useful. If you are a kind but sensitive person, you may be better off not knowing that two particular people really detest you, a piece of knowledge that would only hurt your feelings and make you miserable. Equally true, false beliefs can be useful. For example, an over-inflated view of your abilities may help you navigate a number of challenges and obstacles, though the view is not accurately grounded in reality.

Second, it is clearly true that what is useful varies significantly from person to person. What is considered useful depends in part both on one's personality and on their outlook on life. A wildlife biologist going to Antarctica believes it is true that various penguins inhabit the area. This belief is clearly useful for him to know, thus making it true on James's view. But the average person could care less about the funny-looking birds that waddle thousands of miles away. Its usefulness to them is minimal at best. Thus James's view commits him to claiming that

(P) Penguins live in Antarctica

is true for the wildlife biologist but not for the average person. This is a strange consequence of James's view.

Third, we thus see that James's view tends toward relativism with regard to truth. Truth is no longer *objective* in nature (where *penguins live in Antarctica* is true simply because it corresponds to a particular set of facts concerning penguins in Antarctica), but rather subjective. We now have (P) is true for the biologist and false for most everyone else. Objectively true claims do not depend on what one believes to be true.

The sun exists

is true whether anyone believes it or not. But on James's view it is only true if it is useful to someone.

And fourth, James's view of truth takes *one* common feature of true claims (that they are useful to the believer) and absolutizes it. It may well be generally true that true beliefs are useful, but it is clearly false that all true beliefs are useful.

Peirce's view. So James's version of the pragmatic theory of truth does not survive careful scrutiny. But there is another pragmatist who puts forth an initially more promising theory of truth. Charles Peirce believed that truth should be understood as follows:

> A belief is true if it is fated to be ultimately agreed to by all who investigate it.

Peirce clearly valued both the careful use of scientific method and the community of scientists who use the method in pursuit of truth. So the idea is roughly that one hundred scientists pursuing research on a particular topic, and all committed to the carefulness required by the scientific method, will in the long run arrive at the same conclusion—they will reach a consensus. Peirce was a brilliant and original thinker, but his view of truth runs into serious difficulties.

First, there is no guarantee that people will believe the truth even if they investigated indefinitely.[14] The matter may simply be too complicated, and the long-term scientific community will not necessarily arrive at any common opinion, even after years of careful research.

Second, there are other issues where more than one opinion is fated to occur. If research group A and research group B, using the same method and procedures, arrive at fundamentally different (and conflicting) opinions, then on Peirce's view both groups have the truth, so their "truths" contradict each other. This is a rather unhappy byproduct of Peirce's view, one that often seems "fated" to occur.[15]

Third, Peirce's theory of truth is better seen as what might be meant for a belief to be *justified* (considered rational). Justification about knowledge and truth are related concepts, but they are also fundamentally distinct.[16]

---

[14]See Alvin Goldman, *Knowledge in a Social World* (New York: Oxford University Press, 1999), 46.
[15]The history of science is littered with such examples.
[16]See Goldman, *Knowledge in a Social World.*

Whether or not truth exists depends on the way (mind-independent) reality is. Justification, on the other hand, is essentially about our attempts to have reasonable beliefs *about* that reality. The common-sense view of truth is that truth exists whether a scientific community (or any comparable community) pursues it or not. Prior to there being any scientific investigators, both of the following were true: (1) there were no careful investigators existing; (2) there was a certain way the world was (it had many definite characteristics).

Fourth, Hilary Putnam, a prominent philosopher sympathetic to the pragmatist tradition, recognizes that "truth" is sometimes recognition-transcendent.[17] What does this mean? It means that not all true beliefs require some individual or community to recognize them as true in order to be true. It is probable that there are some truths in mathematics and physics that have yet to be discovered. And they are true whether seen as such by any particular community of investigators. Peirce, like James, latches on to one important component of many truths (that they are discovered after a long period of careful inquiry) and makes it a required feature of truth.

Traditional Christians are committed to a number of beliefs about God: the incarnation, the atonement, the resurrection, and other matters of crucial importance. Pragmatist theories of truth make truth dependent on what certain individuals or communities (come to) think. We want to claim that

(J) Jesus is risen

is true whether anyone recognizes it as such or not! Rather than being mind dependent, truth claims are actually mind independent. So though James and Peirce do capture some important elements intimately associated with truth, they fail to capture what it is that all true beliefs have in common, namely, truth itself.

THE COHERENCE THEORY

In the past two hundred years there have been a number of very capable philosophers who have endorsed what has been come to be known as the coherence theory of truth. J. M. E. McTaggart, Brand Blanshard, F. H. Bradley, and others have endorsed the coherentist view. Blanshard argued that a claim is true along the following lines:

---

[17]See ibid., 47.

> A proposition is true if and only if it coheres or meshes with the other (set of) beliefs held by the individual.

This means we think of our beliefs as similar to a huge puzzle, and each new belief, in order to be recognized as "true," must fit (not conflict with) the other pieces. So if it coheres well it is true; if it doesn't, then it isn't. Coherence itself involves a number of important elements:

1. Logical consistency: If a new belief (N) is logically contradicted by the person's existing set of beliefs, then (N) cannot possibly be true.

2. Some inferential relationship: The belief in some propositions is based on or inferred from the belief in other propositions. For example, a particular perceptual claim (e.g., "I see a tree") is viewed as true based on the general reliability of our five senses in general.

Rather than seeing acquiring knowledge as something similar to the structure of a sturdy building (where we start with foundational, highly probable beliefs and build based on that steady foundation), coherentists see knowledge as more closely resembling someone on a raft who is repairing the raft as he travels. As Otto Neurath writes, "We are like sailors who must rebuild their ship on the open sea, never able to dismantle it in dry-dock and to reconstruct it there out of the best materials."[18] While it is true that true beliefs are logically consistent with other true beliefs, attempts to defend a coherentist view of truth run into four legitimate problems.

First, given that our existing set of beliefs is fallible (since we are mere humans), some beliefs that cohere with our set of established beliefs will be false. Even in situations where we have a significant amount of supporting evidence, it is still possible for a belief to be false. As Alvin Goldman argues, there are both true propositions for which we currently possess no evidence (such as those concerning distant galaxies) and false propositions for which we have ample evidence.[19] So lots and lots of evidence is no guarantee of truth.[20]

Second, coherence as a theory of truth cuts us off from the external world. The point made by Putnam is that some facts are recognition-transcendent (they are true whether anyone recognizes them or not). The

---

[18]Otto Neurath, "Protocol Sentences," in *Logical Positivism*, ed. A. J. Ayer (New York: Free Press, 1959), 201.

[19]Goldman, *Knowledge in a Social World*, 44.

[20]For those familiar with such things, consider how often juries, even after careful and fair-minded deliberation, still get things wrong.

British philosopher Simon Blackburn notes that "our judgment that a cat is in the garden is made true, if it is true, by the cat's being in the garden." He concludes that "we don't, as [it] were, look sideways, either to other people or to [our] systems of belief. We look at the cat and look round the garden."[21] What all this means is that many of our true beliefs don't require the sort of meshing or system fit that coherence theory requires.

Third, coherence theory also allows for contradictory beliefs to be true. Marian David argues that coherence is always relative to particular people at particular times. So what people believe as true is partly conditioned by both who they are and where and when they live. Lots of folks in Europe during the Middle Ages believed the flatness of the earth to be an obvious truth. Nowadays such beliefs are rather rare. Given all this, we can easily imagine the following: Sarah has a set of beliefs we will label A, while Sam has a set of beliefs we will label B. Now suppose that both Sarah and Sam are considering whether a particular proposition P is true or false. Sarah rightly sees that P's being true is inconsistent with her set of beliefs, so she rejects P as false. Sam, on the other hand, believes P is true because it does mesh nicely with his entire system of beliefs. So what we have is Sarah and Sam having a contradictory belief that is, according to coherence theory, true for both people simultaneously. Sarah believes ~P is true, while Sam believes P is true. But logic 101 tells us that contradictory beliefs cannot both be true. This means that something is seriously wrong with the coherence theory of truth.

Fourth, remember that coherence advocates tell us that a true belief is one that is consistent with our entire (or maximal) set of beliefs. This set needs to be large enough to enable us to accurately determine the truth (by way of coherence) of any new belief that comes along. But as William Alston and others have argued, the requirements for such a large set are "far in excess of anything we have on our hands at present or anything we have any real prospect of attaining."[22] So the question arises, how exactly is this large system of beliefs established in the first place? Are these beliefs we know to be true *prior* to their being subjected to the coherence test? If so, then is it

---

[21]Simon Blackburn, *Spreading the Word: Groundings in the Philosophy of Language* (Oxford: Oxford University Press, 1984), 246-47.

[22]William P. Alston, *A Realist Conception of Truth* (Ithaca, NY: Cornell University Press, 1996), 225.

perhaps the case that they are true in virtue of properly corresponding to reality? The upshot is that it seems that coherence theorists need to assume or presuppose a large set of beliefs as true independently of whether they cohere. It is rather difficult to generate a large set here without falling back on some sort of correspondence notion of truth along the way.

For these four reasons, the majority of philosophers, including a large majority of Christian philosophers, have rejected the coherence theory of truth, and have looked elsewhere for a less troubled theory.

POSTMODERNISM AND TRUTH

It is important to begin by pointing out that there is *no single distinctively postmodern view of truth*. It is not true that postmodern thinkers reject any and all meaningful understandings of truth. They are not relativists, in other words, when it comes to the idea of truth. Any basic reading of Foucault, Derrida, or Rorty makes it clear that they believe certain claims are true and others false. They do believe that Descartes's search for complete certainty in knowledge is a project doomed to fail. And they do believe that humans are unable to view the world/reality in a completely objective and impartial manner. But neither of these beliefs, even if true, requires us to give up the idea of truth. So the question arises: whose view of truth do we take to be broadly representative of postmodernism? We think a decent case can be made for choosing the views of Richard Rorty as the best representative of postmodernism. Rorty was very well known in his lifetime, fashionable in many circles, and a thinker of undeniable talent and charisma. Furthermore, his view of truth changed over time, something with which many postmoderns would be comfortable. So in what follows we will focus on two views of truth, what we call his early view and his later view.

Rorty's early view of truth. In 1979 Rorty penned *Philosophy and the Mirror of Nature*, a highly acclaimed and massively influential book. In the book Rorty presents the (now infamous in Christian circles) idea that truth is what our peers will let us get away with.[23] Many philosophers, Christian and otherwise, have not been overly impressed by Rorty's take here. They argue that it is not only false but also nonsense, even plain silly. Okay, so what exactly is wrong with Rorty's early view?

---

[23]See Richard Rorty, *Philosophy and the Mirror of Nature* (Princeton, NJ: Princeton University Press, 1981), 175-76.

As Alvin Plantinga makes abundantly clear, this view of truth has ludicrous consequences.[24] Whether or not it is true that God exists would *depend on* our peers permitting us to say this. In a similar vein, the tragedy of the Holocaust could be averted if a sufficient number of your peers cooperated by denying its existence. One could go on and on showing how many ridiculous (and embarrassing) consequences such a view of truth would allow. The essence of this criticism can be summarized as follows:

1. If Rorty's view of truth is correct, then ridiculous consequences are true.

2. But such ridiculous consequences are not true.

---

3. ∴ Rorty's view of truth is not correct.

Many reading this may think, "Rorty *has* to have a better idea of what truth is than the early view just mentioned." And they would be right. So we move on to Rorty's second attempt to get it right.

Rorty's later view of truth. In some of his later writings Rorty pursues the idea that what truth amounts to is nothing more than what justification aims at in the theory of knowledge.[25] Many traditional epistemologists (those philosophers who focus on the theory of knowledge) claim that knowledge aims at truth. In order to have knowledge we must have beliefs that are *both* justified and true, such that *knowledge = justified true belief.*

Laurence BonJour, a particularly distinguished epistemologist, notes that the aim of all knowledge is truth: we want our beliefs to correctly describe the world.[26] We have many beliefs we think are reasonable in that we have more evidence in favor of them than against them. This still leaves unsettled the deeper question, "Are such beliefs also true?" Rorty simply collapses the distinction between epistemology (what we think is reasonable or justified) and metaphysics (what is in fact true). A belief's being justified is one legitimate test for whether a belief is true; it is a *test* for truth. But a test for truth is *not* the same as the *definition* of truth. As Goldman, Richard

[24]Alvin Plantinga, *Warranted Christian Belief* (New York: Oxford University Press, 2000), 49.

[25]See Richard Rorty, *Truth and Progress: Philosophical Papers* (Cambridge: Cambridge University Press, 1998), especially the essay "Is Truth a Goal of Inquiry?" (19-42).

[26]Laurence BonJour, *Epistemology: Classic Problems and Contemporary Responses*, 2nd ed. (Lanham, MD: Rowman & Littlefield, 2009), 34.

Kirkham, and a cast of thousands have pointed out, truth does not reduce to justified belief. As we argued earlier, there are many beliefs that are reasonable yet false. Anyone who follows sports knows that team A may be better than team B, such that the claim

(T) Team A will beat team B

is reasonable to believe. The odds are 50 percent or better that team A will win. But reality is not always so accommodating. Low-probability events happen with remarkable frequency, showing us that what is reasonable and what is true are two very distinct concepts. So to fix this problem most philosophers think it important to claim both of the following to be true:

(T) Truth ≠ justified belief

and

(K) Knowledge = justified *true* belief*

So we conclude that Rorty's early view deserves to be rejected given that it yields ridiculous consequences, something no adequate theory does. And his later view is deeply flawed in that it collapses the distinction between truth and rational justification, two very distinct concepts. So neither Rorty's early view nor his later view is worthy of our acceptance.

We have now briefly examined the pragmatist theory of truth, the coherence theory of truth, and two versions advanced by Richard Rorty,[27] and found all of them seriously lacking. It remains to ask whether there is a more defensible view of truth yet to be examined. The answer is yes, and the view in question is what has traditionally been called the correspondence theory of truth.

THE CORRESPONDENCE THEORY OF TRUTH

As with the views of truth already examined, the correspondence theory is not a single view, but rather a family of views with enough similarities to be grouped under the same label. Aristotle, Bertrand Russell, Ludwig Wittgenstein, John Searle, William Alston, and Alvin Goldman have all offered some particular version of the correspondence theory as the most defensible theory of truth. The view advanced by Russell and Wittgenstein is sometimes

---

[27]And his highly cooperative peers.

labeled as *correspondence as congruence*, where there is a pretty much perfect fit between the claim (or proposition) being made and the "slice" of reality (a state of affairs or fact) that corresponds to it. The view advanced by Alston and Goldman is labeled *correspondence as correlation*, where it is asserted that there is some sort of accurate mapping occurring between the particular proposition and the particular state of affairs, though the exact nature of that mapping may be left unspecified. The view endorsed by Russell and Wittgenstein is more ambitious (and thus more difficult to defend), while the view endorsed by Alston and Goldman is more modest and thus easier to support. Given how limited human beings are, cognitively and otherwise, and the effects of sin on our ability to think well, we think the Alston-Goldman version of correspondence theory is the best way to go with regard to truth.

At its most basic level, truth involves a particular kind of relationship to reality.[28] So true (or truthful) claims can be understood as those that are faithful to reality, while false claims are those that lack such faithfulness. Similarly, a friend who is faithful is one who is true. Searle makes the point that, "typically when we act, think, or talk, we take for granted a certain way that our actions, thought, and talk relate to things outside us."[29]

Though many points could be made with respect to the correspondence theory, here we will limit ourselves to a list of eight remarks:[30]

1. The correspondence theory of truth is the common-sense or default mode. As Searle writes, "Why would anyone in his right mind wish to attack external realism?"[31] External realism is the belief that there is an external world that exists independently of our minds. This belief serves as a background or presupposition to the correspondence theory. The fact that it is the default position does not guarantee its truth, but it does place a burden of sorts on those who disagree with it. We generally need good reasons to think that common sense is mistaken on a particular matter, and this is no exception.

---

[28]This section is indebted to Goldman, *Knowledge in a Social World*, 41-68.

[29]John R. Searle, *Mind, Language and Society: Philosophy in the Real World* (New York: Basic Books, 1998), 12.

[30]For detailed accounts of correspondence theory, see William P. Alston, *A Realist Conception of Truth* (Ithaca, NY: Cornell University Press, 1997); Goldman, *Knowledge in a Social World*; John R. Searle, *Construction of Social Reality* (New York: Free Press, 1995); and Kirkham, *Theories of Truth*.

[31]Ibid., 14.

2. With the coherence theory in mind, it should be noted that the correspondence theory is a theory about the *nature/definition of truth*. It is not in any way a test (as coherence sometimes is) to see if a particular belief is true or not.

3. Adopting the correspondence theory does not require us to adopt a picture theory of how true sentences work. As Steven Cowan and James Spiegel argue, the statement

(G) George Washington was the first president of the United States

is true because it refers to or because it lines up or corresponds with what actually happened. It is not true in the same sense that a picture corresponds to whatever it is a picture of.[32] It is important to note here that we know full well what it means for a statement to correspond with reality, even though we may not be able to spell out all the details of what that correspondence involves.

4. We can think about truth here in one of two ways:

A. A proposition is true if and only if it is the case.

or

B. A proposition is true if and only if it *maps onto* or *fits* the state of affairs (the fact) to which it refers.

The main point here is that being the case (being true), mapping onto, and fitting are three different ways of expressing the same idea, namely, that of correspondence. To those who think that the idea of correspondence is somehow mysterious or vague, we reply that humans know very well what it means for a statement to fit or map onto a particular state of affairs. If someone says that snow is white, we simply look outside and check the newly fallen snow on the ground. If it is white, then the statement is true; if not, then it is false. Just as good maps accurately refer to what we might call geographical reality, so a true statement accurately refers to a fact or state of affairs outside itself.

5. For those who want a slightly more detailed version of what correspondence involves, Goldman develops the idea that *fittingness* is the basic idea of correspondence.[33] Just as some clothes fit us better than others (and it is

---

[32]Steven B. Cowan and James S. Spiegel, *The Love of Wisdom: A Christian Introduction to Philosophy* (Nashville: B&H Academic, 2009), 37-39.

[33]Goldman, *Knowledge in a Social World*, esp. 41-68.

a matter of degree here, not an all-or-nothing matter), so some statements better fit reality than others. Those with a good fit may be said to correspond and to be true, while those with a poor fit may be said to fail to correspond and thus be false.

6. Our brief examination of the pragmatist, coherence, and post-modern views of truth showed all three to be seriously defective. We therefore have no good reason to think any other version of truth is superior to the correspondence theory.[34]

7. The question occurs, as Searle rightly asks: Why would anyone reject the correspondence theory? Here Searle has some important insights that are well worth considering. He argues that the primary motivation for denying an objectively real external world is not because there are good arguments supporting such a position (he rightly notes how feeble such arguments are), but rather because of what might be called ethical concerns. It is worth quoting Searle at length here:

> The motivation for denying realism is a kind of will to power, and it manifests itself in a number of ways. . . . From this assumption, forms of postmodernism, deconstruction, and so on, are easily developed, having been completely turned loose from the tiresome moorings and constraints of having to confront the real world. If the real world is just an invention—a social construct designed to oppress marginalized elements of society—then let's get rid of the real world and construct the world we want. That, I think, is the real driving psychological force behind antirealism at the end of the twentieth century.[35]

There are at least two points worth making here: (1) if we don't like the world as it is, then we can simply choose to create/invent a different one more to our liking; (2) the common postmodern tendency toward antirealism (the denial that there is an external and mind-independent reality) is a form of sinful rebellion against an external reality that some simply do not want to answer to! If we are both atheists and antirealists[36] then there is not much, philosophically speaking, to which we need to answer. It may seem

---

[34]There are other views of truth, though we submit they are, if anything, *more* problematic than the three alternatives discussed above. See Kirkham, *Theories of Truth*, and Alston, *A Realist Conception of Truth* for sophisticated critiques of alternative theories of truth.

[35]Searle, *Mind*, 19-20.

[36]Let's be clear that many postmoderns do not embrace both atheism and antirealism.

"too awful that our representations [beliefs and the like] should have to be answerable to anything but us,"[37] but it is not something we have any control over. Why not just accept the fact of the reality of the external world as a given and move on from there?

8. There are a number of criticisms of the correspondence theory that have been offered, two prominent examples being the mystery objection and strange entity objection. We will deal with each in turn.

As for the mystery objection, some philosophers have complained that the central idea of the correspondence theory of truth, namely, that true claims somehow correspond with an external reality, is fundamentally mysterious. In other words, we don't know exactly what the idea of correspondence involves here. It is true that the idea of correspondence as congruence (perfect-fit views) championed by Russell and the early Wittgenstein spells out in detail what the correspondence relation is supposed to involve: a point-by-point perfect fit between a statement and a fact or state of affairs. And since it is widely agreed that this (as it was called) structural isomorphism model fails badly, perhaps those who doubt the correspondence theory believe that any version of the correspondence theory needs to be as ambitious in explaining the correspondence relation as Russell and Wittgenstein were. But this is a vain hope. We don't know much about correspondence above and beyond the simple fact that it involves correspondence. But we do know what it means for a statement to correspond with reality.

Consider the following propositions:

(D) The dog is on the mat.

(M) My computer monitor has a black frame.

(C) Columbus sailed west in 1492.

We know what a dog is, and we know what a mat is. So we know that if we look and the dog *is* on the mat, then the proposition *corresponds* with a slice of external reality and is thus true. And if it fails to match up or correspond with the facts of the matter, then it is false. How complicated is that? The answer is, not very. So understanding the basic idea of what correspondence involves is more than enough to ward off this particular objection.

---

[37]Searle, *Mind*, 17.

According to the strange entity objection, holding to a correspondence theory of truth commits us to believing in the existence of some fairly strange things. Remember that a true proposition (or statement) is one that corresponds with a state of affairs (or fact). But what exactly is a fact? For openers, facts are not physical objects. No one has ever tripped over a fact before. Rather, they are abstract entities—they are immaterial (nonphysical) entities. Is this a problem? It is far from clear why it would be. Most philosophers think that numbers exist, and they are certainly not physical objects. So if one class of nonphysical "things" can exist, then why can't another? Many philosophers who are committed to some form of naturalism (the idea that only the physical exists) reject the existence of most if not all abstract entities. But as Christians we have no good, let alone compelling, reasons to think naturalism is true. God exists, angels exist, the human soul exists, and so do numbers. So if it is true that we need to "add" facts or states of affairs to the existing list, then we are fine with that. Suppose we now consider the following claim:

(G) If the Chicago Cubs win the 2016 World Series, then I will be very happy.

This is a *conditional*, or "if . . . then" sort of claim. What exactly makes this proposition is true? Well, the fact (or state of affairs) that *if* the Cubs win, *then* I will be happy. If we believe propositions that make straightforward claims such as

(C) The cat is in the garden

are true because they refer to some abstract fact or state of affairs, then why can't we also acknowledge that some facts or states of affairs that are conditional (or "if . . . then") in nature are true? As Kirkham asserts, "It is not at all clear why there cannot be facts of these sorts."[38] Philosophical naturalists may object to the existence of such entities, but we have already seen we have no good reason to buy into naturalism.

So we can now see that there are good reasons for accepting some version of the correspondence theory as true. It captures the common-sense idea of truth, we know what the basic idea of correspondence involves, and there are no serious objections to adopting it. Finally, it escapes the sort of serious problems that undermine all of the major alternatives we examined.

---

[38]Richard Kirkham, *Theories of Truth: A Critical Introduction* (Cambridge, MA: MIT Press, 1995), 139.

SUMMARY

1. The idea of truth is of crucial importance for traditional Christianity. Christians are committed to many substantive truth claims.

2. Common sense supports the idea that there is such a thing as truth.

3. One leading theory of the nature of truth is the pragmatic view.

   A. William James argued that true propositions are ones useful to the believer.

      i. He is correct that most true propositions are useful.

      ii. But his view has four problems:

         a. Some true beliefs are not useful, while some false beliefs are useful.

         b. What is useful clearly varies from person to person, but it makes little sense to argue that truth varies from person to person.

         c. James's view thus tends toward relativism with respect to truth.

         d. James's view tends toward one important feature of truth and absolutizes it.

   B. Charles Peirce sees truth as the belief fated to be agreed to by all who properly investigate it.

      i. He is correct that this would be generally true.

      ii. But Peirce's view also has troubles.

         a. There is no guarantee that investigators will ever arrive at the truth. And why should we think the end of investigation will ever come?

         b. It is not uncommon for careful investigators to arrive at two or more accepted (and competing) conclusions.

         c. Peirce's view is better seen as focusing on what it means for a belief to be justified (or rational), rather than what is true.

         d. As Putnam argues, truth is sometimes recognition transcendent. This means that its truth in no way depends on any investigating community or the like.

4. A second leading theory is the coherence theory of truth.

A. On this view a proposition is true if and only if it coheres with the entire (or maximal) set of beliefs held by an individual.

B. Coherence involves both logical consistency and some sort of inferential relationship between true beliefs.

C. Coherence theory has (at least) four significant challenges:

  i. Given that our maximal set of beliefs will include false beliefs, some new beliefs that cohere or mesh will also be false. So coherence hardly guarantees truth.

  ii. Coherence as a theory of truth makes the external world irrelevant. Blackburn points out that many of our true beliefs don't require any sort of mesh or fit with other beliefs to be considered true.

  iii. Coherence theory allows for contradictory beliefs to be true. And since two contradictory beliefs cannot both be true, something is wrong with a theory of truth that allows for this possibility.

  iv. The preexisting set of beliefs we need to test any new belief to see if it is true is beyond the capacity of any ordinary human being. Alston argues that all humans lack such a set and have no realistic prospects for acquiring such a set in the foreseeable future.

5. Two views of truth emerge from the work of Richard Rorty, and can be accurately labeled as postmodern.

  A. Rorty's early view advanced the idea that truth is what your peers will let you get away with. Plantinga shows that this view has consequences that are plainly silly and/or morally objectionable. The idea that our peers could eliminate the truth (actuality) of the Holocaust is repugnant.

  B. Rorty's later view proposed that truth is roughly equivalent to what might be called justified belief. Yet many justified beliefs are false, and many unjustified beliefs are true. These two considerations clearly demonstrate that Rorty's later view also deserves to be rejected. So neither of Rorty's two candidates is worthy of acceptance.

6. The final theory we examined is the correspondence theory of truth. The following is worth noting here:

   A. Common sense supports the correspondence theory. This does not establish it as true, but it does place the burden of argument on those who disagree.

   B. This is a theory about the nature of truth, and should not be viewed as a test for truth.

   C. Adopting the correspondence theory does not require that we endorse a picture theory of truth, one readily acknowledged to have many issues.

      i. The version adopted by Russell and the early Wittgenstein, correspondence as congruence, is generally seen to be problematic.

      ii. But the more modest correspondence as correlation view of Alston, Searle, Goldman, and others avoids such problems.

   D. We know what it means for a proposition to correspond with reality.

   E. Alvin Goldman develops the idea of correspondence as "fittingness," which makes the idea of correspondence less mysterious and more substantial. And we have a pretty good idea what it means for something to fit.

   F. The four alternatives to the correspondence theory that we examined were all seen to be seriously flawed.

   G. John Searle argued that many simply do not want to have to answer to the idea of a fixed and unyielding (to human effort) reality, and that some versions of postmodernism on offer advocate the ability to construct and/or modify reality.

   H. Neither the mystery objection nor the strange entity objection seriously challenged the reasonability of correspondence theory.

7. We concluded by noting that the four leading alternatives to the correspondence theory are significantly flawed, while the correspondence theory withstood the major challenges raised against it.

SUGGESTED READINGS

Alston, William. *A Realist Conception of Truth*. Ithaca, NY: Cornell University Press, 1997. This is a brilliant book on a difficult topic. Significant background knowledge is helpful here.

Blanshard, Brand. *The Nature of Thought*. 2 vols. London: Allen and Unwin, 1939. An elegant introduction to the coherence theory of truth.

Goldman, Alvin I. *Knowledge in a Social World*. Oxford: Clarendon, 1999. A brilliant book by a leading contemporary philosopher.

Groothuis, Douglas. *Christian Apologetics: A Comprehensive Case for Biblical Faith*. Downers Grove, IL: IVP Academic, 2011. A long book, but generally accessible to undergraduate students.

James, William. *Pragmatism*. Repr. New York: Dover, 1995. A classic take on pragmatism by one of its founders.

Kelly, Stewart E. *Truth Considered and Applied: Examining Postmodernism, History, and the Christian Faith*. Nashville: B&H Academic, 2011. Contains an extended section on the various theories of truth.

Kirkham, Richard. *Theories of Truth: A Critical Introduction*. Cambridge, MA: MIT Press, 1995. A thorough and well-argued book, though dense at times.

Moreland, J. P., and William Lane Craig. *Philosophical Foundations for a Christian Worldview*. Downers Grove, IL: InterVarsity Press, 2003.

Rorty, Richard. *Philosophy and the Mirror of Nature*. Princeton, NJ: Princeton University Press, 1979. A famous book by a leading postmodern thinker.

Saatkamp, Herman, Jr. *Rorty and Pragmatism: The Philosopher Responds to His Critics*. Nashville: Vanderbilt University Press, 1995. A good introduction to Rorty's version of pragmatism.

Searle, John R. *The Construction of Social Reality*. New York: Free Press, 1995. A readable book on truth and the nature of reality.

———. *Mind. Language, and Society: Philosophy in the Real World*. New York: Basic Books, 1999. A book that complements much of what Searle has to say in the other book cited here.

12

POSTMODERNISM AND THE
CRITIQUE OF ENLIGHTENMENT
RATIONALISM

The universal Disposition of this Age is
bent upon a rational religion.

THOMAS SPRAT, *THE HISTORY OF THE*
ROYAL SOCIETY OF LONDON

INTRODUCTION

The search for knowledge has been a primary goal of philosophers since the ancient Greeks. Socrates, Plato, and Aristotle all sought to determine whether genuine knowledge was possible, and if so, how we acquired it. These Greek thinkers had to contend both with some rather serious skeptics, who doubted that any knowledge was attainable, and the sophist Protagoras, who made both truth and knowledge relative to the culture one lived in. Two modern rivals to the pursuit of knowledge are the skeptics, who claim that all knowledge claims are unjustified, and the classical foundationalists, led by Descartes and Locke. In this chapter we will examine both of these views, and then seek to determine whether there is a via media, a middle way, to be steered between the two.

DESCARTES AND THE SEARCH FOR CERTAIN FOUNDATIONS

René Descartes (1596–1650) is widely considered to be the founder of modern philosophy in the West. His thought marked an important break with the past and helped set the course for the direction of thought for hundreds of years to come. Descartes was troubled by the challenge of skepticism and sought to find a method that would secure certain knowledge and avoid the various pitfalls seen to be associated with skepticism.

In the 1500s there were a number of challenges to traditional thought and to traditional ways of thinking. In the 1560s a number of works written by Sextus Empiricus (AD 160–210) were published. Sextus labels his view Pyrrhonism, in honor of an earlier Greek skeptic named Pyrrho. Pyrrhonists are full-fledged skeptics, and have significant doubts concerning how much humans truly know, whether there are good reasons for belief, and whether there are any genuinely reliable sources for knowledge (such as the senses, reason, and memory). Furthermore, the eloquent French thinker Michel de Montaigne (1533–1592) developed some of the Pyrrhonist lines of thought in a book titled *Apology for Raymond Sebond*. Montaigne, himself a Catholic, expresses grave doubts about the human ability to acquire genuine and certain knowledge, and casts doubt on a variety of methods often thought to yield knowledge

So by the time Descartes came on the scene in the early 1600s, there were a number of major factors that had challenged traditional ideas and traditional ways of thinking. The Protestant Reformation, beginning with Martin Luther in 1517, challenged the Catholic Church's authority and questioned whether they properly understood the Scriptures. Montaigne and the revival of Pyrrhonist skepticism challenged traditional approaches to the acquisition of knowledge. And finally, work in astronomy by Copernicus (1473–1543) and Galileo (1564–1642) demonstrated that the earth was not, as the church had long taught, the center of the universe. Intellectually speaking, there was thus a degree of uncertainty, even chaos, that European culture had not known for centuries. Descartes's ambitious goal was to provide a new (and improved) theory of the universe, specify humanity's place in it, and to describe how humans might adequately respond to Pyrrhonism. He also wanted to show that human knowledge is possible and that certain knowledge can be attained.

Descartes wondered at length how to best respond to the Pyrrhonists. He came up with the idea of trying to beat the Pyrrhonists at their own game— what would happen if we doubted everything? We would either end up showing the Pyrrhonists to be correct, or, as Descartes hoped, we would see that humans cannot truly doubt everything. Why not? Because some things are simply indubitable; it's not possible for human beings to doubt them. So Descartes had a goal, he developed a method, and he set out to show that the marriage of the goal with the proper method will yield fruitful results.

Descartes's goal is *certainty*.[1] Just as Galileo and Copernicus strove for absolute certainty in astronomy, and just as mathematicians did with the new geometry, Descartes thought this the only goal worthy both of a genuine philosophy and an adequate response to the skeptics of his day. Descartes's method is often called the method of doubt. He claims that if we doubt everything we think we know, in the end we will be left with at least one belief that is impossible to doubt—an absolutely certain, indubitable belief. He even entertains the possibility there is an evil demon[2] who consistently deceives us. But, as Descartes eventually realized, can a demon deceive us if we don't exist? In other words, are any nonexisting beings deceived? A strange question, but the answer is no. In order to be deceived, one has to exist. So if I am being deceived, then I exist. More generally, Descartes concludes, *Cogito ergo sum*—"I think, therefore I am." It is impossible to doubt our own existence. Descartes goes on to seek to establish the existence of God, because he needs God to guarantee the general reliability of our ways of acquiring knowledge. So Descartes now thinks he has provided a certain foundation for pursuing human knowledge. We know that we exist, that God exists, and that if we only accept ideas that are clear and distinct[3] we can build a system of knowledge based on these foundational beliefs. Descartes is very confident that humans can attain certain beliefs, that they can rise above the influence of culture and other external factors on our beliefs, and that they can build an edifice (building) of knowledge based on these certain beliefs. Later thinkers would have significant doubts about Descartes's goal, his general confidence in human reason, and his reliance on God to safeguard human knowledge.

---

[1]The following overview of Descartes's theory of knowledge is massively simplified, omitting many specific details that Descartes presents at great length. *Certainty* here is used in its mathematical sense. A certain belief is one where there is absolutely no possibility, however remote, of being mistaken. A belief that was 99.9999 percent probable would not qualify here.

[2]He is not claiming there is such a demon, only that it is not so easy to disprove the existence of such a being. Furthermore, your lack of evidence for there being such a being is entirely consistent with there *actually being* such a being! After all, a well-trained being would deceive us without our knowing it, rather than taking out an ad in the local paper announcing who the demon would try to deceive on a given day.

[3]Descartes claimed that ideas that were *clear and distinct* were true, while ideas lacking such clarity and distinctness were to be rejected.

Rather than beginning with the church, as the Catholic Church advised, or with Scripture, as Luther, Zwingli, and Calvin all promoted, Descartes set human reason as the final arbiter (decision maker) for what is true and reasonable and good. It is this autonomous human reason at the center of his approach that makes Descartes distinctively *modern*. Descartes himself saw reason as supporting Christianity, but many prominent later thinkers would agree with Descartes that whether God existed was an important question, but they would have serious doubts about whether such a being truly did exist.[4] Descartes opens the door to the possibility that carefully applied human reason *may reject* God's existence, or at least seek to make it more palatable to the modern mind. John Locke and Immanuel Kant sought to hold on to God's existence, all the while radically modifying traditional Christianity, making it more about being good than having our sins atoned for by the second person of the Trinity come to earth in human form, namely, Jesus Christ. By the end of the 1700s, 150 years after Descartes's death, intellectuals professing belief in the Trinity were much harder to find than they were in Descartes's day. And some thinkers, such as the Scottish skeptic David Hume, had no problem doing away with virtually all forms of traditional religious belief.

DOUBTS ABOUT DESCARTES AND LOCKE

Descartes and Locke are two major figures in the history of Western philosophy. The question for modern Christians is twofold: What should we think about Descartes's view of knowledge, and what should we think of Locke's idea that divine revelation should answer to human reason? Many modern-day epistemologists are committed to the idea of *foundationalism*— the idea that our beliefs can be divided into basic (or foundational) beliefs and nonbasic beliefs (those that are believed in virtue of their being supported by basic beliefs). Descartes's particular version is widely known as classical foundationalism, which is committed to all of the following:

1. There are basic beliefs that are justified (we have self-evident reasons to believe them).

2. Our other (nonbasic) beliefs are justified by being properly supported or grounded in these basic beliefs.

---

[4]This, of course, is hardly Descartes's fault.

3. Our basic beliefs are *indubitable*, that is, they are impossible to doubt.

Most philosophers specializing in epistemology have had massive reservations about classical foundationalism, including philosophers who are broadly sympathetic to some version of foundationalism.[5] Three of the main problems peculiar to classical foundationalism follow.

First, though classical foundationalism seems initially attractive to many, it "doesn't survive close examination; it is subject to powerful, indeed, fatal objections."[6] Its biggest problem is, to use some fancy terminology, that it is self-referentially incoherent. What exactly does that mean? It essentially means it is self-contradictory, as it violates its own standards. Consider the following two examples:

(A) I don't speak a word of English.

(B) There is no such thing as truth.

Neither one of these statements can be true. If you don't speak a word of English, then you can't speak the words in (A). And if there is no such thing as truth, then (B) is false, in which case it is true there is no truth! This, of course, is nonsense. So how exactly is classical foundationalism self-contradictory? It is because it lays down a standard that it does not (and cannot) meet.[7] The standard is something like

(S) We should only believe what is self-evident or clearly certain.[8]

Well, for starters, what should we think about (S)? Is it self-evident? The short answer is no. Self-evident claims are ones such that by understanding them we also understand they must be true. For example,

(T) $2 + 1 = 3$

(U) If all humans are mortal and Socrates is a human, then Socrates is mortal.

If we understand all the terms in (T) and (U), then we know the claims must be true. So is this the case with (S)? Is it self-evident in the same way as (T) and (U) are? The answer is clearly no. As Alvin Plantinga writes, "I

---

[5]Five prominent examples of modern foundationalists are Roderick Chisholm, Richard Foley, Alvin Goldman, Michael DePaul, and Alvin Plantinga.
[6]Alvin Plantinga, *Warranted Christian Belief* (New York: Oxford University Press, 2000), 93.
[7]We are following Plantinga's take on classical foundationalism fairly closely here.
[8]A simplified version of what the classical foundationalist standard is.

understand it, and I don't see that it is true, and I'll bet the same goes for you."[9] This means that (S) itself is not self-evident. So (S) violates the very standard it lays down by not being self-evident. It is a self-contradictory belief. So contrary to Descartes and his fellow classical foundationalists, his own standard fails to be certain or indubitable.

Second, we have many beliefs. Many of these beliefs are very ordinary and also seem clearly true. Two examples of such beliefs are as follows:

(A) I ate breakfast this morning.

(B) I ate lunch with my friend Jay today.

Both (A) and (B) clearly seem true; I have good evidence in support of them and no decent reason to doubt either. But remember that for Descartes beliefs must either be self-evident (the basic beliefs) or properly based on the self-evident. But both (A) and (B) are *neither* self-evident (there is no contradiction in claiming they are false) *nor* based on other basic beliefs.[10] This means that (A) and (B), and thousands of similar beliefs, are not reasonable for us to believe![11] This strongly suggests that something is seriously wrong—not with us and our beliefs, but with the classical foundationalist approach to knowledge.

If we have to choose between supporting all these ordinary beliefs and classical foundationalism, the ordinary beliefs win every time. So much the worse for classical foundationalism. On Descartes's view we need a number of certain foundational beliefs to build our edifice of knowledge. The pressing problem is that certain beliefs are very hard to come by. Richard Foley writes that "at best only a very few beliefs, or at least only a very few contingent beliefs, are infallible."[12] As such the Cartesian demands "are too limiting," as we simply can't find many candidates that meet the standard of absolute certainty. Paul Moser notes, with a bit of exaggeration, that "radical [classical] foundationalism, then, attracts hardly any contemporary philosophers."[13]

---

[9]Ibid., 294.
[10]We certainly cannot justify (A) and (B) solely on the basic of "I think, therefore I am."
[11]The line of argument here is indebted to Plantinga.
[12]Richard Foley, *Working Without a Net: A Study of Egocentric Epistemology* (New York: Oxford University Press, 1993), 190.
[13]Paul K. Moser, Dwayne H. Mulder, and J. D. Trout, *The Theory of Knowledge: A Thematic Introduction* (New York: Oxford University Press, 1998), 87.

Third, Descartes's foundationalism requires that humans can be infallible about their own mental states (beliefs formed in their own mind). But it is doubtful that humans can have foolproof mental beliefs. Consider the following example, taken from the philosopher Richard Feldman:

> You are walking toward a counter that has an electric frying pan on it. You have just been told to be careful of the pan because it is very hot. As you approach the counter, you trip and put your hand out to stop your fall. Your hand unfortunately comes down right on the pan. You immediately pull it away, thinking: I am now having a sensation of extreme heat. In fact, as you soon realize, the pan is actually not on. You did not feel the heat at all.[14]

If all of the above is correct, then, as Feldman notes, we are not infallible about our own mental states (what is going on in our own minds). But Descartes and classical foundationalism require that we possess this sort of mental certainty.

Thus for the three reasons described above, the majority of contemporary philosophers think classical foundationalism is both false and pretty much hopeless. There are no good reasons to think such a view can be revived and shown to be reasonable.[15] Virtually all postmodern thinkers also agree that classical foundationalism should be rejected.[16] The question for postmoderns is: What view of knowledge and reason should we adopt, given the failure of classical foundationalism?

RADICAL POSTMODERNISM AND HUMAN REASON

It would be true to say that Descartes and Locke (and the Enlightenment in general) had great confidence in human reason and the human ability to know. By contrast, most postmodern thinkers have no such confidence. In fact, many believe that human reason has little if any ability to rise above the various influences of our environment.

---

[14]Richard Feldman, *Epistemology* (Upper Saddle River, NJ: Prentice-Hall, 2003), 55.

[15]A notable exception here is the Christian philosopher Timothy McGrew, who capably defends a version of classical foundationalism. See Timothy McGrew, *The Foundations of Knowledge* (Lanham, MD: Rowman & Littlefield, 1995).

[16]For three prominent examples, see Stanley J. Grenz, *A Primer on Postmodernism* (Grand Rapids: Eerdmans, 1996); John R. Franke, *The Character of Theology: An Introduction to Its Nature, Task, and Purpose* (Grand Rapids: Baker Academic, 2005); and Nancey Murphy, *Beyond Liberalism and Fundamentalism: How Modern and Postmodern Philosophy Set the Theological Agenda* (Valley Forge, PA: Trinity Press International, 2007).

Many postmodern thinkers, both secular and Christian, view the Enlightenment hope for establishing knowledge on certain foundations as an utter failure. In the modern-day philosophical world there is not a huge number of card-carrying classical foundationalists. This much postmodern thinkers are clearly right about. But many postmoderns, such as Richard Rorty (1931–2007) and the evangelicals John Franke and Stanley Grenz go beyond this point. Rorty claims that for foundationalism to be a viable view, it needs to be true that the human mind is capable of mirroring what we find in nature. That is, the mind must be capable of taking a "picture" (of some sort) of the external world, and that we can look in this mirror to see what the external world is really like. The problem, Rorty famously argues, is that the human mind is capable of nothing of the sort. Further, Rorty thinks all humans are radically situated,[17] meaning we are unable to rise about the many external influences that mold, shape, and direct our thought. As such our knowledge merely represents a convenient summary of all these various influences. There is no point of view available to humans which enables us to gather genuine knowledge about the world around us. Rorty should not be understood as denying the existence of the external world (a radical claim), but merely arguing that we humans lack the ability to know it with any degree of objectivity. Rorty's radical situatedness thus rules out genuine knowledge, and we are left with some form of skepticism.[18] Very few postmoderns entirely reject any semblance of truth, but they do reject Descartes and his fellow classical foundationalists' attempt to acquire knowledge that is certain, objective, and universal.

Franke, a well-known evangelical theologian, has written widely on postmodernism and on foundationalism. As a postmodern evangelical, Franke argues that we now live in a postmodern world and that we need to reject the "quest for certain, objective, and universal knowledge."[19] Franke claims that "the expression of Christianity and Christian teachings have taken shape and been revised and reformed in the context of numerous cultural and historical circumstances."[20] Given that we once again live in a new

---

[17]See chap. 4 for a detailed examination of situatedness.

[18]Rorty makes many valiant attempts to restore some degree of objective knowledge about the world, though it is far from clear whether he succeeds.

[19]John Franke, *The Character of Theology: An Introduction to Its Nature, Task, and Purpose* (Grand Rapids: Baker Academic, 2005), 15.

[20]Ibid., 17.

context/set of circumstances, we need to "come to terms with the challenge of doing theology in a postmodern context."[21] Besides rejecting Descartes's classical foundationalism, we also need to reject the underlying view of human reason that Descartes and others promoted. First and foremost we need "to rethink the nature of rationality."[22] Rather than promoting a confident and objective approach to reason, we need to move toward an understanding of rationality that is "chastened, situated, and contextual."[23] We need to give up the idea traditionally known as realism, that the world exists independently of our attempts to think about it. The world simply isn't "out there" in the way we once thought it was. Rather than seeing language as accurately expressing (or mirroring) the external world, we need to see language as helping us to construct or create reality. Foundationalism, Franke assures us, "is in dramatic retreat . . . [and its] assertions have come under withering critique."[24] Franke and Grenz see traditional Christian theology as mistakenly supporting the idea that there are universal truths that apply to all people in all cultures. This is the idea of a worldview, a grand story, or a *metanarrative*, where a metanarrative is a story about reality that claims to objectively ("truthfully") tell us who God is, who we are, what our place is in the world, how we can know, and how we should live.[25] Grenz and Franke suggest that all theology is "local" or "specific."[26] So it is "true" given the specific local culture/context in which it arises. To say more than that, it is implied, is to go beyond what humans are capable of knowing. There are no stories (or worldviews) that are true for everybody everywhere.

The question arises, what should we think of Rorty and Franke, the rejection of all forms of foundationalism, and the idea that the best we can offer with respect to the "truth" of Christianity is that it is "true" in some specific, local contexts. We have significant doubts that Rorty and Franke and their views are compatible with biblical Christianity. Four criticisms are offered here.

---

[21]Ibid.

[22]Ibid., 22.

[23]Ibid.

[24]Stanley J. Grenz and John R. Franke, *Beyond Foundationalism: Shaping Theology in a Postmodern Context* (Louisville, KY: Westminster John Knox, 2001), 24.

[25]For helpful books on worldview, see Ronald H. Nash, *Faith and Reason: Searching for a Rational Faith* (Grand Rapids: Zondervan, 1994), and James W. Sire, *The Universe Next Door*, 5th ed. (Downers Grove, IL: IVP Academic, 2009).

[26]Grenz and Franke, *Beyond Foundationalism*, 25.

First, Franke is certainly correct that all theology arises in a context and that Christians over the centuries have struggled to make the gospel relevant to the particular culture in which they lived. So far so good. The prognosis turns bleak after that. Cultural contexts are *not* neutral (with respect to the Christian faith) outside sources that Christians need to align themselves with. Thoughtful Christians ranging from Augustine to G. K. Chesterton to C. S. Lewis to J. I. Packer and D. A. Carson have always seen culture as a mixture of the good, the bad, and the ugly. The philosopher Paul Helm notes that some cultures are "hellish."[27] The Scriptures, the very Word of God, are meant to be our measuring stick for evaluating the culture we live in. To have the Scriptures answer to culture is to worship culture and to turn our backs on many of the central truths of Scripture. The Scriptures tell us that God exists, that we are sinful, that we need a Savior, and that God has sent one through his Son, Jesus Christ. Modern American culture is, for the most part, hostile to all four of these claims. What are we to say? That we need to accommodate the Scriptures to culture? May it never be! Evangelicals interested in such matters would do well to read D. A. Carson's book *Christ and Culture Revisited*, which seeks to carefully and biblically evaluate the culture(s) in which we live.

Second, Franke (and Rorty) write as if classical foundationalism is the only game in town, that it is the only version of foundationalism out there. This is woefully inadequate, and a bit embarrassing! For years[28] there has been a more modest (and sensible) view of foundationalism known as modest foundationalism. This is a view of knowledge held by many prominent philosophers, both Christian and otherwise. It's as if some American music critic, writing in 1965, heard the music of Gerry and the Pacemakers (who did have a few hits), decided he didn't like their music, and concluded, "There is no good music to be found out of Liverpool." Anyone knowing a little about the history of rock 'n' roll also knows there was another group

---

[27] Paul Helm, review of *The Character of Theology*, by John Franke, *Reformation21*, (blog), October 2005, www.reformation21.org/shelf-life/the-character-of-theology.php.

[28] Modest foundationalism has been a popular (if not dominant) view in epistemology since the mid-1970s and the pioneering work of William Alston, Mark Pastin, Alvin Goldman, and others. See, for example, Goldman, *Knowledge in a Social World*; Roderick Chisholm, *Theory of Knowledge*, 2nd ed. (Englewood Cliffs, NJ: Prentice Hall, 1977); Richard Foley, *The Theory of Epistemic Rationality* (Cambridge, MA: Harvard University Press, 1987); R. Douglas Geivett, "Is God a Story? Postmodernity and the Task of Theology," in *Christianity and the Postmodern Turn*, ed. Myron B. Penner (Grand Rapids: Brazos, 2005), 37-52; and Plantinga, *Warranted Christian Belief*.

from Liverpool who needs to be considered, namely, the Beatles. Only a very uninformed music critic would make such a claim. And only a very uninformed philosopher (or theologian) would make such a claim about foundationalism being dead in the water. Modest foundationalists such as Alvin Goldman, Roderick Chisholm, Richard Foley, Doug Geivett, and Alvin Plantinga[29] all claim that there are some beliefs which serve as a secure foundation for other beliefs. These foundational beliefs can be called basic beliefs, foundational beliefs.

Goldman, in his critique of Rorty, writes that "Rorty's critique . . . simply ignores most theories now under serious consideration. He pays almost exclusive attention to a single historical theory [classical foundationalism] that once enjoyed popularity but was long since exploded, as *everybody* in the field knows. All the currently respected theories, on the other hand, are treated as if they did not exist."[30] Franke and others considering moving away from foundationalism altogether need to, at the least, give us a detailed argument in favor of such a move. As far as we know, that still remains to be done. As knowers we are affected by our context/situation, but that does nothing to rule out the possibility of genuine, objective knowledge.[31]

Third, if the human predicament described in the Scriptures is truthful, then humans are in a very bad way indeed. We are portrayed as sinful, capable of limited knowledge, self-destructive, unable to turn to God on our own, and desperately in need of being reconciled to the one true Creator God. Given all these truths, the gospel (the good news that God sent his Son

---

[29]Plantinga is a vocal critic of classical foundationalism, but this does not mean that he rejects all versions of foundationalism (in the broad sense of the word). Grenz and Franke misunderstand him on this point; see *Beyond Foundationalism*, 230-31. Moser, Fumerton, DePaul, and most modern epistemologists correctly understand him as committed to a form of foundationalism, just not the classical version. See Paul K. Moser and Arnold vander Nat, *Human Knowledge: Classical and Contemporary Approaches*, 3rd ed. (New York: Oxford University Press, 2002); Richard Fumerton, *Epistemology* (Malden, MA: Wiley-Blackwell, 2006); and Michael DePaul, *Resurrecting Old-Fashioned Foundationalism* (New York: Rowman & Littlefield, 2000).

[30]Alvin Goldman, *Knowledge in a Social World* (New York: Oxford University Press, 1999), 27 (emphasis added). Franke fails to inform us who has generated the "withering critique" of foundationalism. Michael DePaul's book *Resurrecting Old Fashioned Foundationalism* (Lanham, MD: Rowman & Littlefield), makes very clear that modest foundationalism is both alive and well. Currently respected theories would include modest foundationalism, reliabilism, coherentism, and various forms of pragmatism.

[31]See James K. Beilby, *Thinking About Christian Apologetics: What It Is and Why We Do It* (Downers Grove, IL: IVP Academic, 2011), 127. See Goldman, *Knowledge in a Social World*, for more on situatedness and knowledge.

that we might be saved) is good news indeed. It is incredibly good news! But if Franke and others are correct, then the good news *is just one local story* competing with other local stories (some of which might reject the gospel, while others might affirm it). Local stories, their value, and their "truthfulness" are all tied to a specific context in a specific culture. It is seen as arrogant to claim that one's local story is somehow true for anyone and everywhere, and that people outside of one's culture are somehow wrong or guilty if they do not accept the particular local story. As Helm notes, when Franke makes everything local he "surrenders the gospel. In dismissing foundationalism he seems (I put the point gently) to be the advocate of relativism, if not skepticism. . . . How can a world in love with cultural relativism . . . be challenged by a relativistic presentation of the Christian gospel?"[32] Genuine hope is always grounded in reality, and a hope that is merely one local story among many is really not much of a hope at all.

Fourth, one can agree with Franke and Grenz that classical foundationalism is worthy of rejection, that humans are very much situated knowers, that our knowledge is always from a particular perspective, and that our knowledge is partial. All of these truths are compatible with seeing traditional Christianity as objectively true and with affirming the possibility of genuine knowledge. The precise nature of truth is a complicated matter, but we still think there are good reasons to affirm the truth of the following claims:

1. God is the Creator of the universe.

2. God exists in three persons (and one substance).

3. Jesus Christ is both the second person of the Trinity and God incarnate.

4. Jesus' death on the cross was a substitutionary atonement for the sins of all who come to faith in him.

5. The Scriptures are the inspired and inerrant Word of God, written by humans under the guidance of the Holy Spirit, who superintended what they wrote.

All five of these claims are true in that they properly correspond (or map onto) reality. And when Jesus says, "I am the way and the truth and the life" (Jn 14:6), he is claiming much more than that one particular local story is

---

[32]Helm, review of *Character of Theology*.

true.[33] Whether God exists is not a matter for local cultures and local stories to decide. As the eternal Creator of the universe, the Creator of humanity, and the Father of our Lord Jesus Christ, the existence of this glorious God is the central truth of the Scriptures and the Christian tradition, and is supported by the testimony of the Holy Spirit in the hearts of all believers.

We have argued that classical foundationalism fully deserves to be rejected, and that the postmodern alternative of rejecting foundationalism altogether doesn't fare any better. We now need to ask the question of whether the third option,[34] modest foundationalism, is superior to the other two. And, thankfully, the answer is a resounding yes.

A MIDDLE ROAD: MODEST FOUNDATIONALISM

Fortunately for us, classical foundationalism and postmodern alternatives that reject foundationalism are not the only games in town. There is another possibility, one richly deserving of our attention and one we think can hold up to careful scrutiny. That other possibility is the view known as modest foundationalism, a view with a long history and an impressive range of scholars who defend the view today.

Let's begin by stating that the view we are defending is not unique, unusual, or merely a byproduct of recent philosophical thought.[35] The dominant tradition in the history of epistemology claims that "it is the quality of the reasons for our beliefs that converts true beliefs into knowledge. . . . By far, the most commonly held view is foundationalism."[36] As Jim Pryor, a leading epistemologist, claims, "Nowadays, most philosophers who are attracted to foundationalism advocate a more modest version of the view."[37] The quote above from Goldman makes clear that Rorty's attack on foundationalism applies only to the Cartesian or classical version, and that most

---

[33]If his story is merely local, then it simply does not apply to us, and we are still dead in our sins. How can a first-century carpenter in Palestine be relevant for twenty-first-century Americans from North Carolina and New Jersey if his story is merely local? We submit it cannot.

[34]We are not claiming that there are three and only three options. We are claiming that in recent years these are three of the most popular options, and that the third option is superior both to the other two and to any other view not discussed here.

[35]*None* of these qualities, even if true, would automatically disqualify any view.

[36]Peter Klein, "Epistemology," in *Routledge Encyclopedia of Philosophy*, ed. E. Craig (London: Routledge, 2014), www.rep.routledge.com/articles/overview/epistemology/v-2/sections/the-normative-answers-foundationalism-and-coherentism.

[37]Jim Pryor, "Foundationalism and Coherentism," personal website, September 8, 2009, www.jimpryor.net/teaching/courses/epist/notes/foundationalism.html.

epistemologists today do not hold to the classical version. Thus Rorty and (too many) advocates of postmodernism are attacking a straw man—a distorted and inaccurate caricature of the most popular (and defensible) version of foundationalism. Michael DePaul, another leading epistemologist, claims that "[modest] foundationalism is alive and well; indeed, at least within Anglo-American analytic philosophy, I think it is safe to say that it remains the dominant position."[38] Finally, Doug Geivett, a leading evangelical epistemologist, notes that "routine caricatures of foundationalism inexplicably associate foundationalism as such with a commitment to absolutely certain foundations."[39] So Peter Klein, Goldman, Pryor, DePaul, and Geivett all make clear the following:

1. There is more than one version of foundationalism.

2. Everyone and their uncle (and their aunt too) reject classical foundationalism.[40]

3. Modest foundationalism has many capable defenders.

4. As argued above, most postmoderns who reject foundationalism aim their arguments at the dead and defeated classical version, and their arguments do not even touch, let alone undermine, the more modest version

5. Since the mid 1970s modest foundationalism has moved to the forefront in views about the justification of knowledge, led by the work of William Alston, Goldman, Chisholm, Foley, Plantinga,[41] Richard Fumerton, and others. It is also noteworthy that one of the leading (and most eloquent) critics of modest foundationalism over the past thirty years, Laurence BonJour, has moved away from his earlier view (known as coherentism) to embrace a version of modest foundationalism. Thus the view casually dismissed by Franke, Rorty, and others is in fact the leading contender today for how to best understand human knowledge.

---

[38]Michael DePaul, preface to *Resurrecting Old-Fashioned Foundationalism*, ed. Michael DePaul (Lanham, MD: Rowman & Littlefield, 2001), vii. Anglo-American analytic philosophy is the dominant approach to philosophy in North America and Britain, both among Christian and non-Christian philosophers.

[39]R. Douglas Geivett, "Is God a Story? Postmodernity and the Task of Theology," in *Christianity and the Postmodern Turn*, ed. Myron B. Penner (Grand Rapids: Brazos, 2005), 48.

[40]There are a few notable exceptions, but very few.

[41]Whom DePaul labels a "newfangled foundationalist." DePaul, preface, xii.

In the few remaining pages of this chapter, we will briefly sketch the view of knowledge that modest foundationalism proposes. This will serve two purposes: the first to present and defend a view on a topic important to evangelical Christians (among others) and the second to show postmoderns there is a viable middle course between Descartes's classical foundationalism and the wholesale rejection of foundationalism by many postmoderns. On a topic that can get complicated and technical in a hurry, we will limit technical jargon and be as brief as possible. In the following pages we will (1) briefly examine the regress argument, one of the best arguments for foundationalism of some sort; (2) examine whether the foundations for our justified beliefs need to be certain or indubitable, as Descartes thought; (3) look at how our other beliefs (those that are not foundational or basic) are *related* to our foundational beliefs; and (4) draw conclusions based on the arguments presented.

THE REGRESS ARGUMENT (AND ITS RELEVANCE)

The regress argument is recognized as one of the strongest arguments for foundationalism.[42] The gist of it is along the following lines:

Suppose that someone, let's call him Wyatt, believes that some claim (A) is true. Should we agree with him? Well, that depends on whether he has good reasons for believing (A), in other words, whether his belief in (A) is justified. Suppose he believes (A) on the basis of (B). And he believes (B) on the basis of (C). And then he says he believes (C) on the basis of (D). Well, if there are good reasons for believing (B), then (A) for now is well supported. But then we want to know whether he has good reasons for believing (C). And if yes, then what about (D)? Can this regress of supporting/justifying reasons go on forever and ever? No, it cannot. Eventually we have to get to a stopping point, which we will label (S). If (S) is unreasonable then the whole chain of reasons collapses and we are not justified in agreeing with Wyatt that (A) is true. Beliefs are only as strong as the reasons that support them. So if (S) is shaky/suspect then everything based on (S) is suspect. Modest foundationalists deny that this chain can go on and on forever. And when it stops, we need to see if (S) is what we might call a foundational (or basic) belief—one that supports other claims but does not itself require any additional support.[43] So what we have so far is the following:

---

[42]Aristotle was aware of some of the issues here in the fourth century BC.

[43]See Ted Poston, "Foundationalism," in *Internet Encyclopedia of Philosophy*, www.iep.utm.edu /found-ep/, accessed on February 1, 2014.

1. For a belief to be justified (reasonable) it either needs to be foundational or to be supported by other premises.

2. If it is supported by other premises, we need to ask whether the supporting premise is foundational.

3. This sort of chain cannot go on forever; eventually we hit a stopping point (a foundational belief). If that foundational belief is a genuinely foundational belief, then we are in good shape. If there are not good reasons for thinking it foundational, then we need to reject it and all other beliefs that depend on it for their justification.

As DePaul makes evident, there are only three possibilities about the chain of beliefs: (1) the chain of beliefs goes on forever (an infinite chain); (2) the chain circles back on itself (in a loop); (3) the regress ends with basic or foundational beliefs, which are self-evident and in no need of further support.

The first possibility seems unreasonable, for if the chain went on forever we would never get to a belief that is justified in and of itself. The person who adopts the second possibility is called a coherentist. They believe that justified beliefs are ones that properly mesh or fit (or "cohere") with the other established beliefs one has. Finally, the person who adopts the third possibility as the most reasonable is the foundationalist, either of the classical or modest variety.[44]

Not many philosophers have adopted the first possibility. This is because an infinite regress of beliefs would mean that we never get to a belief that supported (acted foundationally for) all the other beliefs. As finite beings, we "cannot complete an infinitely long chain of reasoning, and so, if all justification were inferential, no-one would be justified in believing anything at all to any extent whatsoever."[45]

Given the importance of understanding the regress argument in our evaluation of modest foundationalism, consider the following analogy:

You have a job, and you are scheduled to work today at 3:00 p.m. You are sick and aren't sure you can get through the day, so you call one of your coworkers. She is also not sure she can make it, so she also provides a backup, and the

---

[44]As Pryor notes, "Foundationalism's prospects quite generally look better today than they did twenty-five years ago." See Jim Pryor, "Highlights of Recent Epistemology," British Journal for the Philosophy of Science 52 (2001): 100. Pryor writes as a modest foundationalist.

[45]Richard Fumerton, "Theories of Justification," in The Oxford Handbook of Epistemology, ed. Paul Moser (New York: Oxford University Press, 2005), 211.

backup does the same, and so on. So you call your boss and tell her, If I'm not there, then Alice will be there. And if Alice is not there, then Barry will be there. And if Barry is not there, then Charlie will be there. By the time the boss hears "If Yolanda is not there, then Zedidiah[46] will be," he hangs up the phone. It has occurred to him that if this chain of supporting workers goes on forever and forever, that means *no one* will end up showing up for work! Realizing that an infinite chain of backup workers will not solve his need to have one actual person show up, he ends the phone call in anger. He knows having an infinite number of backups will not ultimately solve his problem— that of getting one employee to cover your shift at 3:00 p.m. After explaining all of this to you, the cranky boss fires you for ultimately failing to provide for an actual backup for you at work.

So what is the point of the story about you, your infinite number of work backups, and your angry boss? It is that infinite regresses of this sort don't really address the problem at hand. And just as your plan of an infinite number of backups didn't solve your boss's predicament, so similarly the infinite regress of supporting beliefs never results in a single belief's *actually* being justified. Some one person has to actually show up for work, and some particular belief ultimately has to be foundational for any nonfoundational belief to be justified. As Alston rightly notes, the regress argument is "the most important argument for foundationalism."[47] This regress argument then points us toward foundationalism.

We can divide all our beliefs into two categories: foundational or basic beliefs, and nonfoundational beliefs.

Foundational or basic beliefs are what might be called self-justified.[48] We can also call these directly justified beliefs, as they are justified without appealing to any other belief. Unlike Descartes, who thought these foundational beliefs had to be absolutely certain and indubitable (no way for us to doubt them), modest foundationalists simply require that such beliefs be highly probable (or something of that sort). On Descartes's approach we don't end up with much of a foundation. Descartes's foundation begins with "I think, therefore I am." Note that this is a belief about one of our own

---

[46]And we would start back through the alphabet when Zedidiah called his backup.

[47]William Alston, "Foundationalism," in *A Companion to Epistemology*, ed. Jonathan Dancy and Ernest Sosa (Malden, MA: Blackwell, 1994), 144.

[48]Ibid.

thoughts. It is far from clear how we can get from this starting point to be-liefs about the external world. As Pryor puts it, Descartes's foundation is "*too austere to support the rest of our empirical beliefs.*"[49] Modest foundation-alists, by relaxing Descartes's overly strict standard for foundational beliefs, allow for a much broader and more secure foundation.[50]

Nonfoundational beliefs are justified by being supported by foundational beliefs. These can also be called indirectly justified beliefs,[51] as such beliefs are always justified by appealing to one or more other beliefs. Descartes thought these beliefs had to be deductively based on the foundational beliefs. Modest foundationalists also relax this very strict standard. For example, if direct perception of an object is a generally reliable method for acquiring knowledge, then a particular example of seeing an object will be justified. Generally reliable methods produce, on the whole, generally reliable beliefs.

We begin to see what view of the structure of knowledge foundationalism promotes. Three examples of self-justified beliefs would be

(SJ 1) My belief that you look happy (you are smiling, there is a twinkle in your eyes, etc.)

(SJ 2) My belief that I am presently in pain (it's difficult to be mistaken about this)

(SJ 3) My belief that I am presently looking at my computer monitor (it's a SyncMaster T260)

If we think we see physical objects in front of us and we have no reason to think we're hallucinating or dreaming, then we are justified in believing there is that object in front of us. Perceptual beliefs are often self-justifying, and there is nothing unusual about my computer monitor example.

One other matter deserves our brief attention. Plantinga has argued that one particular foundational or basic belief is the belief in God.[52] He believes that if our cognitive faculties are working properly,[53] we are justified in claiming

---

[49]Pryor, "Highlights," 101 (emphasis original).

[50]As Richard Fumerton argues, "It is hard to come up with uncontroversial examples of infallible beliefs." See Fumerton, "Foundationalist Theories of Epistemic Justification," *Stanford Encyclopedia of Philosophy*, ed. Edward N. Zalta (June 2010), https://plato.stanford.edu/archives/sum 2010/entries/justep-foundational.

[51]The terminology is from Alston.

[52]It goes without saying that many non-Christian philosophers would disagree with Plantinga on this point.

[53]Which might include having enough sleep, taking no mind-altering drugs, not being prone to hallucinations, among other things.

(G) God exists.

Plantinga regards this as a reasonable (or warranted) belief, though it is not indirectly justified. Rather, he sees belief in God as a directly justified belief. He thinks that human cognitive faculties, when working properly, naturally tend to believe in God.[54] Just as memory, sense perception, and other faculties are reliable sources of knowledge, so Plantinga believes that the properly functioning cognitive capacities of a human will allow them to experience the presence and reality of God in a direct and immediate sense. John Calvin taught that humans naturally have what he called a *sensus divinitatis*—a natural ability to believe in God. The results of sin and unbelief have clouded this faculty for those who reject God, but the person of (Christian) faith has their faculties working properly, thus revealing what seems obvious—that God exists. There is a massive literature on Plantinga's idea of belief in God, and it is fair to say that many Christian scholars have been persuaded that Plantinga's approach is worthy of serious consideration, if not substantial agreement.

We have now seen that there is a third option concerning knowledge and that classical foundationalism and the common postmodern approach are not the only possibilities here. Furthermore, we have argued that this third option, modest foundationalism, is a reasonable one, for it makes knowledge possible, avoids skepticism and the problems with classical foundationalism, and also provides a broad framework that is compatible with understanding belief in God along the lines Plantinga suggests.[55] We can now summarize the benefits of the modest foundationalist view.

1. It provides a satisfactory reply to the regress argument.

2. It meshes with common sense—we can hold beliefs that are fairly obviously true as our foundation, and then we affirm other beliefs because they are supported by these bedrock foundational beliefs.

3. It avoids setting the bar too high for knowledge, as Descartes's influential version of foundationalism did.

---

[54]With God, of course, being the creator of our cognitive faculties.
[55]We should note that modest foundationalism does not require that Plantinga's idea of God *as a basic* or foundational belief be true. Further, it is compatible with a broad range of evangelical approaches to belief in God.

4. It also gives us the tools to avoid any version of relativism with respect to knowledge.

5. For all these reasons we believe modest foundationalism is easily the best of the three options presented, and that there are good reasons to adopt it. As such, we heartily recommend this view for the reader's consideration.

Summary

1. Descartes had great confidence in human reason, and argued that Scripture/revelation ultimately is answerable to human reason.

2. Descartes and classical foundationalism
   A. Context of skepticism and religious intolerance
   B. Descartes's search for certainty
   C. Use of the method of doubt
   D. Three problems with classical foundationalism:
      i. Classical foundationalism requires that all foundational beliefs be absolutely certain.
         a. Yet classical foundationalism itself is not a certain belief.
         b. So it fails to meet its own standard.
      ii. Many (most) of our beliefs cannot be supported by the very few beliefs that are absolutely certain.
         a. Thus the great majority of our beliefs are unreasonable/unjustified.
         b. So much the worse for classical foundationalism.
      iii. Descartes's classical foundationalism requires that we know some of our mental states with absolute certainly. But as Feldman and others have argued, there is very little we know with such certainty.

3. Radical postmodernism and human reason
   A. Rorty's attack on the traditional picture of knowledge
   B. Franke, Grenz, and the rejection of foundationalism in all its versions
      i. Franke suggests there is a need for a chastened rationality.
   C. Four criticisms of this position:

    i. Evangelicals should take culture seriously, as Franke suggests, but should part company with him when he suggests that, in some important ways, Scripture is answerable to modern culture.

    ii. Franke and Rorty ignore the obvious fact that there are contemporary versions of foundationalism that are not in the classical foundationalist tradition.

       a. This view is commonly known as modest foundationalism.

       b. They neither acknowledge this fact nor prove any detailed argument that suggests we should reject modest foundationalism.

    iii. If we do away with the traditional idea of (objective) truth and are then left only with local stories (as opposed to a big story that claims to be universally true), it is far from clear how a local story from first-century Palestine is either relevant or "true." Such relativism undermines both the truthfulness of the gospel and the hope that it offers modern humanity.

    iv. We agree with Franke and Grenz that humans are situated knowers, and heavily influenced by our environments. But it does not logically follow that objective human knowledge is somehow not possible. The four authors of the Gospels all wrote Gospels from their particular human perspective. But more importantly their writing was superintended by the third person of the Trinity, namely, the Holy Spirit, whose guidance guaranteed the final product be inerrant Scripture.

4. Modest foundationalism

   A. The two previous views are not the only options out there; there is also a middle road, a view known as modest foundationalism.

   B. Modest foundationalism is a reasonable view of human knowledge.

   C. Main points about modest foundationalism:

     i. The regress argument clearly points toward foundationalism as the most defensible view of human knowledge.

ii. Some of our beliefs, though not certain, are yet basic or foundational for our beliefs.

iii. Other beliefs are justified by appeal to the foundational beliefs.

iv. Alvin Plantinga argues that belief in God should be seen as a foundational or basic belief for Christians.

5. We concluded by commending modest foundationalism as the most defensible view of human knowledge.

SUGGESTED READINGS

Alston, William. "Foundationalism." In *A Companion to Epistemology*, edited by Jonathan Dancy and Ernest Sosa, 144. Malden, MA: Blackwell, 1994. Alston was perhaps the most capable defender of modest foundationalism. Alston cofounded the Society for Christian Philosophers with Plantinga.

DePaul, Michael, ed. *Resurrecting Old-Fashioned Foundationalism*. Lanham, MD: Rowman & Littlefield, 2001. This book convincingly makes the case that modest foundationalism is both alive and well. The contributing essays are best understood by those with some background knowledge.

Franke, John. *The Character of Theology: An Introduction to Its Nature, Task, and Purpose*. Grand Rapids: Baker Academic, 2005. A leading evangelical who is clearly sympathetic to much of postmodernism.

Goldman, Alvin. *Knowledge in a Social World*. Oxford: Clarendon, 2003. A lucid and powerful argument for the possibility of genuine knowledge. Some background knowledge is helpful, though reading Goldman is always rewarding.

Grenz, Stanley. *A Primer on Postmodernism*. Grand Rapids: Eerdmans, 1996. Grenz was a prominent evangelical theologian, and clearly sympathetic to postmodern thought on a number of issues.

Israel, Jonathan. *A Revolution of the Mind: Radical Enlightenment and the Origins of Modern Democracy*. Princeton, NJ: Princeton University Press, 2011. A massively learned book.

Lints, Richard. *The Fabric of Theology: A Prolegomena to Evangelical Theology*. Grand Rapids: Eerdmans, 1993. A leading evangelical thinker presenting a careful response to postmodernism and making the case for a modest apologetic.

McGrath, Alister. *Historical Theology: An Introduction to the History of Christian Thought*. 2nd edition. Malden, MA: Wiley-Blackwell, 2012. An excellent overview of Christian thought through the centuries.

Plantinga, Alvin. *Warranted Christian Belief.* New York: Oxford University Press, 2000. The third book in a trilogy. Plantinga's defense of Christianity is sophisticated and sustained. One of the leading Christian thinkers in the past one hundred years.

Porter, Roy. *The Creation of the Modern World: The Untold Story of the British Enlightenment.* New York: Norton, 2001. A lively and lucid account of the British Enlightenment.

Rorty, Richard. *Philosophy and the Mirror of Nature.* Princeton, NJ: Princeton University Press, 1981. A hugely influential attack on the possibility of knowledge and traditional approaches to philosophy. Rorty's career began in philosophy and ended in comparative literature, a move that illustrates the path his thought took.

13

THE HOPE OF THE GOSPEL

*The heart of the gospel is redemption, and the essence of
redemption is the substitutionary sacrifice of Christ.*

CHARLES SPURGEON, "THE HEART OF THE GOSPEL"

Put simply, the *gospel* is the good news of what God has done in and through
Jesus Christ to reconcile the world to himself. In this chapter we will offer a
brief overview of the gospel, what it is, and how it is genuinely good news
for a lost and dying world. Much of what we write here is indebted to a
number of evangelical scholars, including D. A. Carson, J. I. Packer, John
Stott, and others. We make no claim to be original here, and our goal is to
faithfully present the gospel as laid out in the Scriptures, the authoritative
revelation of the one true God. So we begin by discussing the human condition, as the good news of the gospel does not take place in a vacuum, but
in the context of human sinfulness and the alienation from the one true God
that our sin causes.

A LITTLE ETYMOLOGY

We first need to say a few things about what the word *gospel* means and what
its origins are. The word *gospel* translates the Greek word *euangelion*, which
occurs seventy-six times in the New Testament. *Euangelion* literally means
"good news," or a "good message." The noun *euangelion* in the New Testament "denotes the good news of the saving intervention of God in Christ,
referring usually to the message about Christ (1 Cor 15:1; Gal 1:11; 2:2), and

by extension, to the act of preaching that message (1 Cor 9:14; 2 Cor 2:12; Phil 1:5; 4:3)."[1] The idea of the gospel came to include both the content of the good news (the message) and "the promotion and declaration of it"[2] (the preaching of it).

THE HUMAN CONDITION: SINFULNESS

Understanding human nature is one of the central tasks of Christian theology. John Stott writes, "It is difficult to understand those who cling to the doctrine of the fundamental goodness of human nature, and do so in a generation which has witnessed two devastating world wars and especially the horrors which occasioned and accompanied the second. It is even harder to understand those who attribute this belief to Jesus Christ. For he taught nothing of the kind."[3]

Legend has it that a sweet and elderly woman approached her pastor one day and asked him, "Sir, my question is, how can a loving God send anyone to hell?" "Madam," he replied, "the bigger question is, how can a just God allow anyone into heaven?" If God does not exist then humans have nothing to fear concerning the consequences of their sins (moral wrongdoings).[4] For there would be no God to answer to, and the consequences of sin would be largely limited to what happens in our lifetime. Or, if God did exist and humans were, for the most part, morally upright, law-abiding[5] citizens, we would be feeling good about our long-term prospects and the possibility of an eternity in God's presence. Unfortunately, from the human point of view, both the *diagnosis* (what is wrong) and the *prognosis* (the solution to what is wrong) are much more serious than initially thought. The diagnosis is captured by the apostle Paul in his letters to the Romans and the Ephesians. He writes:

1. "For all have sinned and fall short of the glory of God" (Rom 3:23).

---

[1] Douglas J. Moo, *The Epistle to the Romans*, New International Commentary on the New Testament (Grand Rapids: Eerdmans, 1996), 43n16.

[2] D. A. Carson, "What Is the Gospel—Revisited," in *For the Fame of God's Name: Essays in Honor of John Piper*, ed. Sam Storms and Justin Taylor (Wheaton, IL: Crossway, 2010), 157.

[3] John Stott, *Authentic Christianity: From the Writings of John Stott*, ed. Timothy Dudley-Smith (Downers Grove, IL: InterVarsity Press, 1995), 146.

[4] This does not rule out an individual's long-term sins making it far less likely they achieve happiness on earth.

[5] We mean "law-abiding" *both* in its legal sense and in the sense of following the law of God laid out in the Old Testament.

2. "For the wages of sin is death, but the gift of God is eternal life in Christ Jesus our Lord" (Rom 6:23).

3. "As for you, you were dead in your transgressions and sins" (Eph 2:1).

4. "Like the rest, we were by nature deserving of wrath" (Eph 2:3).

There is a problem here, a sin problem, and Paul recognizes it as such. We are sinful creatures, fundamentally selfish by nature and by choice, who fall radically short of the standard set by the one true God.[6] And the bad news is that being a perfectly holy (morally righteous and unstained by sin) God requires that God hold us accountable for our sins. This is not good. It is not good at all. We exist, we are sinful, and our behavior offends a perfect and holy God who condemns us for these sins. Given who he is, a just and holy God cannot turn a blind eye toward sin. Rather, God's righteousness demands that sin be punished. Jeremiah 9:24 speaks of a steadfast God who delights in exhibiting justice. This is part of what being a child of wrath (under God's judgment) is all about. The reason we sin continually "is that we are sinners by nature, and that nothing we do or try to do for ourselves can put us right or bring us back into God's favor."[7] Some will say they are basically good, for they do not murder or cheat on their spouses, they pay their taxes, and so forth. The problem is that holiness requires we keep the moral law toward our fellow humans *and* toward a perfect and holy God. In other words, moral goodness has both a horizontal and a vertical component. Our best deeds[8] still fall far short of the perfect standard set by a perfect God. There is a chasm, a bottomless abyss between us (and our sins) and the one true God. And as human beings, we lack the ability (and the desire) to bridge this chasm in our own strength.

Many people still cling to the idea that humans are not sinful by nature, but rather are either inherently neutral or inherently good. Such a view can be called meliorism—the belief that humans are by nature good (unselfish), and have the capacity to do moral good apart from the grace of God.[9] In

---

[6]See 1 Pet 1:16: "Be holy, because I am holy."

[7]J. I. Packer, "What Is the Gospel Message?," in *Evangelism and the Sovereignty of God* (Downers Grove, IL: InterVarsity Press, 1991), 59.

[8]Remember that "all of us have become like one who is unclean, / and all our righteous acts are like filthy rags; / we all shrivel up like a leaf, / and like the wind our sins sweep us away" (Is 64:6).

[9]The fifth-century monk Pelagius (390–418) held to a view similar to this, and was later condemned as a heretic.

other words, there is no sin problem and we can do just fine, thank you, without any sort of divine assistance. The legacy of the twentieth century is difficult to square with meliorism. The slaughter and carnage associated with World War I and World War II, along with the massive casualties involved in the Mexican Revolution, the slaughter of the Armenians, the deaths brought about by Joseph Stalin, the mass killing of the Chinese by the Japanese in the late 1930s, Mao Zedong's massacre of millions during the Cultural Revolution in the late 1960s, Pol Pot and the slaughter in Cambodia, the disasters in Rwanda, Biafra, and Serbia, and the murder of the Kurds by Saddam Hussein. The total number killed is staggering, but somewhere in the neighborhood of 150 to 200 million deaths, numbers that boggle the mind and numb the conscience. Humans are the only species to indulge in mass slaughter of their own kind, a dubious distinction if there ever was one. In literary circles, it's hard to do better than William Golding in his *Lord of the Flies*, where highly "civilized" British schoolboys brutally kill each other off, before adults mercifully intervene at the end to ensure that some survive. Many argue that education and the acquisition of knowledge is sufficient for humans to both know and do what is good. Education *does* help humans improve in some important areas. For example, people with college degrees are significantly less likely to be racist or sexist than those who only a high school diploma. But there is little evidence that education by itself is sufficient to change the human heart and to make us able to do that which God requires of us—keep his commandments and love him before all other things. C. S. Lewis once scornfully referred to the humans transformed by education as "trousered apes."[10] Education enables us to polish our rough edges and be better aware of the demands of morality, but it does little to change our hearts such that we seek God on our own or have the ability to please him apart from the empowering of the Holy Spirit.

For those still unconvinced, ask yourself the following question: If you are in a long-term romantic relationship, how difficult is it to make such a relationship work? If the answer is truly "It's fairly easy" or "It's not that hard," then maybe some form of meliorism is yet true. But unlike most answers on the TV show *Family Feud*, neither of those answers is a "good answer." The correct answer, supported by a wealth of data, a high divorce rate, and

---

[10]See C. S. Lewis, *The Abolition of Man* (New York: Macmillan, 1947), 22.

human experience, is "It's pretty hard." Why is this? It is, we submit, because we (and our spouses) are basically selfish and sinful. After a long day of work, both parties in the relationship would (ideally) like to relax and have someone take care of their needs for the rest of the day. The only problem is, the other person is thinking the same thing! We have a real problem here—two selfish people, much to do, and neither one naturally inclined to put the needs of other first. And remember, it is this difficult with people we generally like a lot! The thought of pursuing such a relationship with someone toward whom we are either indifferent or hostile makes our skin crawl.

So we have argued that Scripture testifies to pervasive human sin, that the twentieth century lends massive support for this belief, and that the difficulty of maintaining healthy long-term relationships only adds to the considerable evidence we already have to believe that humans are sinful. Such a view may not be fashionable, but we believe Scripture, human history, and human experience are all on our side here.

So as evangelical Christians, people committed to proclaiming the good news of what God has done through the atoning death of Christ and his resurrection from the dead, we submit that the truths of Scripture do a far better job of explaining human behavior (and atrocities) than any competing theory of human nature. So we believe the bad news is true—we *are* sinful and we come up woefully short before a holy God. The result of all this is that the wrath of God is rightly upon all of us, and, as Romans 8:7 and other passages make clear, we are unable to turn to God in our own strength. Things look bleak, and there is no obvious hope on the horizon. What should we say to all this?

THE EXCELLENT NEWS OF THE GOOD NEWS: CHRIST'S ATONING DEATH

Paul describes the gospel as "the power of God that brings salvation to everyone who believes: first to the Jew, then to the Gentile. For in the gospel the righteousness of God is revealed—a righteousness that is by faith from first to last, just as it is written: 'The righteous will live by faith'" (Rom 1:16-17). Thus the gospel focuses on what God has done to make possible the salvation of human beings; the gospel is "the revelation of God's righteousness."[11] As Thomas Schreiner writes, "The proclamation of the

---

[11]John Webster, "Gospel," in *Dictionary for Theological Interpretation of the Bible*, ed. Kevin J.

gospel is so powerful that it effects salvation in those who believe."[12] Having said that, there are a number of important points that need to be made about the gospel.[13]

1. *The gospel is* Christ centered. The messages of Christmas (that the second person of the Trinity came to earth in the form of a human being) and Easter (that Jesus rose bodily from the dead on the third day) are at the heart of the gospel. It is also crucial to mention Jesus' work on the cross, often referred to as the *atonement.* To "atone" means to make amends, to blot out the offense and give satisfaction for a wrong done.[14] God sends his Son to atone for human sins. Some have referred to this as the Great Exchange, for Jesus receives the full punishment for our sins, while we receive his righteousness. Never has there been a greater gift, a more gracious gift, than Jesus' death on our behalf. As Wayne Grudem writes, Jesus' death on the cross met four fundamental human needs:

A. That we deserve to die as the penalty for sin

B. That we deserve to bear God's wrath against sin

C. That we are separated from God by our sins

D. That we are in bondage to sin and to the kingdom of Satan[15]

Jesus' death can thus be said to be sacrificial, to turn away God's wrath, to reconcile us to God, and to redeem us and free us from our bondage to sin.[16] Paul writes in his first letter to the Corinthians that "God made him who had no sin to be sin for us, so that in him we might become the righteousness of God" (2 Cor 5:21). As evangelical Christians it is difficult to overestimate the importance and the graciousness of Christ's work on the cross on sinful humanity's behalf. We gladly bow the knee before him in thanks and in worship.[17]

Vanhoozer (Grand Rapids: Baker Academic, 2005).

[12]Thomas Schreiner, *Romans*, Baker Exegetical Commentary on the New Testament (Grand Rapids: Baker, 1998), 61.

[13]Most of the following is heavily indebted to D. A. Carson, *The Gagging of God: Christianity Confronts Pluralism* (Grand Rapids: Zondervan, 1996) 433-40.

[14]The terminology is from J. I. Packer, *Concise Theology* (Carol Stream, IL: Tyndale House, 1993), 134.

[15]Grudem, *Systematic Theology* (Grand Rapids: Zondervan, 1995), 580.

[16]Ibid.

[17]See Phil 2:10: "That at the name of Jesus every knee should bow, / in heaven and on earth and under the earth."

2. The gospel is **God-centered.** It is God (the Father) who raised Jesus Christ (the Son) from the dead (see 1 Cor 15:15). It is also important to note that "God sent the Son into the world, and the Son obediently went to the cross because this was his Father's will. . . . If the gospel is centrally christological, it is no less centrally theological."[18] God and Jesus deservedly get all the credit here. It is crucial to note, as D. A. Carson, N. T. Wright, and others do, that these are *historical* events.[19] Someone at that time and place, if they had a video camera, could have taped both the crucifixion and the risen Christ.[20]

3. The gospel is **biblical.** Paul emphatically writes that "Christ died for our sins according to the Scriptures, . . . he was buried, . . . he was raised on the third day according to the Scriptures" (1 Cor 15:3-4). Carson notes that we may not know exactly which Scriptures Paul has in mind here, though Psalm 16 and Isaiah 53 are two distinct possibilities. Also, in Romans 1:2 Paul writes that the gospel was "promised beforehand through his prophets in the Holy Scriptures" (Rom 1:2), indicating that Scripture itself, the inspired Word of God, predicts the atoning death of Jesus.[21]

4. The gospel is **apostolic.** Paul repeatedly draws attention to the apostles: Jesus "appeared to Cephas [Peter], and then to the Twelve" (1 Cor 15:5). The true teachings of the early church are grounded in the message transmitted to and passed on by the apostles.

5. The gospel is **historical.** Christianity is ultimately founded in historical events taking place in time and space. First Corinthians 15 makes clear that Jesus both died and rose again. As Carson notes, "Jesus' death and resurrection are tied together *in history*: the one who was crucified is the one who was resurrected; the body that came out of the tomb, as Thomas wanted to have demonstrated, had the wounds of the body that went into the tomb. This resurrection took place *on the third day*: it is in datable sequence from the death."[22]

6. The gospel is **personal.** Jesus' atoning death and resurrection not only demonstrate the mighty power of God but also make possible the salvation of humans whose situation would otherwise be without any hope whatever.

---

[18]D. A. Carson, "The Gospel of Jesus Christ (1 Corinthians 15:1-9)," a sermon preached on May 23, 2007, The Spurgeon Fellowship website, http://thespurgeonfellowship.org/journal/feature_Sp08.pdf.

[19]See N. T. Wright, *The Resurrection of the Son of God* (Minneapolis: Fortress, 2003), 683-738.

[20]In contrast to the theologian Marcus Borg, who thinks it likely Jesus's body is still in the tomb.

[21]Is 53 is one particularly relevant passage here, especially Is 53:6.

[22]Carson, "The Gospel of Jesus Christ" (emphasis original).

The gospel challenges all to repent of their sins and turn to faith in the one true God who has revealed himself in and through Jesus Christ (see Acts 4:12). In Matthew 4:17 Jesus says, "Repent, for the kingdom of heaven has come near."

7. *The gospel is* **universal.** It is offered to all people irrespective of race, gender, ethnicity, country, and so on. Jesus' death is sufficient to cover the sins of all who believe, past, present, and future. In Galatians 3:28 Paul writes, "There is neither Jew nor Gentile, neither slave nor free, nor is there male and female, for you are all one in Christ Jesus."

This gospel makes possible our salvation (human faith is required), sets us free from the bondage of sin, and enables us, by the indwelling of the Holy Spirit, to act in a manner that truly puts others before ourselves and brings honor and glory to Jesus Christ, our Savior. As Luke puts it in Acts 4:12, "Salvation is found in no one else, for there is no other name under heaven given to mankind by which we must be saved."

OTHER CONSIDERATIONS

Evangelicalism and liberalism. The first point is the contrast between an evangelical (gospel-centered) understanding of the gospel and that of traditional Protestant liberalism. Protestant liberalism is, for the most part, a product of the Enlightenment and of the decline in the belief in miracles, the reliability of Scripture, and the doctrine of original sin. Influenced by the thought of Immanuel Kant (1724–1804) and Friedrich Schleiermacher (1768–1834), many liberal Protestants have reduced Christianity to being a morally good person and obeying the dictates of morality as revealed by our consciences. In the late nineteenth century, Protestant liberalism reached its high point in the work of the German theologian Adolf von Harnack (1851–1930), who saw Christianity as amounting to the universal fatherhood of God and the brotherhood of man. He rejected belief in miracles and reduced traditional (supernatural) Christianity to following the moral commands of Scripture and conscience. The gist of the problem with Protestant liberalism is nicely summarized by the theologian H. Richard Niebuhr (1894–1962), who writes that liberalism promotes the following creed: "A God without wrath brought men without sin into a kingdom without judgment through the ministrations of a Christ without a cross."[23] As such

---

[23]H. Richard Niebuhr, *The Kingdom of God in America* (New York: Harper & Row, 1959), 193.

Protestant liberalism does nothing to address the fundamental human problem—that we are guilty sinners answerable to a holy God. Liberalism shifts the focus from Christ's saving work on the cross (and the subsequent resurrection) to human moral effort and a kindly (and nonjudging) God.

Evangelical Christianity has always been rooted in the miracles presented in Scripture, especially the incarnation of Jesus, his numerous documented miracles recorded in Scripture, and especially in the miracle of his being raised from the dead. The apostle Paul makes clear that if Jesus has not bodily risen, then our faith is in vain, we are still dead in our sins, and we are the people most to be pitied (see 1 Cor 15:14, 17, 19). If one removes all the miracles from Scripture one is not left with much, and certainly not enough to address our basic sin problem. The gospel presented in Scripture is "irrevocably Christ-centered," while the gospel of Protestant liberalism is human-centered and dangerously optimistic about the human ability to please the one true God.

Differences within evangelicalism. It is important to note that there are some important differences within evangelical Christianity on some key points. For example, the Reformed[24] (or "Calvinist") understanding of the gospel is different from the understanding advanced by those in the Arminian/Wesleyan[25] tradition. Those inclined toward a Reformed understanding "will think of the gospel as the good news of God taking action to save men and women by the death and resurrection of his Son,"[26] while those of Arminian persuasion will see God taking action "to provide the possibility of salvation for men and women by the death and resurrection of his Son."[27] The Reformed emphasize God's election of all those who come to believe, while the Arminians believe that all humans have enough ability to respond to God in faith, and not just those who eventually come to faith. Well-known Reformed thinkers include Calvin and Jonathan Edwards,

---

[24]The word "Reformed" here refers to the theology associated with the tradition of Huldrych Zwingli (1484–1531) and John Calvin (1509–1564). It should be noted that the term *Calvinist* is anachronistic (out of place, so to speak), given that Calvin saw himself as following Augustine and (in some ways) Luther (1483–1546) and Zwingli. "Augustinian" would be more appropriate.

[25]"Arminian" refers to the thought of Jakob Arminius (1560–1609), while "Wesleyan" refers to the thought of John Wesley (1703–1791).

[26]D. A. Carson, "The Biblical Gospel," in *For Such a Time as This: Perspectives on Evangelicalism, Past, Present and Future*, ed. Steve Brady and Harold Rowdon (London: Evangelical Alliance, 1996), 82.

[27]Ibid.

while famous Arminians include Arminius, John and Charles Wesley, and Charles Finney. Both positions acknowledge the need for the grace of God, the need for Jesus' death to be a substitutionary atonement, and the need for the indwelling of the Holy Spirit to enable Christians to do that which God requires (see Gal 5:16).

What the gospel is and what it isn't. It is crucial as evangelical Christians to distinguish between the central message of the Bible, which is the gospel, and other beliefs that seem supported by Scripture. Carson notes that some have understood following the greatest two commandments to be the gospel. But Carson correctly makes the point that "the gospel is the good news of what God has done" and "not the stipulation that God requires."[28] With that in mind, here are a few issues of (perhaps great) importance to evangelical Christians, which are better (and biblically) seen as outcomes of following the gospel rather than the gospel itself. Nine such possibilities are:

1. Abortion
2. A particular political party/platform
3. Creation versus evolution
4. Same-sex marriage
5. Social justice
6. Homeschooling (vs. public schooling)
7. End times (eschatology)
8. Nature/authority of Scripture
9. Women in ministry

All of these issues deserve the careful, thoughtful, and biblically based attention of all serious Christians, but they are not the gospel itself. We humbly submit that Scripture and/or human reason may combine to give us good reasons to take a particular position on one or more of these issues. Having said that, it remains true (and biblical) that none of these positions is part of the gospel.

The gospel is fundamentally trinitarian. The Bible presents what rightly may be called a trinitarian approach to the gospel. What does this mean? God the Father is both the co-Creator (along with Jesus) and the

---

[28]Carson, "What Is the Gospel?—Revisited," in *For the Fame of God's Name: Essays in Honor of John Piper*, ed. Sam Storms and Justin Taylor (Wheaton, IL, Crossway, 2010), 159.

orchestrating agent of the gospel. He sends his Son into the world to reconcile all who believe in him (Jn 3:16 is clearly relevant here). Jesus and his
work on the cross are the gracious means by which God's plans are imple-
mented. And the Holy Spirit both convicts us of sin and later, after conversion, indwells all believers, enabling them to pursue holiness and the
various fruits of the Spirit (see Gal 5).

Each member (person) of the Trinity is fully God, though there are good
biblical reasons to believe that the persons of the Trinity have had different
functions (roles) in history. This is sometimes called the "economy of the
Trinity,"[29] where the word *economy* is used in the traditional sense of ordering the affairs of a household. With respect to the doctrine of redemption,
it is biblical to say that *God the Father* planned redemption and sent his Son
into the world with that in mind (see Jn 3:16; Gal 4:4; Eph 1:9-10). *Jesus the
Son* obeyed the Father and accomplished redemption on our behalf (Jn 6:38;
Heb 10:5-7). Jesus the Son died for our sins, not God the Father. After Jesus'
ascension into heaven, the *Holy Spirit* was sent by the Father and the Son to
apply redemption to us (through the conviction of sin and repentance; see
Jn 3:5-8). The Holy Spirit plays a crucial role both in our regeneration (being
born again) and in our sanctification (e.g., Acts 1:8; Rom 8:13; 1 Pet 1:2).

The fancy words for all three persons of the Trinity being fundamentally
equal is *ontological equality*, which literally means equal with respect to existence. But this equality with respect to existence is perfectly compatible with
the idea of economic subordination, meaning that each member of the Trinity
plays a different role, with the Father overseeing and planning[30] and Jesus the
Son and the Holy Spirit carrying out or implementing this agreed-on plan.

Paul, John Newton, and two modern sinners. Scripture clearly teaches
that the natural state of humanity (ever since Adam) is separation from God.
And anyone who has ever seriously examined their own heart may be shocked
and surprised at what they find. Sure, we do some good deeds (actions that
benefit others, for example), we haven't murdered anyone lately, and we regularly pay our taxes, drive carefully, and give to charities. These are not bad
things. But Scripture teaches that God is interested more in our hearts that
underlie our actions[31] than he is the actions themselves. After all, we all are

---

[29]What follows is taken from Grudem, *Systematic Theology*, 248-49.
[30]We are vastly understating what God the Father does here.
[31]The Greeks referred to this as our *character*, a concept that significantly overlaps with the biblical
idea of the human heart.

perfectly capable of helping others only because we hope to get some good thing out of it (money, free pizza, a job offer, etc.). Both Jesus and Paul have some rather unflattering things to say about the human heart. For example, Jesus says, "Out of the heart come evil thoughts—murder, adultery, sexual immorality, theft, false testimony, slander" (Mt 15:19). Not a pretty picture. And Paul paints a similar picture in a passage worth quoting at length:

> What shall we conclude then? Do we have any advantage? Not at all! For we have already made the charge that Jews and Gentiles alike are all under the power of sin. As it is written:
>
> "There is no one righteous, not even one;
>> there is no one who understands;
>> there is no one who seeks God.
> All have turned away,
>> they have together become worthless;
> there is no one who does good,
>> not even one."
> "Their throats are open graves;
>> their tongues practice deceit."
> "The poison of vipers is on their lips."
>> "Their mouths are full of cursing and bitterness."
> "Their feet are swift to shed blood;
>> ruin and misery mark their ways,
> and the way of peace they do not know."
>> "There is no fear of God before their eyes."
>
> Now we know that whatever the law says, it says to those who are under the law, so that every mouth may be silenced and the whole world held accountable to God. Therefore no one will be declared righteous in God's sight by the works of the law; rather, through the law we become conscious of our sin. (Rom 3:9-20)[32]

The upshot of all this is that the human heart is pretty bad, naturally selfish, hostile toward God, and this is the universal human condition, not just the condition of two sinners from North Carolina and New Jersey. Jesus, Paul, Scripture in general, human history, and our personal experiences all combine to paint a depressing picture of the human condition. We are up

---

[32]Paul is quoting Isaiah and the Psalms at various points.

the creek without a paddle, with no way of getting to the shore. Worse yet, the shore is not even in sight! As J. I. Packer has written, "We have no natural ability to discern and choose God's way because we have no natural inclination Godward; our hearts are in bondage to sin, and only the grace of regeneration can free us from slavery."[33] Like Nicodemus before us, our only hope is to be born again, something we are incapable of doing apart from God's grace.[34] The modern evangelist Billy Graham, who preached to millions during his lifetime, has said, "Sin is a disease in the human heart. If affects the mind and the will and the emotions. Every part of our being is affected by this disease," and "there is no other way of salvation except through the cross of Christ."[35]

John Newton (1725–1807) was a man apart from God. He made his living for a long time as a trader of slaves, benefiting from the legal buying and selling of fellow human beings. In 1748 God reached down to Newton and changed his heart. Newton accepted the Christian faith and spent his remaining years calling for the abolition of slavery, writing hymns, and spreading the good news of the gospel. Newton is today best remembered for writing the hymn "Amazing Grace," the words of which are familiar to many:

Amazing grace! How sweet the sound
that saved a wretch like me!
I once was lost, but now am found;
was blind, but now I see.

To some the word "wretch" may seem a bit too pessimistic. We humbly disagree. If one reads the words of Jesus, Paul, and the whole counsel of Scripture, it becomes evident that "wretch" accurately describes the human condition apart from faith in Christ. A "wretch" is an unfortunate or unhappy person; or, more informally, a despicable or contemptible person. Apart from the grace of God, the universal human condition is indeed one of wretchedness.

Finally, both of us testify to the grace and kindness extended to us. One of us grew up in a Christian home, while the other did not. But both of us

[33]Packer, *Concise Theology*, 86.
[34]See Jn 3 for the discussion between Jesus and Nicodemus.
[35]Quoted in Billy Hallowell, "Billy Graham's Powerful Final Sermon to America: 'I've Wept' as 'I've Seen How Far People Have Wandered From God,'" *The Blaze*, November 7, 2013, www.theblaze.com/stories/2013/11/07/billy-grahams-powerful-final-sermon-to-america-ive-wept-as-ive-seen-how-far-people-have-wandered-from-god/.

needed, just as Nicodemus did in John 3, to be born again, to put our faith in Christ, and trust that his death on the cross atoned for our sins, past, present, and future. We thank God the Father for pursuing us unto faith, for Jesus paying the price for our sins, and for the Spirit convicting us of our need to turn to God and giving us the strength to serve God on a daily basis. Here we refer to the apostle Paul, who writes,

> Therefore, there is now no condemnation for those who are in Christ Jesus, because through Christ Jesus the law of the Spirit who gives life has set you free from the law of sin and death. For what the law was powerless to do because it was weakened by the flesh, God did by sending his own Son in the likeness of sinful flesh to be a sin offering. And so he condemned sin in the flesh, in order that the righteous requirement of the law might be fully met in us, who do not live according to the flesh but according to the Spirit. (Rom 8:1-4)

Postmodernism teaches that there is no fixed human nature, that moral standards are at best local in nature, that Christianity is ruled out by its exclusive nature and oppressive past, and that there is no genuine hope beyond the grave. By contrast, we affirm a fundamentally sinful human nature, a universal moral standard grounded in the God revealed in Scripture, a gospel available to all people of every nation, and the hope of a much better existence beyond the grave. Our hope is that those who have read to this point consider the truth claims of this very gospel.

SUMMARY

1. The gospel is the good news of what God has done in and through Jesus Christ and his work on the cross.

2. The word *gospel* comes from the Greek word *euangelion*, meaning "good news" or "good tidings."

3. The human condition/the bad news is as follows:

    A. All humans are sinful.

    B. Our sin merits the punishment of a just and holy God.

    C. We are dead in our sins, unable to commend ourselves to God apart from his grace.

    D. We are entirely unable to meet the demands of the moral law.

    E. Meliorism, the belief that humans are fundamentally decent/good creatures, does not hold up to careful scrutiny. Some supporting reasons are listed:

       i. The carnage of the twentieth century

      ii. The difficulty of maintaining healthy long-term relationships

     iii. Human experience

     iv. The overwhelming testimony of Scripture

        a. Isaiah 53

        b. Romans 3

4. The (very) good news of the gospel is as follows

    A. Gospel as Christ-centered; the Great Exchange

    B. Gospel as God-centered

    C. Gospel as biblical

    D. Gospel as apostolic

    E. Gospel as historical

    F. Gospel as personal

    G. Gospel as universal

5. Other Considerations

    A. Contrast between evangelicalism and liberal Protestantism

    B. Differences between Reformed and Arminian views of the gospel

    C. Distinction between the content of the gospel message and other important issues that are separate from the gospel

    D. Gospel as fundamentally trinitarian

       i. Though being equally God, the three persons of the Trinity have had different functions/roles in human history.

         a. God as Creator and the planner of our redemption

         b. Jesus as the Son whose substitutionary death on the cross made redemption a reality

         c. Holy Spirit to convict us of sin and to indwell us and make progress in sanctification possible

    E. Paul, John Newton, and two modern sinners

       i. All sinners are lost apart from God's grace.

      ii. All are saved by God's grace through the death of Jesus Christ, who died for our sins that we might live.

Suggested Readings

Carson, D. A. "The Biblical Gospel." In *For Such a Time as This: Perspectives on Evangelicalism, Past, Present, and Future*, edited by Steve Brady and Harold Rowdon, 75-85. London: Evangelical Alliance, 1996. A clear overview of what the gospel is and what it involves.

———. *The Gagging of God: Christianity Confronts Pluralism*. Grand Rapids: Zondervan, 1996. A detailed and persuasive defense of the God of Christianity in the face of pluralism.

———. "What Is the Gospel?—Revisited." In *For the Fame of God's Name: Essays in Honor of John Piper*, edited by Sam Storms and Justin Taylor, 147-70. Wheaton, IL: Crossway, 2010.

Grudem, Wayne. *Systematic Theology*. Grand Rapids: Zondervan, 1995. A leading systematic theology from a Reformed perspective.

Jeffery, Steve, Michael Ovey, and Andrew Sach. *Pierced for Our Transgressions: Rediscovering the Glory of Penal Substitution*. Wheaton, IL: Crossway, 2007. A careful and detailed defense of a crucial doctrine, including thoughtful replies to a variety of objections.

Machen, J. Gresham. *Christianity and Liberalism*. 1923. Reprint, Grand Rapids: Eerdmans, 2009. A brilliant and passionate defense of traditional Christianity against Protestant liberalism. Should be required reading for all evangelical Christians.

Mazower, Mark. *Dark Continent: Europe's Twentieth Century*. New York: Vintage, 2000. One historian's take on all the war and slaughter of the twentieth century. Little background knowledge needed.

Morris, Leon L. *The Atonement: Its Meaning and Significance*. Downers Grove, IL: InterVarsity Press, 1984. A classic statement of the doctrine of substitutionary atonement. Highly readable.

Oden, Thomas C. *Classic Christianity: A Systematic Theology*. San Francisco: HarperOne, 2009. A learned systematic theology from a church historian working in the Wesleyan tradition.

Olson, Roger E. *The Journey of Modern Theology: From Reconstruction to Deconstruction*. Downers Grove, IL: IVP Academic, 2013.

Packer, J. I. *Concise Theology: A Guide to Historic Christian Beliefs*. Carol Stream, IL: Tyndale House, 2001. A brief introduction to the central doctrines of Christianity by a leading British evangelical.

Stott, John. *The Cross of Christ*. 1986. Reprint, Downers Grove, IL: InterVarsity Press, 2006. A classic defense of the doctrine of substitutionary atonement and its importance to the gospel.

WHERE DO WE GO FROM HERE?

We have covered a lot of ground in the preceding thirteen chapters. In this chapter we will briefly review where we have been, offer some suggestions for the direction we are heading, and make some final comments intended to challenge and encourage those who seek to better understand postmodernism from a perspective that is both biblically grounded and philosophically informed. We conclude the chapter with suggestions for further research, a challenge to the reader, and some final thoughts.

We believe we have demonstrated a few central truths about the worldview known as postmodernism:

1. *It is a bit more complicated than many people think.*

    A. It includes a large collection of claims.

    B. Postmodernism is not a monolithic movement, but rather broad and diverse.

    C. Claims by postmodern thinkers range from the eminently sensible to the downright ludicrous, and everything in between.

2. *It is not committed to relativism with respect either to truth or to morality.*

    A. The idea that all (or most) postmoderns are metaphysical and moral relativists does not hold up under scrutiny.

    B. Nietzsche, Foucault, Derrida, and Lyotard all make substantive claims about what is good and what is not.

    C. Many postmoderns see the dominant metanarratives in Europe and the United States as inherently oppressive and deserving of rejection.

D. There are postmoderns (such as Latour and Jenkins) who say some pretty silly things, but they do not represent all postmoderns.

3. *It has (much) more to offer than many Christians believe.*

   A. Its critique of classical foundationalism has significant merit.

   B. The observer is significantly situated—the sociology of knowledge needs to be taken seriously.

   C. The writing of history is significantly ideological, though this does not entail any sort of skepticism or relativism.

   D. Truth does have a therapeutic element.

   E. Many metanarratives have been oppressive, and both the American and the European pasts are replete with examples of oppression.

   F. The chastened view of human reason is consonant with the emphasis on the noetic effects of sin.

4. *Though some of its claims are not compatible with traditional Christianity, a number of its claims fit rather well with the truth claims of the Christian faith.*

5. *In many ways it is a moral and political critique of European and American exceptionalism.*

   A. Many Americans and Europeans have turned a blind eye to the omnipresence of oppression in their collective pasts.

   B. The number of people groups who have been excluded and/or marginalized is simply embarrassing.

   C. This oppression makes the call for charity and inclusion all the more important in a world increasingly divided by race, gender, politics, and religion.

All of the above clearly suggests that Christians need to read more broadly, reason more carefully, act more inclusively, and live out the good news of the gospel in all that we say and do. Our hope is you join us in these commitments. May God be glorified.

We end with some suggestions for further research.

First, can postmodernism maintain its moral and political critique of what it sees as exclusion and oppression without lapsing into some form of moral relativism? It is hard to see how evangelical Christians will take this moral critique seriously if the idea of objective truth is abandoned. It needs to be carefully examined how truth, a commitment to social justice, and the central claims of biblical Christianity can all be integrated into a single coherent whole.

Second, can Christians reach out to a postmodern culture and world without also significantly compromising some of the exclusive claims of the faith—for example, the traditional Christian claim that faith in Jesus Christ is the only genuine path to salvation?

And third, more research is needed on the question of whether a commitment to biblical Christianity means that serious Christians should endorse some version of political conservatism. We suspect that the connection between politics and biblical faith is more heavily influenced by culture than many Americans imagine.

APPENDIX

CHART ON MODERNISM AND POSTMODERNISM

MODERNISM		POSTMODERNISM		CHRISTIAN
MAIN CLAIMS	EVALUATION	MAIN CLAIMS	EVALUATION	EVALUATION
Confidence in human reason as exemplified by Descartes; Hume as exception	Too much confidence in reason	Rejection of confidence in reason	Rejection of both modernism and postmodernism	Via media between modernist and postmodernist views
Commitment to progress: science as driving force	Much too optimistic: twentieth century as a disaster	Observer as radically situated	Observer is situated but still a capable knower	Observer is situated but still a capable knower
Rejection of doctrine of original sin; Locke as key figure; affirmation of meliorism	Affirmation of the traditional doctrine of original sin	Language as inherently unstable and nonreferential	Language as stable and referential	Language is both stable and referential
Eurocentric moral exceptionalism	Rejection of both European and American moral exceptionalism	Truth as constructed, not discovered	Truth as more discovered than constructed	Ultimately truth is a matter of discovery
Major Enlightenment thinkers rejected traditional Christianity	Affirmation of the truth and relevance of traditional Christianity and the Christian view of the self	No stable enduring self	Stable and enduring self	Christianity affirms a stable and enduring self made in the image of God
		Writing of history as essentially ideological	History can be selective and partial and still attain modest objectivity	Modest objectivity is humanly attainable
		Rejection of both European and American exceptionalism	Praise for science and technology; otherwise in significant agreement	Affirmation of human dignity and worth, and value of all cultures
		Truth as more therapeutic than objective	Objectivity trumps therapeutic value	Truth as both objective and therapeutic
		Metanarratives as inherently oppressive	Some metanarratives are oppressive, but Christianity is not	Christianity as the one true metanarrative
		Rejection of omnicompetence of human reason	Much agreement, though chastened rationality is defensible	See row one above

AUTHOR INDEX

SUBJECT INDEX

SCRIPTURE INDEX

Finding the Textbook You Need

The IVP Academic Textbook Selector
is an online tool for instantly finding the IVP books
suitable for over 250 courses across 24 disciplines.

---

ivpacademic.com